LITERATURE AND THE *Child*

LITERATURE AND THE *Child*

ROMANTIC CONTINUATIONS,

POSTMODERN CONTESTATIONS

Edited by James Holt McGavran

University of Iowa Press   Iowa City

University of Iowa Press,
Iowa City 52242
Copyright © 1999 by the
University of Iowa Press
All rights reserved
Printed in the United States of America
Design by Richard Hendel
http://www.uiowa.edu/~uipress

Printed on acid-free paper

The Calvin and Hobbes cartoons, copyright © 1992,
1993, 1995 by Bill Watterson, are reprinted with
permission of Universal Press Syndicate. All rights
reserved.

Library of Congress
Cataloging-in-Publication Data
Literature and the child: romantic continuations,
    postmodern contestations / edited by James Holt
    McGavran.
        p.   cm.
    Includes bibliographical references and index.
    ISBN 0-87745-690-9
    1. Children's literature, English—History and
criticism.   2. Children's literature, American—
History and criticism.   3. Children—Books
and reading.   4. Postmodernism (Literature).
5. Romanticism.   I. McGavran, James Holt.
PR990.L58   1999
820.9'9282—dc21   99-24458

99   00   01   02   03   C   5   4   3   2   1

The editor dedicates

this book to Anita Moss,

without whose help and

encouragement it would

not have appeared.

Contents

4. ROMANTIC IDEAS IN CULTURAL CONFRONTATIONS

LITERATURE AND THE Child

James Holt McGavran

ROMANTIC CONTINUATIONS, POSTMODERN CONTESTATIONS, OR, "IT'S A MAGICAL WORLD, HOBBES, OL' BUDDY" . . . CRASH!

n imaginative, withdrawn boy roams wild in a rugged natural setting that becomes a site of instruction in human mortality and morality. Learning as he goes, he revels in the world's beauty, cowers before its ugliness and pain, or retreats to the sometimes snug but often conflicted institutions of home and school, where he plays power games in order to control those he considers his adversaries—practically everyone, in fact. Curiously, this boy possesses a kind of double vision, seeing people and things as they exist both in their material reality and in his imagination. And even more curiously, he both is and is not alone: accompanying him like a shadow is a bigger-than-life being of his own creation that is alternately stronger and weaker, more civilized and more brutal than he is. This creature, sometimes his closest friend and ally, acts just as often as a stalking nemesis, waiting to pounce on him and demand his rights.

I have, of course, just listed some key elements of Bill Watterson's brilliant and very popular comic strip *Calvin and Hobbes*. Readers of British Romantic literature, however, will also recognize in the preceding paragraph key elements of three of the most important texts of that period: William Wordsworth's *Prelude*, where the mature poet recalls and reconstructs his boyhood, spent in the rural Lake District, as both sublime and savage; William Blake's double-visioned *Songs of Innocence and of Experience*, where both material and imaginative values are simultaneously celebrated and interrogated; and Mary Shelley's *Frankenstein*, where Victor first obsessively, adoringly produces his creature/child and then heartlessly rejects him when he finds him ugly, thus driving his alter ego to evil and locking both of them into a love-hate relationship that ends only with their deaths. Throughout its ten-year history, *Calvin and Hobbes* confirms Alan

Richardson's argument, in the first essay in this volume, that American childhood at the end of this century continues to be haunted, for better or worse, by Romantic conflicts of identity which polarize an autonomous, imperial self and an Other located variously in nature, in society, and/or within that same self.

Granted, Calvin's enslavement to television and his channel-surfing mentality, his fragmented verbal echoes of contemporary commercial and political discourse (sound-bytes he has presumably heard on the tube), and his fear-driven fascination with schemes of vengeance and mass destruction certainly reveal other, more recent influences than those of early-nineteenth-century England. Indeed, Lois Kuznets has brilliantly analyzed him and Hobbes in terms of post-Freudian psychoanalysis and postmodern, poststructuralist de-centerings and fractures. However, Kuznets also historicizes the strip in regard to Romantic tradition (35, 45–46; see also Singer 115), which she, like Richardson, finds simultaneously subversive and conservative with regard to social change (57–58); later in the present volume Richard Flynn links the fracturings of postmodern adult poetry with a revitalization of the image of the Romantic child, and Dieter Petzold finds Romantic irony in postmodern fictions for children.

Thus one can see postmodernism itself as a long-term result of Romantic prophecies, and I will suggest, following not just Flynn and Petzold but Chris Baldick and Warren Montag, that in creating a new myth of the monstrous powers and dangers of science and technology first unleashed on the world by the Industrial Revolution and of the resulting reconstruction of society into bourgeoisie and proletariat, Mary Shelley in *Frankenstein* anticipated these fractures between and within individuals on both the societal and domestic levels. Certainly William Blake did in his relentless attacks on the "mind-forg'd manacles" societies produce when they rely on reason and technological progress instead of imagination ("London," l. 8, *Works* 102), and Wordsworth did also in a well-known passage in his 1800 Preface to *Lyrical Ballads*:

> For a multitude of causes, unknown to former times, are now acting with a combined force to blunt the discriminating powers of the mind, and, unfitting it for all voluntary exertion, to reduce it to a state of almost savage torpor. The most effective of these causes are the great national events that are daily taking place, and the increasing accumulation of men in cities, where the unifor-

mity of their occupations produces a craving for extraordinary incident, which the rapid communication of intelligence hourly gratifies. (*Poetical Works* 735)

Writing almost two hundred years ago, Wordsworth uncannily seems to anticipate what we now know as the mass media, telecommunications, and the information highway—and the couch potatoes, like Calvin himself when hypnotized before the screen, who passively sit back and receive the "communicated intelligence." But the Romantic heritage of *Calvin and Hobbes* manifests itself more positively in Calvin's joyously imaginative but usually disastrous explorations of the wooded ravine behind his house, his love of the way fresh snow changes the landscape, the double vision that leads him to endless clashes with the (ironically) mostly female upholders of his still-patriarchal society, his always-intense but always-changing relationship with his other self, Hobbes, and even the manner of the strip's disappearance from the newspapers on Sunday, December 31, 1995.

Wordsworth's statement in *The Prelude* that his rural childhood was "fostered alike by beauty and by fear" (Book I [1805]: 306) is illustrated perfectly when he tells of the raising of a drowned man from the lake of Esthwaite:

There came a company, and in their boat
Sounded with iron hooks and with long poles.
At length the dead man, 'mid that beauteous scene
Of trees and hills and water, bolt upright
Rose with his ghastly face.
   (*Prelude*, Book I [1799]: 275–79)

Wordsworth here in this grim parody of a forceps-assisted birth restates the ancient dichotomy between the bright and dark sides of maternal nature that, as Camille Paglia notes (230–47), was reinscribed in late-eighteenth-century France in the roughly contemporaneous writings of Jean-Jacques Rousseau and the Marquis de Sade. In the *Social Contract* and also in his educational treatise *Emile*, Rousseau had reversed the Judeo-Christian doctrine of original sin to argue that man in nature is innocent and good and that it is our social institutions of home, school, church, and state that corrupt us. De Sade in his actual behavior and his writings represented human life in its most bestial condition where libido is totally unrestrained

FIGURE 1.

and pain is inseparable from pleasure. This dichotomy is perfectly illustrated in a two-frame daily strip where Calvin first recites six lyrical lines about a spider web in tall grass (fig. 1):

> Like delicate lace,
> So the threads intertwine,
> Oh, gossamer web
> Of wond'rous design!
> Such beauty and grace
> Wild nature produces . . .

These lines, interestingly, both echo and mock Robert Frost's poem "Design" (see *Complete* 396). Then, in the second frame, Calvin's face contorts with revulsion as he adds his own commentary to the verses: "Ughh, look at the spider suck out that bug's juices!" (*Observer*, June 29, 1993).

In a Sunday strip that examines the same issue (fig. 2), Calvin and Hobbes are walking through fresh snow as Calvin rather glibly comments: "We have houses, electricity, plumbing, heat. . . . Maybe we're so sheltered and comfortable that we've lost touch with the natural world and forgotten our place in it. Maybe we've lost our awe of nature" (he's obviously been reading either Wordsworth or perhaps a mass mailing from the Sierra Club). Then he turns and looks earnestly up at Hobbes: "That's why I want to ask *you*, as a tiger, a wild animal close to nature, what you think we're put on Earth to do. What's our purpose in life? Why are we here?" With a sweet grin Hobbes replies, "We're here to devour each other alive." For three small frames Calvin considers this wordlessly; then in the final drawing we see him inside, perched on a chair back in order to reach the thermostat as he calls out: "Turn on the lights! Turn up the heat!" (*Observer*, February 23, 1992). Thus Calvin realizes again, like Wordsworth, that the life and innocence of nature are also the death and

FIGURE 2.

corruption of nature—that the beauty and fear are inseparable, and that much of everyday life in society consists of artifices and distractions that help us to deny both our own mortality and our cruelty to others. The lesson parallels that presented below by William Scheick in his analysis of Mary Austin's stories of conflict between the Native American closeness to nature and the Anglo obsession with technology and "progress." In *The Prelude* Wordsworth shows a similar awareness when, after retelling several of his outdoor adventures, he brings the outdoor and indoor worlds together as he recalls skating on the frozen lake while all around the shore the cottage windows light up to call him and his friends home for study, food, or rest (Book I [1799]: 150–59). Then later, having reentered the indoor world, Wordsworth describes the simple but passionately pursued "home-amusements," mostly card games, with which he and his friends distracted themselves inside when bad weather prevented outdoor play. Thus Watterson and Wordsworth seem to agree that the various social activities and conflicts that take up so much of our energy—vital and dangerous as they may be—are trivial in comparison to the moments of vision and insight one may have when outdoors and alone.

Canonical Romantic poetry always stresses the importance of the writer's creative imagination, which sees through these trivial encounters and conflicts of everyday life in society to confront deeper issues of identity and spirituality. Blake epitomizes the double vision in a much-quoted passage from his November 22, 1802, verse-letter to Thomas Butts:

> For double the vision my eyes do see,
> And a double vision is always with me.
> With my inward eye, 'tis an Old Man grey,
> With my outward, a Thistle across my way.
>   (ll. 27–30, *Works* 188)

Texts like the companion "Chimney Sweeper" poems in *Innocence* and *Experience* work similarly by presenting opposing views of the London sweeps' terrible, often fatal working conditions. In *Innocence*, with touching but dangerously naive faith, the child-narrator trusts in his father, who sold him, and in God and the Church: "So if all do their duty they need not fear harm" (l. 24, *Works* 74). In *Experience* the same child has come to recognize his exploitation, and he bitterly blames his poor parents, who "are gone to praise God and His Priest and King, / Who make up a Heaven of our misery" (ll. 11–12, *Works* 104). Calvin shows this Blakean Romantic privileging of the double vision not just by animating his stuffed tiger but every time he sees his parents as dinosaurs or robots, himself as Spaceman Spiff, or the green blob of food on his plate as an attacking enemy.

Explaining his battles with his syndicate over licensing, Watterson further aligns himself with this aspect of Romantic tradition as he writes: "My strip is about private realities, the magic of imagination, and the specialness of certain friendships" (*Tenth* 11). Praising three other strips that have influenced him, Watterson clearly values the individual vision of each of these precursors. Of Charles Schulz's *Peanuts* he says, "I think the most important thing I learned from *Peanuts* is that a comic strip can have an emotional edge to it and that it can talk about the big issues of life in a sensitive and perceptive way" (*Tenth* 17). He admires Walt Kelly's *Pogo* for its visual richness, "lushly drawn . . . , full of bombast and physical commotion," and the rich stew of its dialogue (*Tenth* 17). But he bestows his highest praise on George Herriman's *Krazy Kat*: "*Krazy Kat* is more poetic than funny, with a charm that's impossible to describe. Everything about the strip is idiosyncratic and peculiar . . . For me, the magic of the strip is not so much in what it says, but how it says it. In its singular, uncompromised vision, its subtle whimsy and odd beauty, *Krazy Kat* stands alone" (*Tenth* 18). Like Schulz, Watterson uses childhood to explore the big issues of life; and in his restless experiments with formats (and the resulting battles with newspapers about space) and with lushly visual fantasy sequences such as those involving dinosaurs, deserts, and Spaceman Spiff, Watterson has followed Kelly and Herriman to achieve his own singular, uncompromised vision.

But he speaks even more specifically about the importance of imagination when he writes of his own relationship to Calvin and of Calvin's relationship to Hobbes. He writes, "I was a fairly quiet, obedient kid—almost Calvin's opposite. One of the reasons that Calvin's character is fun to write is that I often don't agree with him" (*Tenth* 21). As with Mary Shelley's Victor Frankenstein and his monstrous creature, Calvin thus functions in Jungian terms as a shadow self, a projection of Watterson's repressed desires that both does and does not have objective reality: Calvin, in other words, at least some of the time is Watterson's Hobbes. Continuing, Watterson speaks of Calvin as his inner child in terms that are perhaps less Blakean than Wordsworthian: "Calvin is autobiographical in the sense that he thinks about the same issues that I do, but in this, Calvin reflects my adulthood more than my childhood. Many of Calvin's struggles are metaphors for my own. I suspect that most of us get old without growing up, and that inside every adult (sometimes not very far inside) is a bratty kid who wants everything his own way" (*Tenth* 21). *The Prelude* similarly is not just about childhood but rather the conflict between Wordsworth's adult and childhood selves, "two consciousnesses—conscious of myself, / And of some other being" (Book II [1799]: 30–31) that merge in moments of high mental intensity but that split into fear, jealousy, confusion, and frustration much of the time. This doubleness, with its inevitable ironic instability and tensions, repeats itself in the Calvin-Hobbes relationship. Watterson seems somewhat ambivalent on the subject of the double existence of Hobbes. He sounds a bit like Victor Frankenstein trying to deny responsibility for his strange creation when he almost testily asserts, "I don't think of Hobbes as a doll that miraculously comes to life when Calvin's around. Neither do I think of Hobbes as the product of Calvin's imagination. The nature of Hobbes's reality doesn't interest me, and each story goes out of its way to avoid resolving the issue." But he concludes the same paragraph by reaffirming the importance of private vision: "None of us sees the world in exactly the same way, and I just draw that literally in the strip. Hobbes is more about the subjective nature of reality than about dolls coming to life" (*Tenth* 22). Nevertheless, just as Mary Shelley deals with the double reality of Victor and his creature or Blake with both material and spiritual frames, Watterson is dealing with *both* the objective nature of reality, whereby Hobbes's "real" presence, words, and actions in the strip have to "make sense" to his readers, *and* the subjective nature, whereby Calvin is always projecting his own unspoken thoughts into his alter ego.

Watterson reveals more disingenuousness regarding Romantic origins in a daily strip published in 1993 (fig. 3), where he has Calvin recite to Hobbes (who is trying to sleep and ignore it) Blake's famous *Song of Experience* about the combined objective and subjective nature of a tiger's reality: "Tiger! Tiger! burning bright / In the forests of the night" ("The Tiger," ll. 1–2, *Works* 85). Ironically, Watterson makes Calvin take these lines literally and thus perversely misunderstand Blake's emphasis on the combined danger and seductiveness of the revolutionary energy his mentalized beast embodies: "Blake wrote that. Apparently the tiger was on fire. Maybe his tail got struck by lightning or something." Calvin walks off muttering, "Flammable felines—what a weird subject for poetry"; Hobbes wakes from his nap, exasperated with human intelligence, or rather the apparent lack of it, to sigh, "This is why I try to sleep through most of the day" (*Observer*, March 27, 1993).

That Romantic childhood or, for that matter, Romanticism itself, with all its internal and external conflicts, is largely a "guy thing" has been emphasized in the recent work of Romantic feminist critics such as Mitzi Myers, analyzing Maria Edgeworth below, and Anne Mellor, who argues that while Wordsworth, Blake, and other male Romantic poets were using their imagination to explore these conflicts, women writers of the period, including Edgeworth, Dorothy

FIGURE 3.

Wordsworth, and Mary Shelley, were creating a feminine Romanticism in a literary art that emphasized the opposing qualities of rationality, community, and cooperation (2–3). Certainly it is true that while Wordsworth takes his own process of self-formation very seriously in *The Prelude* and Blake stresses over and over again the importance of maintaining one's personal vision, Mary Shelley uses Victor Frankenstein and his creature to show how monstrously destructive such egotism can be both to others and to oneself. Late-twentieth-century American society may still be patriarchal, but except for his father, the community forces against which Calvin does battle daily are represented almost exclusively by the numerous women in his life: his almost anachronous stay-at-home mother; his teacher, Miss Wormwood; his babysitter, Rosalyn; and especially his classmate and neighbor, Susie Derkins. Again and again Calvin despises Susie just for existing, grosses her out in the lunchroom, or lobs snowballs at her—until Susie has had enough, and then she shows she is extremely dangerous when aroused and easily able to outdo him in schemes of vengeance: when Calvin steals her doll, she steals Hobbes (*Tenth* 136–44). Calvin never learns from this in the strip, and in his own comments on it, Watterson emphasizes the primacy of this antisocial masculine imagination to both himself and Calvin. This is not to critique Watterson himself as chauvinistic. In fact, he makes clear in his written comments on Susie that he admires and likes her: "Susie is earnest, serious, and smart—the kind of girl I was attracted to in school and eventually married. . . . Neither . . . [Calvin nor Susie] quite understands what's going on, which is probably true of most relationships" (*Tenth* 24). In his final comment on Susie, Watterson again shows sympathy with feminist viewpoints: "I sometimes imagine a strip from Susie's point of view would be interesting, and after so many strips about boys, I think a strip about a little girl, drawn by a woman, could be great" (*Tenth* 24).

In no way does *Calvin and Hobbes* more clearly reveal its Romantic cultural baggage than in the manner of its departure from the newspapers in December 1995. The production and distribution of Watterson's strip, with its economic and psychological tensions, both reinscribe and interrogate the efforts of the librarians in Anne Lundin's study in this volume to further the reputation of Kate Greenaway's illustrations and the efforts of both A. A. Milne and the Disney empire, as recounted below by Paula T. Connolly, to use Winnie-the-Pooh to market Romantic childhood. Watterson became increasingly frustrated over time by his long wars with Universal Press Syndicate over licensing rights (Grossberger)—the syndicate wanted to put Calvin and Hobbes onto coffee mugs and T-shirts—and with newspapers about his sabbaticals (Astor, "Mixed") and about getting sufficient space to reproduce his increasingly large and unorthodox Sunday formats (Astor, "Cartoonists"). Rather than agree to what he perceived as these limits to his control and his creativity, Watterson ended newspaper appearances of *Calvin and Hobbes* on New Year's Eve 1995 with a powerful strip that almost literally sends Calvin and Hobbes sliding off the confining medium of the comic pages and into the as-yet-uncharted visions and unfinished business of Watterson's ongoing creative career (fig. 4). Mary Shelley's doomed pair, Victor and his creature, cannot transcend their division or escape their fate, and they perish in arctic wastes, but Calvin and his creature seem to find new life and hope in the snow they have always loved. As the strip begins, Calvin is forging a new path through deep snow, and Hobbes follows, carrying their sled. Both look euphoric as they speak through three frames:

Calvin: Wow, it really snowed last night! Isn't it wonderful?
Hobbes: Everything familiar has disappeared! The world looks
      brand-new!

FIGURE 4.

Calvin: A new year . . . a fresh, clean start!
Hobbes: It's like having a big white sheet of paper to draw on!
Calvin: A day full of possibilities!

Then, as they get onto the sled, Calvin continues: "It's a magical world, Hobbes, ol' buddy"; and in the last, long, nearly empty white frame, which stretches across the bottom of the strip, we see them in midair as Calvin says, "Let's go exploring!" Never has Watterson been more "in your face" with his syndicate and his editors, never more Romantic in his protestation against societal constraints and confinements than here. Blake, whose engravings, like newspaper comics, are always framed in boxes, ends "The Tiger" by asking ironically: "What immortal hand or eye, / Dare frame thy fearful symmetry?" (ll. 23–24, *Works* 86). Like the ironically self-conscious writers for children that Dieter Petzold discusses below, Watterson similarly imputes to his creation a metafictional life beyond the frame, beyond the page (and the T-shirt) altogether. In the greatest climactic passage of *The Prelude*, Wordsworth similarly interrupts his poetic re-creation of crossing the Alps to celebrate the power of human imagination to lead beyond memory and even beyond poetry:

> In such strength
> Of usurpation, in such visitings
> Of awful promise, when the light of sense
> Goes out in flashes that have shewn to us
> The invisible world, doth greatness make abode,
> There harbours whether we be young or old.
> Our destiny, our nature, and our home,
> Is with infinitude—and only there;
> With hope it is, hope that can never die,
> Effort, and expectation, and desire,
> And something evermore about to be.

Then, as if anticipating Watterson's lonely battles with syndicate and newspapers and their appeals to both his reason and his greed, Wordsworth immediately continues:

> The mind beneath such banners militant
> Thinks not of spoils or trophies, nor of aught
> That may attest its prowess, blest in thoughts
> That are their own perfection and reward.
> (*Prelude*, Book VI [1805]: 532–42, 543–46)

Yet while the mind in such moments of power may eschew spoils or trophies, Watterson, like Blake and Wordsworth, simultaneously realizes that his imagination must accept material realities and the framing discipline of his medium in order for his visions to be communicable and thus useful to others—otherwise his doubled heroes, like Mary Shelley's, would indeed be lost in the snow. Calvin and Hobbes's sled is floating in midair in that last frame, but it is descending, and it is headed for the woods, where, if past strips are any guide, they will soon crash. These same woods may also remind Watterson and us of the great numbers of trees that must be cut down, at steadily increasing prices, to produce newspapers and all they contain, including comic strips; they are in another, broader sense the woods none of us, in this world at least, will ever be out of. Thus the euphoria of idealized Romantic transcendence contains in its very assertion, in Watterson's comic strip as in the poetry of Blake and Wordsworth and the fiction of Mary Shelley, the counterassertion that more compromise must occur not just for artistic production and distribution to continue but for life itself to be faced and lived.

Ever since the publication of *Romanticism and Children's Literature in Nineteenth-Century England*, I have envisioned a second collection that would pursue the question of the continuing influence and importance of the Romantic reconceptualization of childhood up to our own time. As the foregoing study of Calvin and Hobbes was intended to illustrate, that question has become even more conflicted since the first volume appeared. The Romantic myth of childhood as a transhistorical holy time of innocence and spirituality, uncorrupted by the adult world, has been subjected in recent years to an increasingly serious interrogation developing on at least two fronts. First, as the field of English studies has been increasingly influenced by the interactions of poststructuralism, feminist and gender studies, Marxism and its extensions into cultural studies, the new historicism, and postcolonial theory and criticism, the myth has been deconstructed and rehistoricized as an often sentimental, sexist, but socially useful ideological manifestation originating in Western Europe in the late eighteenth century which tended to support, but could also subvert, the rise of the bourgeois nuclear family. Simultaneously, children of this period have come to be seen less as potential seers and saviors of corrupt adults and more as victims—along with women, colonized native populations, and slaves—of the imperialistic textual, sexual, and political-economic practices of a power structure that enforces a hierarchical organization of home, society, and state and uses education and training as means of indoctrination, brainwashing, and crowd control. Hugh Cunningham's *The Children of the Poor* (1992), Anne Mellor's *Romanticism and Gender* (1993), and Alan Richardson's *Literature, Education, and Romanticism* (1994) have been major contributors to this revisioning of Romantic childhood, as are the numerous feminist essays of Mitzi Myers and the introduction and several essays in *Infant Tongues*, edited by Elizabeth Goodenough, Mark A. Heberle, and Naomi Sokoloff (1994).

Second, and concurrent with this refocused academic debate, the relentless pace of late-twentieth-century demographic and technological change exceeds our ability to conceptualize about it ourselves, let alone prepare our children for it, while the increasingly acrimonious tone of public debate over family- and child-related issues often seems to threaten more than it advances the well-being and future of children in America today. Given this confusion of theory and practice, masters and servants, change and instability in the world, the home, and the school, can myths or ideologies of childhood, Romantic or otherwise, still be worth talking about? Isn't it at best—if it ever existed at all—a luxury only affluent, well-educated parents can offer their children? On the other hand, was there ever a time, then or now, when ideals were simple, pure, and uncomplicated, or a time when children—and their parents, caregivers, and teachers—didn't make dreams and schemes for a better life?

The contributors to this book contend as I do—though in widely differing ways—that our culture is still pervaded, in this postmodern moment of the late 1990s, by the Romantic conception of childhood that first emerged two hundred years ago as, in the wake of the French Revolution and the Industrial Revolution, Western Europe experienced another fin de siècle similarly characterized by overwhelming material and institutional change and instability. The continuing and sanative paradox of the rhetoric of Romanticism (Knoblauch 127, 133), then and now, is that it democratically privileges individual consciousness at the precise historical moment when the chaos of the world outside—whether read in terms of nature, gender, or politics—threatens such consciousness, thus producing Bakhtinian dialogics and psychic/political commitment both within individuals and between those individuals and others.

In the first section, "Romanticism Continuing and Contested," leadoff essays by Alan Richardson and Mitzi Myers interrogate both the origins and ends of Romantic childhood. Richardson argues that Western concern for childhood precedes Rousseau and Wordsworth by centuries; paralleling Cunningham's argument in *The Children of the Poor*, Richardson also affirms that Wordsworth's apotheosis of prepubescent childhood benefited the sons and daughters of the rich and privileged long before it trickled down to improve the lives of poor children by arousing the conscience of Victorian social activists. But he concludes "Romanticism and the End of Childhood" by emphasizing that in spite of the dangers and limitations of Romantic-based anxieties for the child, to destroy the myth of childhood would be to abandon twenty-first-century children entirely to the unchecked depredations of late capitalism and the collapse of both the public and the private will to protect and nurture them. Because young children especially need protection in ways that adult women, racial minorities, and subjected peoples do not, Richardson cautions against seeing them as just another disadvantaged or marginalized group.

While Richardson thus almost grudgingly allows that the ideology of Romantic childhood not only continues to exist but may actually play an advocacy role in the current political debate over children and families, Myers unites feminist, postcolonial, and poststructuralist theory in "Reading Children and Homeopathic Romanticism" to question whether Romantic childhood came into existence during the Romantic period at all or was instead, as she suggests, a later invention of a male-dominated academic literary establishment and one that can and should now be dismissed or at least very extensively revised. Analyzing a once-popular but now little-read story by the Anglo-Irish writer Maria Edgeworth, "The Good Aunt" (first published in 1801, just three years after Wordsworth's and Coleridge's *Lyrical Ballads*), Myers argues that Edgeworth parallels men's colonization of women and the feminine with England's colonization of Ireland and the British Empire's establishment of slaveholding colonies in the Caribbean. One of the story's main characters is an English boy raised on a plantation in Jamaica who has returned to England to go to school. What he learns is, first, that the grandiose, powerful masculine self that the Romantic poets apotheosize is the dictatorial force that requires female submission in the home, "fagging" in the public school, and imperial domination in international affairs; and, second, that domestic, institutional, and national models of control must be replaced by opposing models of cooperation and shared power if a society is to be fair to all its inhabitants. Thus Myers both lends support to and extends Anne Mellor's argument in *Romanticism and Gender* that while male poets like Wordsworth and Shelley were creating a masculine Romanticism of the transcendent, nonrational self, women writers of the period were forging a feminine Romanticism of rationality and community in a struggle for self-empowerment.

The next section of the book, "Romantic Ironies, Postmodern Texts," includes Dieter Petzold's "Taking Games Seriously," Richard Flynn's "Infant Sight," and my own "Wordsworth, Lost Boys, and Romantic Hom(e)ophobia." All of us problematize historical Romanticism, in somewhat opposed but complementary ways, to analyze postmodern texts about children written for either children or adults. Petzold begins by reminding us of the undercurrents of irony that lie embedded in the canonical Romantic texts themselves. He argues that although we may carelessly assume that Romantic writers, and their twentieth-century followers, take childhood altogether seriously, in fact Romantic writers glorified both the innocent child and the unifying power of the experienced, controlling adult writer. Thus texts were produced, and still are being produced by recent fantasy writers working in the Romantic tradition, which encourage their readers to suspend their disbelief and experience the fantasy while simultaneously revealing, by means of what today are termed metafictional interruptions, that the writer is playing games with them. Insisting that children like and learn from this, Petzold closely examines "metafantasy" in Peter Beagle's *The Last Unicorn*, Michael Ende's *The Neverending Story* (*Die unendliche Geschichte*), and Salman Rushdie's *Haroun and the Sea of Stories*.

Flynn in effect extends Petzold's argument by linking Romanticism with mainstream adult postmodern poetry in "Infant Sight"; he argues that after World War II poets in America consciously reverted to the Romantic figure of the child in order to free themselves from what they found to be the emotional sterility and formal conservativism of the New Critics and Agrarian poet-critics who had immediately preceded them. He contrasts the cold reification and voyeurism he finds in John Crowe Ransom's "Bells for John Whiteside's Daughter" with texts by Randall Jarrell, Robert Lowell, Elizabeth Bishop, and Lyn Hejinian, all of whom use the figure of the child in personal, autobiographical—that is, Romantic—lyrics.

My essay links ironies of Romantic childhood and postmodern texts for children and young adults in yet another way. Concern for homeless children is my starting point, but "Romantic Hom(e)ophobia" focuses on the homeless boys who, in far greater numbers than the girls, either fall through or intentionally escape from the safety nets set for them by professional caregivers in the psychological, social work, and educational communities. Searching to account for this deliberate and potentially deadly self-exiling of runaway boys, I outline a homoerotic element which I argue is inherent in the Romantic exaltation of boyhood, show to what degree Wordsworth in *The Prelude* in effect prewrites *Huckleberry Finn* and *Peter Pan*, and use queer theory to argue that some well-respected books about homeless boys, written for children and adolescents (Virginia Hamilton's *The Planet of Junior Brown*, Felice Holman's *Slake's Limbo*, and Maurice Sendak's *We Are All in the Dumps with Jack and Guy*), may actually be doing young readers a grave disservice by refusing to engage seriously with the same-sex tensions that often complicate their lives.

Next come two articles which deal, though in differing ways, with "Romanticism and the Commerce of Children's Books" or, more specifically, the conflicted interaction of the Romantic ideology of childhood with the marketing of some of its best-known icons. Anne Lundin's essay uses theoretical perspectives derived from Jane Tompkins, Michel Foucault, and Anne Mellor to examine the role that engravers, publishers, critics, librarians, and imitators have had on establishing, canonizing, and promulgating the feminine Romantic aesthetics of Kate Greenaway's picture books. The growing popularity in America of the "Greenaway tradition" of sentimental, preindustrial, community-centered, pretty, pastoral Romanticism found two powerful advocates in Anne Carroll Moore, the early-twentieth-century director of the children's room of the New York Public Library, and Bertha Mahony, founder of the *Horn Book*, the first journal of children's books. Largely through their influence, Lundin shows, Greenaway's substance and style have been so often reproduced as to become truly internationalized during the course of the twentieth century.

Paula T. Connolly's essay provides a fine close reading of the divided, ironicized Romanticism of A. A. Milne's Winnie-the-Pooh books, establishing that it is not the knowledgeable, manipulative, part-playing Christopher Robin but the blundering, dreamy Pooh —the stuffed toy that will inevitably be left behind when the boy grows up—that actually embodies the Romantic ideal of innocent childhood. She also shows how Milne's highly successful marketing of his stories, originally written for his son Christopher, ironically made them impossible for either father or son to leave behind; indeed, Milne's commercial success acted as a kind of metafictional curse upon Christopher's life and career (so, at least, Christopher maintained), and Milne himself found himself similarly trapped in the role of children's writer that he very much wanted to shed. Connolly concludes after taking a close look at the Walt Disney empire, currently the official merchants of images of Christopher, Pooh, and their cohorts, and at the entrapments and betrayals operating whenever a beloved childhood icon becomes subjected to contemporary mass-marketing techniques and strategies.

Concluding the volume is a final section, "Romantic Ideas in Cultural Confrontations," which contains two essays examining the richly evocative interactions of Romantic childhood, which these writers take as a given in the twentieth century regardless of its date of origin, with other major cultural systems. First William J. Scheick demonstrates how turn-of-the-century writer Mary Austin united transcendental Romantic thought about nature, spirit, and childhood with Native American culture and a protofeminist insistence on the importance of women as storytellers in her story collection *The Basket Woman*. In these stories, which sometimes implicitly, sometimes overtly criticize the materialistic, patriarchal Anglo civilization of the Southwest, Scheick shows that a child narrator or character both embodies and comes to understand Austin's belief in the interpenetration or integration of dream and reality, the human with the animal and the spiritual, myth and history, art and ethos. Scheick concludes by examining two late-twentieth-century novels for children, Jean Craighead George's *Julie of the Wolves* and Whitley Strieber's *Wolf of Shadows*, which reaffirm Austin's Romantic synthesis.

Finally, Teya Rosenberg both examines and interrogates the interaction of Romantic transcendence (what M. H. Abrams has called "reconstituted theology"), archetypes, and multicultural perspectives (including reincarnation) in Canadian fantasy author Ruth Nichols's 1976 novel *Song of the Pearl*. In the novel a woman dies young, learns she has lived before and will live again, and undergoes a series of experiences that lead her to greater and greater self-knowledge—but only, and troublingly, within the limits imposed upon her by her sex.

It would be naive to imagine that the essays in this book can in themselves have much impact on the current cultural and political debates over children's issues—education, health care, the family. Nevertheless, like the other recent books already mentioned which historicize various aspects of Romantic childhood by tracing its specific conflicts with political-social-economic forces at work over the last two hundred years, these essays too show us, when we compare the past with the present, how little these forces, so often dangerous to children's lives and minds, have changed over time. We hope that our readers may see further yet into these forces and into the creativity—often subversive—of the writers responding to them that first produced childhood as we still know it in Europe two hundred years ago and that continue to underlie, and to offer useful perspectives upon, the present situation. As if anticipating today's bumper stickers, writers working in the tradition of Romantic childhood "practiced random acts of kindness and beauty"; they also saw the need to "question authority" and even to "question reality." Historically conscious study of them and their writings can enrich the current highly politicized public debate over which sorts of competing literacies—functional-technological, cultural-intercultural, and/or critical-revolutionary (Knoblauch and Brannon 17–24)—children and teachers need in order to be empowered rather than merely trained or indoctrinated. Wordsworth inscribed the epigraph of a redefined personal, family, institutional, and national/international life when he wrote that "the Child is father of the Man"; we believe that continued study of Romantic writers and the tradition that began around them can both father and mother safer, stronger children in the twenty-first century.

WORKS CITED

Astor, David. "Cartoonists Discuss 'Calvin' Requirement: Some of the Creators Interviewed by *E&P* Support Bill Watterson's New Sunday Size/Format while Others Oppose It." *Editor and Publisher*, March 7, 1992, 34.

———. "Mixed Response to Second Sabbatical: Artists and Editors Discuss

Bill Watterson's Decision to Take Additional Time Off from 'Calvin and Hobbes.'" *Editor and Publisher*, March 26, 1994, 30.

Baldick, Chris. *In Frankenstein's Shadow: Myth, Monstrosity, and Nineteenth-Century Writing*. Oxford: Oxford UP, 1987.

Blake, William. *Poetical Works*. Ed. John Sampson. London: Oxford UP, 1913.

Cunningham, Hugh. *The Children of the Poor: Representations of Childhood since the Seventeenth Century*. Oxford: Blackwell, 1991, 1992.

Frost, Robert. *Complete Poems*. New York: Holt, 1949.

Goodenough, Elizabeth, Mark A. Heberle, and Naomi Sokoloff, eds. *Infant Tongues: The Voice of the Child in Literature*. Detroit: Wayne State UP, 1994.

Grossberger, Lewis. "Hold That Tiger: Bill Watterson Stops Creating His Comic Strip 'Calvin and Hobbes.'" *Mediaweek*, December 4, 1995, 30.

Knoblauch, C. H. "Rhetorical Constructions: Dialogue and Commitment." *College English* 50 (1988): 125–40.

Knoblauch, C. H., and Lil Brannon. *Critical Teaching and the Idea of Literacy*. Portsmouth, NH: Boynton Cook Heinemann, 1993.

Kuznets, Lois Rostow. *When Toys Come Alive: Narratives of Animation, Metamorphosis, and Development*. New Haven: Yale UP, 1994.

McGavran, James Holt., Jr., ed. *Romanticism and Children's Literature in Nineteenth-Century England*. Athens: U of Georgia P, 1991.

Mellor, Anne K. *Romanticism and Gender*. New York: Routledge, 1993.

Montag, Warren. "'The Workshop of Filthy Creation': A Marxist Reading of *Frankenstein*." Mary Shelley, *Frankenstein*. Ed. Johanna M. Smith. Boston: St. Martin's Bedford, 1992. 300–311.

Paglia, Camille. *Sexual Personae: Art and Decadence from Nefertiti to Emily Dickinson*. New York: Random Vintage, 1991.

Richardson, Alan. *Literature, Education, and Romanticism: Reading as Social Practice*. Cambridge: Cambridge UP, 1994.

Singer, Armand E. "Annotating Calvin and Hobbes." *Popular Culture Review* 7 (1996): 111–20.

Watterson, Bill. *The Calvin and Hobbes Tenth Anniversary Book*. Kansas City: Andrews and McMeel, 1995.

———. "Calvin and Hobbes." *Charlotte Observer*, February 23, 1992.

———. "Calvin and Hobbes." *Charlotte Observer*, March 27, 1993.

———. "Calvin and Hobbes." *Charlotte Observer*, June 29, 1993.

———. "Calvin and Hobbes." *Charlotte Observer*, December 31, 1995.

Wordsworth, William. *Poetical Works*. Ed. Thomas Hutchinson, rev. Ernest De Selincourt. London: Oxford UP, 1961.

———. *The Prelude: 1799, 1805, 1850*. Ed. Jonathan Wordsworth, M. H. Abrams, and Stephen Gill. New York: Norton, 1979.

PART ONE

Romanticism Continuing and Contested

Alan Richardson

ROMANTICISM AND
THE END OF CHILDHOOD

dolescents regularly bring weapons to school, and the daily violence occasionally erupts into knife fights; a thirteen year old beats another student to death at a prestigious academy. Less affluent urban children spend more time on the streets than at school and drift unthinkingly into criminal activity, and an anxious public allows children to be prosecuted and sentenced as adults. Gangs of inner-city children battle one another for turf, so economically desperate that they fight over scavenging rights to the scrap metal at burnt-out building sites. Teenage pregnancy is epidemic; alarmingly large numbers of unplanned, unwanted infants stand at severe risk of undernourishment, neglect, and abuse. In rural areas, impoverished children of casual agricultural laborers, who often lack literacy skills and political rights, are shamefully and openly exploited, working alongside their parents beginning at ages as young as six or seven.

This list, which could easily be extended, sounds all too familiar and might have been culled from a month's reading of any major urban newspaper in the United States. It provides ample evidence (if any further evidence is needed) of the fall, disappearance, or erosion of childhood which sociologists, social historians, and educationalists have been warning us about for the past dozen years or so (Sommerville, Postman, Suransky). Yet all these examples are taken from accounts of late-eighteenth- and early-nineteenth-century England, a period during which the modern notion of childhood as a discrete, protected, innocent state devoted to schooling and recreation rather than productive labor was first being widely disseminated across class lines (Chandos 133–54; Pinchbeck and Hewitt 2: 351–53; Place; Liu 251–66). Ironically, as the Romantic ideal of childhood loses its social purchase, the condition of contemporary children begins to resemble more and more that of the majority of their real Romantic-era counterparts. A Romantic childhood may soon again become an elite experience, mainly limited to middle- and upper-class families with the economic and cultural capital to afford it—as it was until our own century.[1] In its threatened dissolution, childhood brings us up against the limits of certain canonical forms of Romanticism even in registering their cultural force. It may equally, however, raise questions regarding both the limits of a postmodern devaluation of Romantic values and the potential for finding something to recuperate in a discourse that, as it recedes from us in time, throws our own cultural practices into sharper outline.

Not everyone would agree, of course, that the demise of the Romantic child is anything to lament. Before considering the case against cultural nostalgia (if not exactly for social complacency), however, I should be more specific about why I use the adjective "Romantic," a notoriously vexed term which recently has again come under assault (Perkins 85–119). After all, an extended childhood considered as a unique period of life, intimately bound up with schooling and other forms of intellectual and moral development, can be traced back to Renaissance humanism or even earlier and had already succeeded in generating a new world of children's toys, books, games, and clothing in eighteenth-century England (Ariès, Plumb). This notion of childhood, perhaps best called "educative," was still, however, an avant-garde ideal largely confined to a social elite (the upper and, especially, the "middling" classes) at the beginning of the Romantic era. What was it that enabled and propelled the democratization of this ideal, particularly at a time when, because of industrialization, children's labor was becoming more rather than less economically valuable (Zelizer)? In his recent and important study *The Children of the Poor*, Hugh Cunningham suggests that the extension to all children (in theory if not always in practice) of the rights and enjoyments previously associated with the children of the dominant group was inextricably bound up with a "change in the representation of childhood" (7) in the early nineteenth century. More specifically, it was the emergence of a "romantic concept of the child" and a "sensibility and rhetoric" among social reformers "unquestionably informed by an internalized acquaintance with the Romantic poets" that made this unprecedented and (in crudely economic terms) unlikely extension of the educative ideal viable (Cunningham 51, 90).

What was novel about the representation of childhood in canonical Romantic writing? In many ways, nothing. The literary "sentimentalization" of childhood, which may have been a necessary condition for taking children out of the workforce (Zelizer 6–12), can be found throughout eighteenth-century poetry before Wordsworth; even the image of the transcendentalized infant, which Wordsworth seems single-handedly to have revived from the works of such (then) obscure seventeenth-century Anglican writers as Vaughan and Earle, turns out to have been anticipated by several eighteenth-century women poets whose works have only recently been recovered (Babenroth; Cunningham 48). But the Romantics, particularly Wordsworth, Coleridge, Lamb, and De Quincey, succeeded at popularizing an image of the child which was no less powerful for being somewhat incoherent, intermingling the sentimentalism of eighteenth-century verse, the transcendentalism of Vaughan, a Lockean emphasis on the child's malleability, and a Rousseauvian faith in original innocence and "natural" principles of growth. Barbara Garlitz has shown in compelling detail that a single poem by Wordsworth—the "Immortality" ode, with its image of the child as "Best Philosopher," fresh from a heavenly preexistence and "trailing clouds of glory"—functioned throughout nineteenth-century British culture as at once synechdoche and authority for the new conception of childhood, appearing via citation, quotation, or allusion not only throughout poetry but also in sermons, journal articles, polemics for children's rights, and the writings of pioneering social workers like Mary Carpenter and Thomas Barnardo (see also Cunningham 145). Wordsworth's powerful and eminently memorable articulation of the child's "heaven-born freedom" could be readily deployed within progressive and egalitarian tendencies in British nineteenth-century social thought (Garlitz 649). According to Neil Postman, the "Romantic vision of childhood" similarly facilitated the beginnings of the progressive education movement in the United States, as well as inspiring "America's greatest book," *The Adventures of Huckleberry Finn* (60–61).

Postman's citation of Twain reminds us that works of children's literature perform no less important cultural work, geared as they are to aid, however directly or indirectly, in the formation of certain kinds of subjectivities, than do the sermons, polemics, and poems for adults surveyed by Garlitz. And nineteenth-century children's literature, both in Britain and America, is pervasively indebted to canonical Romanticism. Here too the "Immortality" ode alone had an extensive influence and is cited prominently in works as diverse as Kingsley's *Water Babies* (19: 50) and Hughes's *Tom Brown's School Days* (33), not to mention its importance for George MacDonald (McGillis). Wordsworth's "child of nature," a Rousseauvian cousin to his "Best Philosopher," becomes an important and recurring figure throughout Victorian children's fiction, as well as crucially shaping "adult" fiction about childhood (Knoepflmacher). The Romantic construction of the child, in its various permutations, was relied upon and further varied throughout nineteenth-century children's literature both in Britain and America (McGavran, MacLeod). As a result, the popular image of the child has long manifested, at least within the Anglo-American tradition, a distinctly Romantic cast.

The culturally dominant construction of childhood, one that becomes more visible as its dominance begins to recede and its inevitability is called into question, can usefully be termed a Romantic phenomenon. Though its various features can mostly be found in works written prior to or outside of what we ordinarily call Romanticism (in seventeenth- and eighteenth-century British poetry, in Evangelical children's fiction, in Rousseau, in some facets of Enlightenment education theory), the constellation of those features and the popularization of the resulting overdetermined construction belong to the mainstream Romantic tradition (Plotz; Richardson, "Childhood"). The Romantic child may owe its freedom to heaven or to a benevolent nature; its growth may be guided by a providentially arranged natural environment or by innate principles of growth (or both); its innocence may have supernatural origins or may instead proceed from its apparent lack of socialization. Either way, the Romantic child makes a strong claim upon us. If we guarantee it a sufficiently benign environment and then, aside from continuing to provide it with ample physical and emotional nurture, we pretty much leave it alone, the child will flourish, may well come to surpass us in its intellectual, ethical, and creative development. If we interfere too extensively and too self-confidently with its growth, we risk producing, as Wordsworth will have it in Book V of *The Prelude*, a "monster." If, on the other hand, we simply abandon it to the streets, or to early immersion in the workforce, or to inadequate institutions, we have blighted the image of God or of our own best selves. In the wake of Romanticism, the arguments for state-supported, progressive education, for social legislation to assure child welfare, and for the curtailment of child labor could rest on that simple, and that powerful, a foundation.

For all its visceral force, however, did the Romantic image of the child really provide an adequate foundation for social discourses aimed at improving the child's status? Did it elide—or even help to create—conditions as pernicious as those which, armed with Romantic rhetoric, social and educational reformers set out to remedy? Recent work on children's literature and the social construction of childhood, as well as recent critiques (particularly from new historicist and feminist perspectives) of Romanticism, suggest that we should think hard about these questions before we celebrate, with Geoffrey Summerfield and a host of critics before him, the Romantic defense of the child. Perhaps most fundamentally, Jacqueline Rose has unmasked the fiction of childhood innocence as a function of "adult desire": an imaginary space for enacting our denial of the "anxieties we have about our psychic, sexual and social being in the world" (xii, xvii). The sentimental construction of childhood innocence codified and endorsed by Romantic authors (here working in conjunction with their un-Romantic contemporaries, from Thomas Day and Anna Barbauld to Legh Richmond and Sarah Trimmer) can be seen as yet another "burden" which children are forced to take up, one that added to their repression even as it diminished their economic exploitation (Sommerville xv, 255). Children, in this reading, were freed from productive labor only to play a different, perhaps no less demanding, role within the capitalist economy as bearers of moral and religious value and as obligatorily blithe denizens of a domestic sphere in which economic man could find respite and emotional renewal (Cunningham 152). Cut off from the productive sphere and expected to enact an impossible fiction, the innocent child experiences a kind of social death, as Wordsworth himself seems to acknowledge with his profusion of dead or spectral children: Lucy, Lucy Gray, the Danish Boy, the Boy of Winander (Spiegelman 50–82).

If the domestic and private role enjoined upon children during the Romantic era (and since) links them with women within bourgeois ideology, however, Romantic childhood remains, as Mitzi Myers has insisted, as "male-determined" as it is influential ("Little Girls Lost" 135). Canonical Romanticism is a notoriously masculine phenomenon, and our cultural enshrinement of the Romantic child has ignored a number of women's alternative romanticisms (not to mention alternatives to Romanticism) which might route us past the dead-end that one repeatedly runs up against in Wordsworth's lyrics of childhood, in Lamb's essays, or in De Quincey's fantasies of dead angelic girls (Myers, "Little Girls Lost"). In its distance from the social world, its seeming immateriality, in a word, its transcendence, the Romantic child seems deliberately formed to underwrite the wishful autonomy, the privileging of consciousness, and the devaluation of bodily experience for which feminist critics like Marlon Ross and Meena Alexander have disparaged male Romanticism. In this sense, the Romantic child is indeed father of the man.

That canonical Romanticism relies upon and disseminates an illusion of autonomous individuality and an equally wishful evasion of the social and material world lies, of course, at the heart of Marxist and new historicist critiques of what Jerome McGann influentially christened the "Romantic ideology." Deftly and remorselessly working a hermeneutic of suspicion, such analyses suggest that behind the illusion of disinterested transcendence lurks one or more interested agendas, from the occlusion of real social and economic life to the support of capitalist and imperialist forms of domination. In relation to the historical transformation of childhood in the late eighteenth and early nineteenth centuries, the Romantic construction of childhood as a discrete, unique, critical phase of life has been linked to the programs of discipline, surveillance, and normatization which Foucault delineates in *Discipline and Punish*. Its very susceptibility to democratic applications meant that the Romantic ideal could be readily enlisted in ambitious and unprecedented programs to "embrace and regulate" *all* children, not just those of the bourgeoisie (Sommerville 224). As Clifford Siskin has argued in his Foucauldian study of Romantic discourse, the Romantic emphasis on growth and on the self as a "mind that grows" participated in a larger cultural enterprise to place individuals within developmental schemas subject to internalized observation and self-regulation (3). Thus the Romantic cult of childhood can be linked with its apparent contrary, the rationalist and progressive child-centered discourse which insures the reproduction of "self-regulated, rational and autonomous subjects" required for the self-perpetuation of modern capitalist economies (Walkerdine 212).

Perhaps, then, the recent spate of jeremiads over the end of childhood, over the demise, that is, of an identifiably Romantic construction of the child, are misguided. Shouldn't we instead be breathing a collective sigh of relief, trusting (as Rose seems to) that the twilight of the Romantic child may prove the dawn of "other, freer sexualities" and a "more radical social critique" which the myth of Innocence has helped to keep in check (xvii)? Or would this simply constitute an updated, more theoretically sophisticated exercise in construing childhood along the lines of adult desire, now raised to a millennial pitch?[2] In any case, before altogether consigning childhood to some ideological landfill, we might pause to weigh the social costs of a world without children in the Romantic sense—or, more troubling, a world with only affluent children. If the case can no longer credibly be made for a Romantic childhood in all its Wordsworthian obscurity and splendor, is there nevertheless something valuable, perhaps invaluable, to be salvaged from the Romantic model?

In a critique of the socially debilitating self-isolation of canonical Romanticism, Terry Eagleton notes as well the "revolutionary force" of the Romantic sympathetic imagination, the "production of a powerful yet decentred human subject which cannot be formalized within the protocols of rational exchange" (41). If a residue inheres within Romantic representations of childhood that manages to evade the subordination to social discipline that critics like Siskin have analyzed so trenchantly, it lies in moments of decentered subjectivity that have few if any contemporary analogues outside Romanticism: the suspension of habitual consciousness which has struck readers so forcibly in the "Boy of Winander" passage of *The Prelude*, the insistence of Wordsworth and Coleridge that the child sometimes "forgets itself" in play or imaginative reading, the sense, shared by Wordsworth and De Quincey, of childhood as at once discontinuous and continuous with the adult self. Latent within the Romantic representation of childhood remains a "radical ideal" (Cunningham 96) that has historically served to counter its implication in disciplinary programs and its utter subordination to adult wishes for a pristine origin and a sacrosanct private sphere. We have noted already how, even in a popularized and somewhat saccharine form, this ideal could help to advance liberal democratic reforms in relation to child labor and welfare. It may be helpful to recall that, contrary to its current bad eminence in Marxist and new historicist circles, Romantic poetry was valued by radical reformers as well; writers in the Chartist press, for example, celebrated the politics of poets like Wordsworth, Coleridge, Shelley, and Byron as akin to their own (Shaaban). That Romantic representations of childhood have continued to be read for their radical implications has recently been attested to by Edgar Freidenberg, a veteran of the alternative schools movement who, though sharing Eagleton's negative assessment of Romantic individualism, like Eagleton registers its oppositional force as well.

It might also be worth recalling just how harsh pre-Romantic childhood could be and usually was, particularly for lower-class children, that is, by far the majority of children (Pinchbeck and Hewitt 2: 387– 413). The sheer amount of work, often under dismally abusive conditions, loaded upon children (at least in the Western world) throughout much of the past, in preindustrial periods as well as in the high era of industrialization, is widely deemed indefensible now and helps explain why a social historian like Lloyd de Mause can persuasively describe the history of childhood, in contrast to Philippe Ariès's pessimistic, retrograde account, as a progressive and optimistic one (Stone). If a protected, educative childhood is all too easily sentimentalized, so, apparently, is a childhood of labor, as when Valerie Suransky laments the passing of the household as a "productive unit" and criticizes compulsory schooling for "denying the child the right to participate in meaningful labor" (19). In fact, home labor was often *more* arduous than factory work, since, especially in the case of cottage industries like spinning, it could expand to fill nearly every waking moment (Pinchbeck and Hewitt 2: 403)— and why should we expect otherwise of the "electronic cottage" industries that Alvin Toffler hopes will redeem children from their "nonproductive" social roles (220)? "Paradoxically," Suransky declares, "in a capitalist society, education is separated from work while ostensibly training the child for work" (20), a paradox noted long ago by Bernard Mandeville, who recommended accordingly that the "children of the poor" be kept out of Charity schools and inured to hard labor and coarse living as early as possible (311). Although, as Suransky notes, the English working class sometimes defended child labor, this was not "precisely" because it helped preserve "traditional" parent-child bonds (19) but more commonly out of sheer economic necessity, as Sommerville points out (197) and as the most superficial reading of nineteenth-century working-class polemical and autobiographical writings would amply evidence. Cunningham demonstrates that working-class parents often *resisted* the new demands placed on child laborers in the early industrial era, making common cause with liberal reformers (226).

Fantasies of liberated children achieving economic independence as free agents in the marketplace can as quickly be dispelled by a few pages of the *Memoir* of Robert Blincoe, who begged to be taken as a chimney sweep and could barely wait (at around the age of seven) to begin work at a cotton factory, credulously believing the recruiters' promises that "they were all, when they arrived at the cotton-mill, to be transformed into ladies and gentlemen: that they would be fed on roast beef and plum-pudding, be allowed to ride their masters' horses, and have silver watches, and plenty of cash in their pockets" (Brown 17). Any argument that, noting the historical infantilization of women, slaves, the working classes, racial minorities, and colonized peoples within modern social discourses, attempts uncritically to portray children themselves as a colonized group (Nodelman), which child-centered discourses "infantilize" (Suransky 8), loses sight of the undeniable fact that children, unlike the various adult groups oppressed in their name, *are* in legitimate need of protection and guidance, though just when their period of dependence ends can vary (within limits) from one culture and historical era to another.[3] It is altogether too easy for adults to trick, cajole, seduce, or simply beat children into doing what they want, whether such exploitation is masked by a contract freely entered into or not. That that exploitation has historically and does currently take place within the family is, of course, undeniable. That there would be much more, rather than less, exploitation of children without the protection of the family and of family-oriented legislation is strongly suggested by the history of industrialization under the rising star of laissez-faire capitalism. If child labor laws are relaxed, this will much more likely proceed from a resurgent laissez-faire ideology (already claiming massive deunionization and the scaling back of social welfare programs among its trophies) than out of legitimate support for children's rights.[4] And it will again be predominately working-class children who will be "liberated" in this way.

In framing her notorious and still provocative vision of a world without patriarchal oppression—and without childhood—in *The Dialectic of Sex*, Shulamith Firestone avoids the problem of child labor by doing away with the need for labor altogether through something called "cybernetic socialism." It is instructive, then, that her vision of a postchildhood society nevertheless remains, as Suransky puts it, "adultist" (189), grossly underestimating the physical, emotional, and cognitive needs of children, whose long period of dependence on parents (now unequally delegated to mothers) would magically give way to a "greatly shortened dependence on a small group of others in general" (Firestone 11).[5] Her vision of licensed child sexuality similarly (and more creepily) proceeds from wishful adult projection: "Relations with children would include as much genital sex as the child was capable of—probably considerably more than we now believe" (Firestone 240). Firestone's dehumanizing, technocratic fantasy (she also looks forward to the replacement of childbirth by "artificial reproduction" [230]) is easy enough to dismiss (Suransky 9–11), but her feminist critique of the repressive, patriarchal character of the bourgeois family strikes closer to, well, home. Even some of her more extreme positions have found echoes among more careful feminist thinkers: Juliet Mitchell, for example, similarly (though less directly) heralds the breakup of the nuclear family and the repeal of the incest taboo, with the nurture of children apparently to be taken over by mass institutions (406–16). The dilemma remains, however, that no alternative to the family (however precisely it is constituted) has yet proved viable on a large scale for the rearing of children in modern industrialized societies. Between the lack of alternatives and the steadily increasing number of children who live in single-parent households and are therefore inordinately condemned to beginning their lives in poverty, the "problem now," as Sommerville remarks, is to provide children with "*any* kind of family situation" (264)—configured along traditional lines or otherwise—that will allow them a fair start.[6]

Given that, whether desirable or not, the "cultural revolution" called for by Mitchell seems still farther off now than it did in 1974, how will we protect children for the duration? For children are at risk, not from overt "Down with Childhood" slogans such as Firestone's but from the tacit, remorseless logic of late capitalism, whose agents have grudgingly welcomed women back into the workforce (as they had been enlisted during the early industrial era) but resist providing truly adequate daycare, extended parental leave, and reliable healthcare; whose adherents will not only agree to employ both members of a couple but will lower wages until two-career families are all but mandatory, blanching, however, at the shorter hours and flexible work schedules which would make humane child rearing more viable under such conditions and crying out against the social welfare programs necessary to foster the children of those deemed unemployable. Yet capitalism, like the nuclear family, has proved easier to criticize than to replace. For the present, a sufficiently powerful rhetoric is required if we are to resist the full demands of a triumphant capitalism on behalf of the children who are increasingly regarded as expendable.[7] And, if we don't wish to see an extended, protected childhood again become an elitist preserve, available only to those who can pay an increasingly high price for it, this rhetoric will have to include a democratic appeal.

Those who are presently attempting to frame such a rhetoric have relied, self-consciously or not, on the distinctively Romantic construction of childhood which facilitated the democratization of an extended, educative childhood in the first place. Postman, who openly values the Romantics, unabashedly adopts their vision of childhood "spontaneity, purity, strength, and joy" and sets out to defend children's "charm, malleability, innocence, and curiosity" (59, xiii). Sommerville, who can be critical of the "sentimentalization" of childhood, nevertheless attributes to (modern) children a power of "imagination" superior to that of adults (160) and asks us to feel intimations of "immortality in fostering the young" (160, 296). Suransky, in a familiar (and no less persuasive) Romantic move, asks whether "any 'theory' can adequately explain such complex and nonoperationally defined experiences as love, attachment, bonding, clinging, and warmth," drawing on recent child development theory to argue that children require the "*irrational* involvement of one or more adults" over and above basic care and instruction (200). These writers are not arguing as conservative apologists for the patriarchal family or seeking to roll back the gains of the women's movement but rather are asking important and disturbing questions about the status of childhood within a late capitalist order which more radical analyses tend to evade. Far from discrediting them (in Mitchell's terms) as "romantics of the family and of the intimate and of the private" (411), I would ask whether their reliance on Romantic discourse says more about the staying power of the Romantic construction of childhood than it does about the limitations of liberal thought.

Still, one must acknowledge that the Romantic rhetoric of childhood has historically proved no less problematic than the Romantic ideology as a whole. It is not simply that, as social historians like Sommerville (200) and Cunningham (96) point out, what is most radically democratic in the Romantic vision has readily become hackneyed and inertly nostalgic in later adaptations. Rather, there is a blind spot in the Romantic approach to childhood that allowed the canonical Romantics themselves to support repressive practices and institutions (the Madras system of Andrew Bell is a particularly stark example) even as they opposed the increasing brutalization and progressive indoctrination of children in an era of industrialization, burgeoning nationalism, and agricultural improvement.[8] I would locate this blindness specifically in the transcendental element of the Romantic construction of childhood, one which had significant cultural uses but could also serve to obscure the child's implication in a social and material world, one moreover that seems to have lost whatever force it once had.[9] But if Wordsworth's "Mighty Prophet" and Lamb's "child angel" have lost their valence, other tendencies within the Romantic representation of childhood remain, as the work of Postman, Sommerville, Suransky, and others attest, vital, perhaps even indispensable.

Attending to writers on the periphery of Romanticism may help in framing a post-Romantic approach to childhood which avoids transcendentalism but provides an alternative to exclusively self-regarding (adultist) or narrowly instrumental views of the child.[10] Blake—canonized only in the twentieth century and notoriously difficult to fit into period definitions—criticizes more consistently and more trenchantly than Wordsworth or Coleridge the child's implication in a social net of oppressive discourses. Yet he also, in *Songs of Innocence* like "Holy Thursday," "The Chimney Sweeper," and "The Little Black Boy," implies that the child's very naïveté can provide it with a potentially saving distance, enabling it to ingenuously probe the various and competing discourses that define its conceptual horizons for rifts and contradictions, playfully deranging them in search of less constricting alternatives.[11] Mary Shelley, in *Frankenstein*, portrays the construction of childhood within a masculinist society quite graphically and yet no less subtly for that. Her monster-child's unnatural physical autonomy (he learns to feed himself in a few hours and can soon find fuel and shelter on his own) only underscores his need for the irrational nurture which, as an abandoned infant, he is denied, eventually falling victim to an intense and compulsive hatred which inversely mirrors the love and sympathy that he has desperately and unsuccessfully pursued. Shelley's father, William Godwin, argues in *The Enquirer* that without transcendentalizing the child ("I do not say that a child is the image of God") or abstracting it from the adult world ("Let us never forget that our child is a being of the same nature with ourselves") one can nevertheless affirm its uniqueness—the peculiarity and excess acknowledged by even so diehard a social constructionist as Godwin—and oppose the despotism of authoritarian education on that basis (60, 87, 142). And, as Mitzi Myers has argued to great effect, even Maria Edgeworth, many of whose works seem so antithetical to Romanticism, develops in certain of her tales (particularly those like "Lazy Lawrence" and "Simple Susan" concerned with lower-class children) a representation of childhood which achieves "affective power" through unsettling the "binaries of adult and child, agency and communion, logic and love" that Blake, Shelley, and Godwin all put into question as well ("Romancing" 102, 105).

Godwin was mocked in his time (among other reasons) for theorizing that scientific progress and better living conditions could eventually render death a thing of the past. Now quite recent advances in the medical sciences (particularly in human genetics) have led some biologists to believe that Godwin may indeed have been right. Apparently, a number of species (sea anemones and bivalve mollusks among them) suffer nothing comparable to our built-in senescence; they don't die unless something kills them. Human death could prove to have been merely an artifact of evolution, and rearranging a strand of genetic code here or there might grant human beings the prospect of immortality. No less eminent a scholar than Hans Jonas has argued that it is already time to begin contemplating the effects of so mind-numbing a development, particularly the possibility that childhood, not simply as a social but as a biological category, might become obsolete, preservation of the self taking precedence over reproduction of the species. His ethical case for continuing to bear children (and, therefore, to avoid overcrowding, continuing to accept a maximum human life span of familiar dimensions) is, not surprisingly, steeped in Romanticism, beginning with his stipulation of feeling as the "mother-value of all values" and his Romantic (and democratic) affirmation of the "different and unique" (Jonas 36, 39).[12] Jonas's argument for maintaining the system of mortality and "natality" depends on our acknowledging the importance of each generation "seeing things for the first time," challenging "habit" with "wonder," bringing a spirit of "eagerness and questioning" to human affairs (39)—ideals that seem natural to us because they make up part of a distinctively post-Romantic culture.

These, as Jonas remarks, are "weird fantasies" (40), and perhaps it is best to conclude by returning to children's literature and its active role in the history of childhood. In a review of several end-of-childhood books published in *Children's Literature* several years ago, Janice Alberghene asked whether "children's books help create childhood for us, not the other way around" (193). I think it is obvious that they do stand in a productive and not simply reflective relation to the constructed aspects of childhood and that, moreover, the Romantic heritage of much nineteenth- and twentieth-century writing for children has played and continues to play a key role in this process. But in many cases children's books modify their Romantic legacy, and not always in a watered-down or hackneyed manner. Some children's writers who seem to owe most to Romanticism—Maurice Sendak and Eric Carle especially come to mind—do not limit themselves to the purely imaginative and securely innocent matter endorsed by Coleridge, Wordsworth, and Lamb and best exemplified by the traditional fairy tale. They also acknowledge, in a manner more reminiscent of Barbauld or Edgeworth, the cognitive needs of child readers, their more than understandable desire for discursive maps and conceptual grids as they work through the arduous and lengthy process of piecing out the densely coded world of adult discourse.[13] It was the canonical Romantics' signal failure in relation to children's reading not to register these needs as well or to see how traditional children's matter—hornbooks and counting rhymes, bestiaries and illustrated alphabets, riddles and other exercises in building linguistic competence—had long met them in a lively, imaginative manner.

Perhaps here the Romantics might have forged common ground with their more sensible female contemporaries, the group of innovative writers Lamb all too memorably termed the "cursed Barbauld crew" (Lamb and Lamb 2: 82), who might themselves have better learned to appreciate traditional children's culture.[14] Sendak, Carle, and others writing in the latter half of this century—which may well be recorded as the golden age of writing for younger children—reassert the rational dame's feel and compassion for the child's cognitive demands in playful, fantastic formats and tonalities which owe more to a distinctly Romantic mode of children's writing. And yet they also understand that, as the Romantics enjoyed pointing out, children don't need to understand everything they read; that children need, on the contrary, to sometimes have their capacities stretched and their expectations broken, to proceed on occasion from words of one syllable to words of five syllables, to fail to quite comprehend why the bestiary features a hippogriff and one of the riddles has no answer. The child needs, in a phrase, the odd "gentle shock of mild surprise." But this need is secondary to the material, affective, and more basic cognitive needs which, as I have been suggesting, the Romantic construction of childhood made it harder than before to ignore, or to see in one group of children and not another, or to make light of or simply shrug off. If the ingenuous, questing, unique, emotive, dynamic child of the Romantics has lost its power to move us, we may well have lost more in terms of cultural power than we think to have gained in terms of critical sophistication.

NOTES

I wish to thank the editors of *Nineteenth-Century Contexts* 21.2 (1999), where this essay first appeared, for permission to reprint it here.

1. Ellen Goodman, in her satirical critique of attacks on social welfare mechanisms ("Let's go all the way and rescind childhood"), worries about just such a development: "Of course, we could retain childhood as a luxury item for those who could afford it. Sort of like an Ivy League college. The rest, the poor especially, will have to do without childhood the way they do without so much else" ("A New 'Modest Proposal'").

2. James Kincaid, in a recent book (*Child-Loving*) which rehearses in diluted form some of Rose's arguments (yet, oddly, makes no mention of her work), hopes similarly that by "deconstructing" childhood as it has been constituted since the early nineteenth century, "we can . . . act strategically and politically, act to devise ever more flexible, subversive, even liberating modes of perceiving and acting" (7). For a trenchant critique of "postmodern" attitudes toward childhood and the way they implicitly favor the needs of adults over those of children, see Elkind.

3. Shahar's compelling statement of this point is worth quoting at length: "Although it cannot be valid to discuss childraising and parent-child relations purely in terms of instinct and natural conduct, there are certainly immutable factors involved. A considerable part of the developmental process is biologically determined, and the continued existence of a society is impossible without the acknowledgement (and conduct attuned to this acknowledgement) that, up to a certain stage in its life, the child has need of nurturing and protection in order to survive. No society could physically survive without a

tradition of child-nurturing. And no society with any awareness of its own essence and aims could endure as a society without ways of transmitting knowledge and cultural traditions during the late stages of childhood, and without an effort on the part of those entrusted with the task of socialization of the young generation" (1).

4. Coleridge, ardently supporting legislation to curb at least the worst excesses of child factory labor, recognized the irony—and the implicit collusion with laissez-faire ideology—in considering children "free agents" in a supposedly "voluntary labour" market at the outset of the *first* great era of unfettered capitalism. "Now, nobody will deny that these children are free agents, capable of judging, whether their labour be commensurate with their strength, and whether or no the term of their employment be prejudicial to their health and comfort. Undoubtedly they are free agents; and as they have neither individually, nor collectively, petitioned Parliament to step forward for their protection, we have a right fairly to conclude, that they are well satisfied with their present condition." Coleridge's ironic laissez-faire apologist also disparages the "tearful" reformers of the "age of sensibilities" who would "open the door to legislative interference" in "cases of free labour" (*Essays* 2: 485–88). His most powerful argument for supporting the legislation lies in a Romantic injunction to "individualize the suffering, which it is the object of this Bill to remedy: follow up the detail in some one case with a human sympathy" (*Shorter Works* 1: 722).

5. That Firestone's speculations owe as much allegiance to futurist as to feminist discourse is suggested by the close parallels in Toffler's *Third Wave*, which similarly finds child-labor laws "anachronistic," heralds a "Child-Free Culture," and advocates a "shorter childhood and youth but a more responsible and productive one" (213, 220, 384). The complicity of such thinking with resurgent laissez-faire ideology is made overt in Newt Gingrich's well-known championing of Toffler's "third wave" vision.

6. My skepticism regarding alternatives to the family should not be taken to imply any opposition to "nontraditional" families (adoptive, variously extended, headed by same-sex parents, etc.), which, to the contrary, seem more needed now than ever. It is heartening to learn that the "principle of the best interest of the child" is being cited in legal decisions that give adoption rights to nontraditional parents such as the domestic partners of lesbian birthmothers (Moskowitz).

7. For a recent assessment, see the Children's Defense Fund's 1997 yearbook. One figure that speaks for many is that the federal government in 1994 was spending eleven dollars (per capita) on Americans over the age of sixty-five for every dollar it spent on Americans under the age of eighteen (Miller 242),

a trend that has continued. For a global perspective, consult the annual UNICEF reports on *The State of the World's Children*; the report for 1995 includes a particularly trenchant articulation of the child's "right to develop normally in mind and body" (2).

8. On these issues, see Richardson, *Literature*, esp. 91–108.

9. James McGavran similarly argues in his introduction to this volume that the Romantic imagination must be tempered with an ongoing recognition of "material realities" if its insights are to exert any appreciable social force.

10. A critical reading of the Romantic canon that pays equal attention to writers at its conventional margins might be seen as a variant on Richard Flynn's insistence (in " 'Infant Sight,' " his essay in this volume) on keeping the "conflicting propositions of Romanticism" in play, understanding it as a dynamic "contradictory field" rather than a unified tradition.

11. For readings of Blake along these lines, see Larissy; Richardson, *Literature*, esp. 153–66.

12. Jonas's insistence on the value of human difference brings out the potentially totalitarian implications of the widespread institution of "artificial reproduction" called for by Firestone: "Such is the working of sexual reproduction that none of its outcome is, in genetic makeup, the replica of any before and none will ever be replicated after. (This is one reason humans should never be 'cloned.')" (39). Mary Shelley, who seems to have shared her father's prophetic gift in regard to the biological sciences, suggests throughout *Frankenstein* that the fantasy, now becoming a reality, of artificially creating life out of dead matter is rooted in the same masculinist desires for autonomy and depreciation of the body and the feminine that feminist critics have located within canonical Romanticism.

13. Moreover, in texts like Sendak's *Pierre* or Carle's *The Rooster Who Set Out to See the World*, these authors manage to combine not only a Romantic appreciation of fantasy with a template for overcoming developmental hurdles (grasping the format of "chapter books" and understanding prime numbers as sets, respectively) but do so in a manner that approaches the "metafantasies" ("fantasy texts that employ Romantic irony") described in this volume by Dieter Petzold, all without leaving the very young child behind.

14. For a groundbreaking, sympathetic survey of this important group of women writers for children, see Myers, "Impeccable Governesses."

WORKS CITED

Alberghene, Janice M. "Childhood's End?" *Children's Literature* 13 (1985): 188–93.

Alexander, Meena. *Women in Romanticism: Mary Wollstonecraft, Dorothy Wordsworth and Mary Shelley*. London: Macmillan, 1989.

Ariès, Philippe. *Centuries of Childhood: A Social History of Family Life*. Trans. Robert Baldick. New York: Vintage, 1962.

Babenroth, A. Charles. *English Childhood: Wordsworth's Treatment of Childhood in Light of English Poetry from Prior to Crabbe*. New York: Columbia UP, 1922.

Brown, John. *A Memoir of Robert Blincoe*. Firle, Sussex: Caliban Books, 1977.

Carle, Eric. *The Rooster Who Set Out to See the World*. New York: F. Watts, 1972.

Chandos, John. *Boys Together: English Public Schools 1800–1864*. New Haven: Yale UP, 1984.

Children's Defense Fund. *The State of America's Children Yearbook 1997*. Washington: Children's Defense Fund, 1997.

Coleridge, Samuel Taylor. *Essays on His Times in the* Morning Post *and the* Courier. Ed. David V. Erdman. 3 vols. Princeton: Princeton UP, 1978.

———. *Shorter Works and Fragments*. Ed. H. J. Jackson and J. R. de J. Jackson. 2 vols. Princeton: Princeton UP, 1995.

Cunningham, Hugh. *The Children of the Poor: Representations of Childhood since the Seventeenth Century*. Oxford: Blackwell, 1991.

Eagleton, Terry. *The Function of Criticism: From the Spectator to Post-Structuralism*. London: Verso, 1984.

Elkind, David. *Ties that Stress: The New Family Imbalance*. Cambridge: Harvard UP, 1994.

Firestone, Shulamith. *The Dialectic of Sex: The Case for Feminist Revolution*. New York: Bantam, 1971.

Foucault, Michel. *Discipline and Punish: The Birth of the Prison*. Trans. Alan Sheridan. New York: Vintage, 1979.

Freidenberg, Edgar Z. "Romanticism and Alternatives in Schooling." *The Educational Legacys of Romanticism*. Ed. John Willinsky. Waterloo, Ont.: Wilfrid Laurier UP, 1990. 175–87.

Garlitz, Barbara. "The Immortality Ode: Its Cultural Progeny." *Studies in English Literature* 6 (1966): 639–49.

Godwin, William. *The Enquirer: Reflections on Education, Manners and Literature*. New York: Augustus M. Kelley, 1965.

Goodman, Ellen. "A New 'Modest Proposal.'" *Boston Globe*, August 8, 1996, A21.

Hughes, Thomas. *Tom Brown's School Days*. New York: New American Library, 1986.

Jonas, Hans. "The Burden and Blessing of Mortality." *Hastings Center Report* (January–February 1992): 34–40.

Kincaid, James R. *Child-Loving: The Erotic Child and Victorian Culture*. New York: Routledge, 1992.

Kingsley, Charles. *The Water-Babies: A Fairy Tale for a Land-Baby. The Life and Works of Charles Kingsley*. 19 vols. London: Macmillan, 1901–03. 19: 1–202.

Knoepflmacher, U. C. "Mutations of the Wordsworthian Child of Nature." *Nature and the Victorian Imagination*. Ed. U. C. Knoepflmacher and G. B. Tennyson. Berkeley: U of California P, 1977. 391–425.

Lamb, Charles, and Mary Lamb. *The Letters of Charles and Mary Lamb*. Ed. Edwin A. Marrs, Jr. 3 vols. to date. Ithaca: Cornell UP, 1975–.

Larissy, Edward. *William Blake*. Oxford: Blackwell, 1985.

Liu, Alan. *Wordsworth: The Sense of History*. Stanford: Stanford UP, 1989.

MacLeod, Anne Scott. "From Rational to Romantic: The Children of Children's Literature in the Nineteenth Century." *Poetics Today* 13 (1992): 141–54.

Mandeville, Bernard. *The Fable of the Bees: or, Private Vices, Publick Benefits*. Ed. F. B. Kaye. 2 vols. Oxford: Clarendon P, 1924.

McGann, Jerome J. *The Romantic Ideology: A Critical Investigation*. Chicago: U of Chicago P, 1983.

McGavran, James Holt, Jr., ed. *Romanticism and Children's Literature in Nineteenth-Century England*. Athens: U of Georgia P, 1991.

McGillis, Roderick. "Childhood and Growth: George MacDonald and William Wordsworth." *Romanticism and Children's Literature in Nineteenth-Century England*. Ed. James Holt McGavran, Jr. Athens: U of Georgia P, 1991. 150–67.

Miller, Ken. "Fixing the Capitalist Road." *The Nation*, February 21, 1994, 242–44.

Mitchell, Juliet. *Psychoanalysis and Feminism: Freud, Reich, Laing and Women*. New York: Vintage, 1975.

Moskowitz, Ellen. "Two Mothers." *Hastings Center Report* (March–April 1995): 42.

Myers, Mitzi. "Impeccable Governesses, Rational Dames, and Moral Mothers: Mary Wollstonecraft and the Female Tradition in Georgian Children's Books." *Children's Literature* 14 (1986): 31–59.

———. "Little Girls Lost: Rewriting Romantic Childhood, Righting Gender and Genre." *Teaching Children's Literature: Issues, Pedagogy, Resources*. Ed. Glenn Edward Sadler. New York: Modern Language Association of America, 1992. 131–42.

———. "Romancing the Moral Tale: Maria Edgeworth and the Problematics of Pedagogy." *Romanticism and Children's Literature in Nineteenth-Century England*. Ed. James Holt McGavran, Jr. Athens: U of Georgia P, 1991. 96–128.

Nodelman, Perry. "The Other: Orientalism, Colonialism, and Children's Literature." *Children's Literature Association Quarterly* 17 (1992): 29–35.

Perkins, David. *Is Literary History Possible?* Baltimore: Johns Hopkins UP, 1992.

Pinchbeck, Ivy, and Margaret Hewitt. *Children in English Society.* 2 vols. London: Routledge and Kegan Paul, 1969–73.

Place, Francis. *The Autobiography of Francis Place.* Ed. Mary Thrale. Cambridge: Cambridge UP, 1972.

Plotz, Judith. "The Perpetual Messiah: Romanticism, Childhood, and the Paradoxes of Human Development." *Regulated Children/Liberated Children: Education in Psychohistorical Perspective.* Ed. Barbara Finkelstein. New York: Psychohistory P, 1979.

Plumb, J. H. "The New World of Children in Eighteenth-Century England." *Past and Present* 67 (1975): 64–93.

Postman, Neil. *The Disappearance of Childhood.* New York: Delacorte P, 1982.

Richardson, Alan. "Childhood and Romanticism." *Teaching Children's Literature: Issues, Pedagogy, Resources.* Ed. Glenn Edward Sadler. New York: Modern Language Association of America, 1992. 121–30.

———. *Literature, Education, and Romanticism: Reading as Social Practice, 1780–1832.* Cambridge: Cambridge UP, 1994.

Rose, Jacqueline. *The Case of Peter Pan, or The Impossibility of Children's Fiction.* 2nd rev. ed. London: Macmillan, 1993.

Ross, Marlon B. *The Contours of Masculine Desire: Romanticism and the Rise of Women's Poetry.* New York: Oxford UP, 1989.

Sendak, Maurice. *Pierre: A Cautionary Tale.* New York: Harper and Row, 1962.

Shaaban, Bouthaina. "The Romantics in the Chartist Press." *Keats-Shelley Journal* 38 (1989): 26–29.

Shahar, Shulamith. *Childhood in the Middle Ages.* London: Routledge, 1990.

Siskin, Clifford L. *The Historicity of Romantic Discourse.* New York: Oxford UP, 1988.

Sommerville, C. John. *The Rise and Fall of Childhood.* New York: Vintage, 1990.

Spiegelman, Willard. *Wordsworth's Heroes.* Berkeley: U of California P, 1985.

Stone, Lawrence. "The Massacre of the Innocents." *New York Review of Books,* November 14, 1974, 25–31.

Summerfield, Geoffrey. *Fantasy and Reason: Children's Literature in the Eighteenth Century.* Athens: U of Georgia P, 1984.

Suransky, Valerie Polakow. *The Erosion of Childhood.* Chicago: U of Chicago P, 1982.

Toffler, Alvin. *The Third Wave.* New York: Bantam, 1981.

UNICEF. *The State of the World's Children 1995.* New York: Oxford UP, 1995.

Walkerdine, Valerie. "On the Regulation of Speaking and Silence: Subjectivity, Class, and Gender in Contemporary Schooling," *Language, Gender and Childhood*. Ed. Carolyn Steedman, Cathy Urwin, and Valerie Walkerdine. London: Routledge and Kegan Paul, 1985.

Zelizer, Viviana A. *Pricing the Priceless Child: The Changing Social Value of Children*. New York: Basic Books, 1985.

Mitzi Myers

READING CHILDREN AND HOMEOPATHIC ROMANTICISM: PARADIGM LOST, REVISIONARY GLEAM, OR "PLUS ÇA CHANGE, PLUS C'EST LA MÊME CHOSE"?

his two-part essay is about reading children—the historical and contemporary narratives we've constructed about them—and about reading children reading in texts.[1] It's a story about competing representations of literary childhood: its admittedly Utopian closure positions the cross-writing linking child and adult as central to revisionist theories of aesthetic and social representation, as well as to the new academic field of cultural studies. My story moves from "big" history as currently organized, the children's literature version of those grand metanarratives deplored by postmodernists like Jean-François Lyotard, the ways we habitually map, traverse, and colonize vast sweeps of juvenile territory, to a "local" narrative which thematizes—and makes uncanny—the reading child within a story that children once read. It's thus about two ways of spatializing narratives of childhood. The first part interrogates the Romantic explanatory paradigm of childhood and children's literature which organizes the discipline we practice and still inflects what we inscribe under the sign of the child. The second part shows how a postmodern perspective on the child's reading and the child character's reading of real cultural secrets within a fictional tale, Maria Edgeworth's "The Good Aunt" (1801), offers a revisionary gleam (or at least flicker). Via a metafictional and somewhat vertiginous regress of textual spaces (readers reflecting on books they read in books we read about them), I'll suggest how reading children in past texts can be construed to question the readings of children we're so used to that we think of them as inevitable and only "natural." My aim is to denaturalize the masculinist high Romantic discourse of childhood—the commonplaces essentializing The Child as imaginative, intuitive, spontaneous, free (we can all fill in the remaining blanks)—and to contextualize a Revolutionary child who

simultaneously embodies the historian's "moment of danger" and the postmodern and postcolonial theorist's crisis of representation (Benjamin 255).[2]

How does Romanticism help or hinder the development of theoretically sophisticated children's literary studies in a postmodern age? What do we mean when we talk about Romanticism or the Romantic child anyway? If adultist Romanticists are currently engaged in interrogating, rethinking, and rediscovering the multiplicities of their discipline, how does (or should) that problematize our own task of establishing our academic viability and scholarly standing? After all, the Romantic child is our foundational fiction, our originary myth, and just how hard it is to distance ourselves from the "always already" saidness of the Romantic literary discourse on childhood almost any critical analysis or historical overview that comes to hand readily (if sometimes inadvertently) testifies. It's a given that overviews of childhood and Romanticism for a child-oriented venue will direct their energies toward adult male poets, but the grown-up critical establishment doesn't take turns. Introducing a collection of essays on children's moral and political status, Geoffrey Scarre observes that the problem with children in philosophical thinking is that they haven't been a problem. The same thing might be said for adultist criticism of the Romantic canon. With notable exceptions, what officially counts as children's literature is remarkable for its absence from adult Romantic critique. If juvenile poems or prose do appear, they typically function like Cinderella's ugly stepsisters — the puerile or, if religious, senile foils who glamorize Wordsworth or Blake, those founding fathers who (along with Locke, Rousseau, and occasionally Coleridge and Lamb) gave birth to modern literary childhood.

This erasure of certifiable children's literature in Romantic criticism is nothing new, but is the genealogy we revere equally venerable? Or might we more fruitfully consider ourselves foundlings in search of a history? Maybe the orphan trope works as well for us as it does for so many of our favorite authors. Let's consider one of the funnier discards in the everybody-read-it-then-but-nobody-reads-it-now bin of literary history, a little work that first appeared anonymously in 1812. *Rejected Addresses* delighted English readers for years and was soon claimed by its owners, Horace and James Smith. Often reissued, it was noticed in the *Edinburgh Review* (a big honor — not many literary works were). When Francis Jeffrey reprinted his contributions to the journal in the 1840s, he updated his original remarks by reiterating his praise and noting how well the parodic poems stood up: the intervening decades hadn't dated the satire. Although *Rejected Addresses* isn't a work for young readers (but then neither were Wordsworth's or Blake's poems), it's important to children's literary history all the same as an indicator of environing cultural attitudes. With glee and accuracy, the parodists seize on every literary figure's style and idée fixe. The Wordsworth entry is "The Baby's Debut," little Nancy Lake's account of intrafamilial affairs, catching with "very extraordinary merit and felicity," in Jeffrey's phrase, the author's "maukish affectations of childish simplicity and nursery stammering" (4: 470n, 475). Drawn on stage in a child's chaise by her uncle's porter, Nancy recounts her quarrel with her nine-year-old brother over a new wax doll and a top: "Jack's in the pouts —and this it is, / He thinks mine came to more than his," so he melts off the doll's nose, literally defacing the toy (Smith and Smith 48).

Barbara Garlitz argues that Wordsworth's "Immortality" ode "had a far more profound influence on nineteenth-century thought than is generally realized," but it's surely a gross overstatement to suggest that the ode was "as powerful an influence on nineteenth-century ideas of childhood as Freud . . . on present day ones"; had she consulted sales figures and numbers of editions, Garlitz could never have made the unfounded claim that Wordsworth "was the favorite poet of most people in the nineteenth century" ("The Immortality Ode" 639, 646).[3] To Romanticists who revere Wordsworth's dialogues between child and adult as serious canonical poetry, it may be disconcerting to find the poet's representations of child language and the natural child adjudged his weakest link, a defacement of the poetic persona as well as Nancy's doll, especially when reprints explain that the Smiths admire Wordsworth's *real* poems: it's just that his sentimentalized Romantic child is ridiculous (xxiv). It is of course precisely this puerile and juvenile Wordsworth who's the target of the reviewers' long-running campaign against the "Lakers." Clearly, however much different schools and factions may have newly valued child life, what currently canonized Romantics thought about childhood wasn't what everybody thought (nor were Romantics themselves, including Wordsworth, of one mind).

Yet no children's literary history can forbear quoting Charles Lamb's letter to Coleridge on what children should read as if it voiced a cultural consensus; it so vividly sets up a dichotomy between Science and Poetry and so rhetorically dragoons the reader into endorsing fairy tales and deploring women writers (Marrs 2: 81–82). But, leaving aside Lamb's gender bias and his misremembering of *Goody Two Shoes* (hardly the amoral classic he recalls), does this discussion really record the baby's debut in children's literary history? When did the Romantic child emerge? Does the nineteenth century express the smoothly developing and coherent pattern we've assumed it did? How do questions of literary production and consumption enter into all this? We've hardly begun to ask, much less answer, fundamental questions about publishing history, literacy, gender, canon formation, or cross-writing (the multiple positionalities of child and adult in works, authors, and audiences).[4] Could it be that Lamb's binary oppositions and Romantic ideologies play a much bigger role in children's literary histories of the *twentieth* century than they do earlier? Did *modernism* in fact fashion a unified Romantic child, projecting it back onto the past and producing a fallaciously coherent narrative from the illogical and the illegible?[5] And if we increasingly view with suspicion Romantic ideologies distinguishing adult works, don't we also need to be alert to the covert Romantic premises that undergird much critical thinking about children's literature?

By situating the formation of subjectivity in history, in language, in story, in the lived realities of social existence, recent reinterpretive work helps us rethink the *grands récits* of children's literature history along lines more contemporaneously relevant *and* more historically referential than the customary Romantic mythologies. Sharing Lyotard's suspicion of the large and the universalizing, feminist, postmodern, and postcolonial theorists image the little narratives that they oppose to conventional big history in local, spatial terms: a "space of translation: a place of hybridity"; the site of "border crossings" and "border pedagogy"; a postnationalist cultural locale that is "multidimensional" and "deterritorialized." Especially relevant for educators, children's literature specialists, and the historical school story that is my exemplary text is Mary Louise Pratt's formulation of the sites and techniques that embody the "all-important concept of *cultural mediation.*"[6] As social spaces where cultures meet and clash, "contact zones" necessitate pedagogical places—safe houses —where groups can construct themselves as communities through shared understandings, including exercises in storytelling and in identifying with the "ideas, interests, histories, and attitudes of others" and in engagement with "suppressed aspects of history (including their own histories)": the disturbing home truths that Freud stages as uncanny dramas of self-reflexivity, the discovery of the psychological and political secrets in "remote corners of [one's] own being" that render home unhomelike (Pratt 40; Freud 243).

The dialogic, multiply situated, and, on occasion, counterhegemonic subjectivities valorized by postcolonialists can be discerned in past fictions as well as present theories, especially in the doubly marginalized genres of women's writing for children. In re-viewing the ways that children's subjectivity is constructed and represented in past literature, conversational scenes of instruction and depictions of reading prove especially helpful, because the character's interaction with others and with text models for child readers of the story as well as for modern critics how the world and the work interact, how a narrative educates as well as what it discusses. If all stories for young people inevitably teach ("ideology," "didacticism," same difference), then what representational strategies do different genres, genders, and periods maneuver? Because Maria Edgeworth's tales for youth as well as adults are chock-full of books and because her allusions so often link the characters' fictional activity of reading to the larger social contexts within which the author writes, her scenes of reading and writing function as notably privileged, potentially uncanny textual spaces. As Commonwealth theorist Helen Tiffin observes, postmodernism and postcolonialism as often designate certain reading strategies, ways of isolating and examining cultural topoi and techniques, as they do time periods, so my model of a Revolutionary *petit récit* is a pioneering story for adolescents, one of the first specifically composed for that audience (vii–viii). Written in 1797, amid the unrest that exploded in the French invasion and the Irish Rebellion of 1798, when the Edgeworths fled home as exiles, "The Good Aunt" appeared in *Moral Tales for Young People* (1801), a collection of young adult novelettes rightly advertised by its publisher as something "new." A feminist and theoretically informed "cross-reading" of a problematic tale for a problematic audience, I believe, allows us to re-vision the female author's cross-writing as simultaneously an interrogation of her own period's master narratives and of conventional juvenile literary history's Romantic metanarrative.

In masculine narrative history as in the male writer's historical romances and Romantic poetry, "man's truth" depends on the relocation of the woman and the nurturant activities she encodes above, below, beyond, someplace other than the public and political narrative of the past that (like lots of other juvenile readers) Jane Austen's Catherine Morland can't abide: the "real solemn history" full of "good for nothing" men, hardly any women, and, she might have added, no children at all.[7] Yet for critics who want to rethink the cultural relationships between past and present, public and private, or self and Other, childhood and its literatures—the *sub*culture par excellence—might seem the obvious place to start. After all, as historians specially concerned with children's use of the past remind us, "The particular usefulness of childhood . . . is that it represents in itself an explanatory narrative; childhood is about how we got to be the way we are" (Steedman 27). Nevertheless, despite the theoretical bombardment to which we have long been subjected, despite the recognition that all texts (and interpretations) are historically and ideologically conditioned, despite the preoccupation with Difference, the Other, the Colonized, the Repressed, and the Marginal, it seldom occurs to the contemporary critical elite that works for, about, and/or by children are ideal investigatory sites for posing questions about alterity and the dynamics between the metropolitan center and its peripheries.

Although postmodern and postcolonial theorists often brilliantly illuminate the tortured symbiosis of the colonizer and the colonized, recent critical discourses can also reveal disturbingly reductive attitudes toward the child as signifier and historical construct, as well as inattention to multiple traditions of cross-cultural criticism in children's literary studies—by both critics *and* writers of juvenile literature. Nevertheless, if our methodology and empathy are agile enough to read *back* across time, we can enter into cross-cultural rapprochements *of* that time which haven't been hitherto noted—perhaps because, as with some postmodern theorists, work self-consciously constructed under the sign of the child and construing that sign positively gets erased as an ideological impossibility, perhaps because, as with some children's literature critics, the survey genre chosen forecloses richer possibilities than the juridical mode of indictment or exculpation. In one staple metanarrative, the juvenile historian ransacks a vast body of writing for imperialist or racist quotes that earn the collective authors a critical spanking, as with boys' adventure novels. In another overview format, sentiments extracted from a heterogeneous array of writers win them a gold star, as with juvenile genres expressing antislavery sentiments. The question of color in past children's books—how that culture read color and how we should read that culture's reading—seems especially prone to produce evaluative assessment rather than contextualized interpretation.[8] However much we need revisionary, culturally situated accounts of literary childhood, thinking of representations of children only as unproblematic socialization narratives which "Other," smother, and colonize the child subject may prove as reductive as the commonplaces of idealizing Romantic regression or the currently modish voyeurism of the erotic gaze.

The temptation of the postcolonial children's literature survey is to fall into the same style of oppositional "Othering" that rigidifies some current theory. Take, for example, Edward W. Said's monolithic *Orientalism* (1978) and *Culture and Imperialism* (1993), still the most influential figurations of the imperialist West versus the Other, or Abdul R. JanMohamed's taxonomy of colonialist discourse, "The Economy of Manichean Allegory: The Function of Racial Difference in Colonialist Literature," originally published in *Critical Inquiry* in 1985 and reprinted in the much-cited anthology *"Race," Writing, and Difference*, a compendium of postmodern and postcolonial theoretical approaches variously configuring the titular topics.[9] Said's critics challenge Orientalism because it posits a rigid binarism of the West versus the rest (the rational male adult versus the childish feminized Other); because it reduces messy histories and heterogeneous traditions of representation to one "totalizing" and univocal metanarrative; and because its depiction of colonial domination and hegemony allows no possibility for the subordinated Empire to talk or write back, much less for critical intervention or border crossings by Western intellectuals of the past.

Almost as often cited as Said's discourse of Orientalism, JanMohamed's influential argument similarly reads all colonialist literary representation as the discursive analogue of material exploitation, a commodification of the native subject that preempts the alien Other as a resource for the white man's fictions. Although it assumes multiple allegorical forms (good/evil, white/black, and so on), the "manichean opposition between the putative superiority of the European and the supposed inferiority of the native" proves inescapable, drawing even writers critical of imperialism "into its vortex." Theoretically, Europeans can respond to the Other in terms of identity or difference. Practically, moral superiority grounded in power relations typically erases any notion of community or collectivity: "instead of seeing the native as a bridge toward syncretic possibility, it uses him as a mirror that reflects the colonialist's self-image" (JanMohamed 82, 84). Gender has little presence and no contestatory valence in these arguments from alterity. The Manichean Allegory is, among other things, a paradigm of the heavy father and the oppressed child which replicates and recycles the negativity it finds in recurrent colonialist and imperialist alignments of the nonwhite with the juvenile and the feminine. Revisionary genealogists of twentieth-century children's literary studies can agree with Satya P. Mohanty that "the separate world of childhood registers and refracts crucial political anxieties of imperial Britain" without also discovering in "the values of childhood a thin allegory for imperial ideology," a pedagogic project which pits the juvenile subject in training for imperial selfhood against the infantilized native Other (22, 31).

Whether we choose to label the current multifaceted critique of the Western master narratives which privilege abstract reason and imperial domination as Orientalism or Manichean Allegory, much cross-cultural, postcolonial, or non-Eurocentric critical theory is ultimately predicated on a model of the child and the world. Paradoxically, one way to evade the homogenizing hegemony and binary discourse of the Manichean opposition might be to transvalue the customary denigration of "native" as child, to take the feminized juvenile seriously as a syncretic locus of revisionary community. We are all natives of somewhere; we have all been children.[10] Paradoxically, too, I suggest, the revisionary way forward in children's literary studies is backward. Rather than re-viewing our disciplinary genealogy as an unproblematic Romantic legacy, a simple story with one identifiable plot, what do we see if we follow out Walter Benjamin's notion of history as an unstable past contingent on present consciousness, if we try to grasp "the constellation which [our] own era has formed with a definite earlier one" (263)? Read postcolonially, colonial scenes of writing and reading challenge academic feminism and children's literary studies to transform the way we tend to view children's and women's literary history. The notion that we discover who we are through encounters with an Other—sometimes empathetic, sometimes exploitative—is as much a commonplace of Enlightened travel writing and tales as it is of postcolonial theory and postmodern anthropological critique. As James Clifford succinctly puts it, "every version of an 'other' . . . is also the construction of a 'self'" ("Introduction" 23). In some more recent work, even Said invokes "identitarian thought" and calls for a "new and more inclusive counternarrative of liberation" that evades both Lyotard's postmodern amnesia (the rejection of history) and the monovocal story of domination and hegemony that Said's own Orientalism has popularized. Perhaps influenced by feminist and postcolonial critics who are developing the heterogeneity of the Other within as well as outside Western configurations, he invokes "exile, immigration, and the crossing of boundaries" as "experiences that can provide us with new narrative forms or, in John Berger's phrase, *other* ways of telling" ("Representing" 225).

Read as a problematic textual space, at once brutal contact zone and regenerative safe house, "The Good Aunt" is a local narrative with transcultural implications, a gendered "little" history which enables other ways of constituting adultstream feminism and literature as well as men's metanarratives of Romantic childhood. Produced at a highly charged political moment marked by domestic insurrection in Ireland and Revolutionary wars abroad, its Enlightened narrative of domestic and public schooling is also a paradigm of colonial encounters, of difference and dislocation: it is as remarkable for its obsession with exploitation, secrets, and torture as for its celebration of affective community and its democratization of educational and cultural representation.[11] Maria Edgeworth's tale foregrounds the interconnections among reading, writing, and affectivity and their foundational role in constructing juvenile subjectivity and cultural community. At the micro level of textual politics, the story represents via personal interrelationships and literary intertextuality the ongoing process through which notions of subjectivity and agency develop and continually change. Cross-writing genders, generations, and ethnicities, Edgeworth as authorial good aunt moves easily among the empathic identifications the fiction seeks from adolescent readers: with Frances Howard, the tale's surrogate mother (once a needy child herself); with her orphan protégé, Charles Howard; with "little Oliver," the parentless exile from Jamaica, as scarred by the failings of his mother country as by the brutalities of British educational custom; and with Cuba, the uncanny "figure of the mulatto woman" who haunts the story (74). A mediatory and liminal freed slave whose dignity, love, and gratitude enable her to gaze and to speak back, Cuba is at once the childhood "best friend" of Frances

(96), the reminiscence of Oliver's beloved Jamaican nurse, and (along with little Oliver) the tale's unlikely solver of mysteries, including perhaps the story's darkest secret, the ghastly groan occasioned by Oliver's reading: the climactic moment that any revisionary cross-reading must account for.[12]

Almost every page of "The Good Aunt" mentions some work's being read or written. Like most of Edgeworth's tales (including those for children and adolescents), it is a strikingly allusive and intertextual narrative; unlike what one might expect from the author's "utilitarian" reputation, few of the references serve solely to relay information, though the reader learns where to go for smoky chimneys, hummingbird habits, and horrific scenes of mutilation and murder. Actual books engender the narrative line of "The Good Aunt," but men's accounts are re-dressed by an Anglo-Irish female writer who creatively exploits her ambiguous status as child and adult, colonized and colonizer, a woman telling tales about a boys' world, a provincial from a country conventionally "feminized" in British political rhetoric. "The Good Aunt" cites Edward Gibbon's autobiographical vignette of his aunt Catherine Porten, "the true mother of my mind," and develops his account of his troubled schooling at Westminster into a complex and complexly gendered critique not just of England's great public schools and the "manly" boys they produce but of Britain's emergent classed, commercial, and colonialist empire as well.[13] Similarly, recycling Thomas Day's originary masculinist myth of the bad little West Indian boy re-educated into emancipationist English ways, Edgeworth simultaneously regenders and revisions Day's *Sandford and Merton* (1783, 1786, 1789) and his famous abolitionist poem "The Dying Negro" (1773), humanizing his suicidal Noble Savage into the living and loving Cuba.[14]

Pragmatically accepted as the passport to a man's world, the disciplinary space of boys' classical public school training figures, like much else in the tale, as a suspect paternal inheritance. Russell, Charles Howard's classics tutor and friend, follows him to Westminster School when the good aunt must turn from privately teaching her nephew to keeping a dame's house for boarders; all her fortune was lost at sea when she disentangled herself from the Jamaican plantation and hence complicity in slavery her grandfather had left her; baby Charles had originally become her charge after his father dissipated his fortune and died "in a duel, about some *debt of hon-*

our, which had been contracted at the gambling table" (1). Edgeworth's subacid wit shapes the representation of the world men have made throughout. Westminster (at that time among the most prestigious and most brutal of the great institutions) is the site for a school story developing the relationship between two heroes, Howard, whose strength in challenging the masculinist, hierarchical ethos of the public school derives from the good aunt of the title, and little Oliver, among the most lovable of Edgeworth's many displaced young persons. He's a Creole sent to England for education: insecure, semiliterate, afflicted with the colonialist habits of thinking endemic to Jamaica's white planters, assaulted by the brutality of the bully Augustus Holloway, an alderman's son, whose fag he is. The appropriately named Holloway and his idol, Lord Rawson, son of the earl of Marryborough, who pillages the youth just as the dubiously aristocratic earl pillages the boy's father, exemplify Edgeworth's class (and gendered) worry that the independent and intellectually renovative values of the aspiring middling orders would be stifled by the reliance on rules and caste privilege synonymous with public school education. Despite his skill with "elegant Latin verses," the alderman's son cares nothing for literature or relationships unless they can be commodified to "*solid gold*" (78). Sycophantic toward dissolute aristocrats, whose "manly" ways with horses and gambling he burns to emulate, the nouveau riche Holloway routinely abuses Oliver, and since his tyranny leaves the child no time to memorize Latin lessons, Holloway's sadism insures Oliver's regular official flogging for stupidity as well: "I will make a slave of him, if I chuse it —a negro slave, if I please!" (33). And, backed by the thoughtless followers who also make the suffering Oliver their butt, Holloway delivers on his boast.[15]

Through Oliver's interactions with peers and superiors, helpers and villains, and figures as anomalous as himself in England's insular society, such as the manumitted Cuba (who emblematizes the bonds of love) and the Jewish peddler (who stands for the competing cash nexus), the story structure explores the Jamaican boy's multiple significations as colonizer and colonized. Moving, troubling, and complexly used, Edgeworth's Oliver is a striking variant of this period's stereotypical Creole brat shipped to the mother country to be schooled and reformed: a familiar feature in children's stories from Day's *Sandford and Merton* in the 1780s to the early twentieth century when Frances Hodgson Burnett's Mary supplies the Indian equivalent. Little monsters spoiled rotten by misguided parents and corrupted by the tyranny inevitable in a slave society, they embody the evils that colonialist culture wreaks on the white masters as well as the black victims. Greedy, illiterate, proud, simultaneously lazy and tumultuous, the terror of the well-ordered English households which take them in, they usually transgress gender norms as well: the boys are effete and sickly; the girls, boisterous and physically violent. Day's terrible Tommy Merton leaps upon the tea table to gorge himself faster but is always puny and afraid of spoiling his fine clothes. Lucy Peacock's Arabella, enraged when a virtuous black thwarts her schemes for illicit nocturnal pleasures, insists that "Negroes have no souls," so "the more they are beaten, the better servants they are" (August 1788: 468–70). Before she gets religion, Barbara Hofland's exuberantly wicked Matilda shrieks for "[s]ome beer, you black beetle!" and dashes her glass in the face of Zebby, simultaneously demonstrating to the reader that she's a "young vixen," and her obsequious and loving former slave is a saint (10–11). If the mother country exports moral evils as well as material goods, the repatriation of rotten progeny brings it all back home. Yet the tensions of these stories are as typically unresolved as their characters are one-dimensional; content to reform the youthful colonial sinner, few children's writers venture on Day's searing indictment of England's class and commercial society.[16] Fewer still enlist such narrative complexities as the intertextuality and metafictional episodes which not only unravel the mysteries of "The Good Aunt" but also work as models for decoding both the fictional strategies that construct it and the real-life world that environs and intrudes upon it. Nor does the usual Creole conversion tale invite young readers to inhabit multiple subject positions, to appreciate shrewd social satire as well as generous feeling, to examine their own hearts of darkness, or to be the engaged interpretants who carry the story's cultural work back into the real-life world.

Most surveys of school stories proceed as if Thomas Hughes had invented them; when overviews of historical children's literature do address early examplars like "The Good Aunt," the generalizing commentary normalizes dissonances and complexities.[17] Situating the tale within a generic context rather than its historical milieu, commentators notice only the six bruising fights between the novice Howard and the accomplished Holloway. The conventional boy hero's triumph over the school bully as well as a woman writer's mock-epic version of the Homeric battle and the aristocratic duel of honor, the marathon is a small though crucial part of Edgeworth's tale.[18] It emancipates Oliver from fagdom to friendship, mocks the public school ethos Holloway embraces, and validates as virile Howard's capacity to think for himself, his challenging of outmoded customs, and his assumption of his aunt's role as nurturing teacher. Sneered at because he's "of *woman bred*," teased as a "saint," a "quiz," and a "prig" by the Westminster rowdies, Charles Howard is nevertheless the unlikely hero of a Rebellion narrative. When he transgresses school custom and impertinently interferes with Holloway's authority as fagmaster, Howard is following his aunt's parting advice and that of Cicero's oracle as well: "making his own genius, and not the opinion of the people, the guide of his life" (37, 24). Both the friend and the innovative mentor of an adoring pupil, Howard, like his strong-minded and unsentimental aunt, demonstrates the conceptual instability of this period's discourses of maternity, of masculinity, and of subjectivity as well.

As was his aunt before him (and her creator), Howard is insatiably curious about everything from travel books to daily life, not just the Westminster boy culture of Latin grammar and "the mysteries of trap-ball and marbles" (26). He too is an inspiriting instructor, privileging conversation and vernacular language and, significantly for the story's larger themes, democratizing "genius": once disabused of the masculinist, elitist, and Romantic notion of innate genius, once convinced that everyone is educable, Oliver is transformed to a "new creature" (39, 58–63). Most important, Howard is an aspiring author who makes things happen in the world. At first a lively writer of domestic letters, he then earns money with his translations that helps transform the community, and his English essay wins him a Westminster medal which little Oliver, another embodiment of Howard's achievement, gets to present. Oliver identifies the author from the older boy's signature motto, "HE, WHO ALLOWS OPPRESSION, SHARES THE CRIME"—the last couplet of Erasmus Darwin's antislavery set piece to Britannia's laggard "BANDS OF SENATORS!" (2: 165). When the governmental figures "high in power" see the boy's work in print, their recognition of its merits underlines what so many of the story's episodes illustrate: the power of the book, the permeable boundary between literature and history, and the dialogic interplay of public and private spheres. Offered a munificent reward, the good aunt and her well-taught pupil turn it down; Howard will make his own way; he isn't for sale (79, 99).[19]

As reader and writer, Charles Howard is, like his aunt Frances, associated throughout with the affiliative, the enabling, and the liberatory. Like her, too, he is positioned within a symbolic structure which domesticates the world into family and transforms contaminated living spaces into healthy environments. As Frances Howard rescues her baby nephew and manumits her childhood friend, the mulatto Cuba, so Charles in turn liberates Oliver and earns the passionate gratitude he also demonstrates: "You first made me love you, by teaching me that I was not a blockhead, and by freeing me," exclaims Oliver, who becomes a boarder in the good aunt's extended household, as will Cuba eventually (140). But in the interim, even before he knows who she is, Howard gives the mulatto woman a clean, tidy English room of her own. No longer the "smoky, dismal, miserable place" where she was carried when flung from the top of the coach Holloway was racing in manly frolic, all is now transformed, not "by magic" but by a boy's "industry and abilities" (94).

Much of the story's wit and charm come from its transgression of sexist, ageist, and racist stereotypes, worked out through Edgeworth's emblematic contrasts, empathic identifications, and dazzling plot contrivances: the agentic children who, ironically, manifest manly honor because they're enmeshed in everyday life and vernacular language versus the impressionable Latinist Holloway, flattered and duped by the masculinist rhetoric of coachmen and gamesters; the interwoven fates of the two commodities lost in the coach crash, Cuba, who doesn't count, dumped in a ditch, and the gold muslin "booked" (insured) gown, which does; the purposive, industrious, and grateful Cuba (she's traveled all the way from Jamaica to find Frances) versus young Holloway's brutality ("I shan't stir for a *mulatto*, I promise you"); and the comically bigoted yet sympathetic postilion and gardener who help the "poor copper-coloured soul" because "she belongs to nobody, she's quite a stranger in these parts, and doesn't know no more than a child where to go." Although she can't speak "good English" (like them), that's her "only fault . . . but we can't be born what we like, or she would have been as good an Englishman as the best of us" (51, 54, 94). In refiguring the child's story from a master myth statically demarcating an economy of complicity and guilt, Edgeworth's multiple and shifting alignments of gender and generation cross-write race too. As threshold or "becoming" figures, the young are proverbially liminal—marginal beings who traverse boundaries and thus unite disparate states—but, as much recent work in diverse disciplines attests, "liminars" also include territorial, gender, ethnic, racial, and intellectual border crossers, as well as the tortured and the dying. However oppressed or exploited, liminars are inherently political, for their peripheral status simultaneously encodes potential communal power.[20]

Neither the Child of Nature nor the Noble Savage beloved by early-twentieth-century literary historians and Romanticists, Oliver and Cuba elude the binaries of the Manichean opposition through their figuration as liminars and revenants, those who cross over and come back. Demonstrating how cultures make, mar, and revitalize children, Oliver starts with the conventional Jamaican vices (indolence, a passionate temper, linguistic disabilities—the so-called Quashiba mentality and syntax derived from omnipresent slave attendants), but his generous affection and capacity for gratitude go beyond the usual Creole openheartedness. Just as we never see Cuba embodying the stereotypes of laziness, frivolity, evasiveness, and lying, we never see Oliver knocking his "inferiors" about as does the typical West Indian product. Understanding marginality and vulnerability, the orphaned Oliver favors Cuba before he meets her because she recalls his mulatto surrogate mother. Emotionally as well as bodily, "the figure of the mulatto woman" thus interrogates the separatist logic of slavery by melding together the West and the Other. Despite the subaltern linguistic dialect they initially share as Jamaican immigrants, the child Oliver and the reborn Cuba are positively coded as liminal and revisionary characters, and not merely in terms of the passionate gratitude and affiliative power—the richly communicative emotional literacy—they manifest. In culture's symbolic logic, as Orlando Patterson notes, the "release from slavery is life-giving and life-creating," undoing the natal alienation and cultural death of enslavement through a complex mode of gift exchange.[21] Postcolonial critics have recently made much of the silenced Other, especially of the black female Other, and of the objectified "native," the looked at who cannot return the patriarch's colonizing gaze, who cannot tell her own story or interpret the white man's world. Like the mutes of melodrama, who function as pure signs of virtue, Cuba's actions are mostly gestural, but she also looks and describes "so accurately" that her words unmask Holloway, disclosing to the boy's silly mother and to Mr. Supine, his neglectful tutor, that their lad of spirit, not Howard, is the villain of the stage-coach mystery, the reckless driver who lamed and abandoned Cuba and cost the coachman his job (114).[22]

Just as Holloway is about to be publicly exposed at Westminster as a brute, a liar, and a cheat (he's involved in an illegal lottery with the Jewish pawnbroker, Mr. Carat, among other schemes), there's a violent rupture in the narrative—thematically and literally—which positions the child reader, along with Oliver, as the involved inter-pretant who must simultaneously decode this textual mystery and the real-life world that produced it. While the progressive comic plot works through the tangled events by which Oliver solves the mystery of Cuba's odd golden thimble, thus restoring to the good aunt her lost childhood friend, her grandmother's jewels, and her hijacked fortune, Edgeworth's uncanny scene (115–20) stops the narrative dead, disrupting the tale's Enlightenment values as well as its tem-poral progression. Readers reveling in child power and morally de-termined action, in the heady sense that the young shape their own fate, must, like the protagonist, negotiate a startling shift of perspec-tive: an intertextual (indeed, metafictional) moment that, in thema-tizing reading, appeals to a poetics and politics of identity even as it traumatizes ideologies of universal kinship and virtue rewarded. By this point in the tale, Oliver is, thanks to Howard's nurturing and teaching, the "new creature" whose reclamation functions meto-nymically in the story's reconstitution of viable community. For instead of the cold cash currently governing both England's old hi-erarchies and the newer commodity culture that calls itself the fash-ionable world, "The Good Aunt" redefines a British cultural identity predicated on vernacular education, democratized "genius," and af-filiative gift exchange. No longer an indolent and despairing "block-head," Oliver is now aligned with the enlightened Howards, who "hate secrets" and "hate mysteries" (74, 111). He's become a gener-ous and capable friend, a close reader of cultural texts and symbols, and a clever intellectual sleuth who brings to light the *unheimlich*, Freud's telltale "forces" in "remote corners" of the self as well as the social (243).

Because representations of the child reading commingle the ma-terial and imaginative worlds, depicting a physical presence whose mind is someplace where the adult viewer cannot travel, such depic-tions tend to become iconic for interpretation itself. Far from simple nostalgic reminders of childhood's pastness, they signify both the child's struggles to make the world make sense and the grown-up viewer's struggles to make sense of the child. The original frontispiece for this volume dramatically depicts a voyeuristic tableau of the boy reading, the cynosure of all eyes who watch him as he explores the ideological and psychic spaces his "large book" discloses. Thus the little Creole's scene of instruction is the penultimate climax for which the child reader has been primed from the start. If "The Good Aunt" associates the arts of education with generous gifts, reciprocal gratitude, and the consequent formation of an inclusive social community, a domesticated public sphere, Edgeworth's emblematic representation of Oliver's reverie unflinchingly links scenes of reading and writing with colonial revolt and repression too. Embedded within the sanctioned insurgency narratives of schoolboys and strong women challenging British things as they are is a bloodier rebellion report. Surrounded by the communal space of Frances Howard's drawing room, with its very relevant chat of imagination, Warton's ode to Fancy, and the "never ending debate upon original genius; including also the doctrine of hereditary temper and dispositions," Oliver's "little table" embodies a spatial metaphor of complex enclosures, a dramatization of the political uncanny as challenging to contemporary postcolonial critics as to the original teenage audience (fig. 1).[23] Freud's famous essay spells out what Edgeworth's interlude implies, the way that the *heimlich*, the protective domestic space, melds into the horrors of the *unheimlich*, the word that ought to be its opposite: *"everything that ought to have remained . . . secret and hidden but has come to light"* (224, quoting Schelling). Mostly cited to explicate psychic allegories of the return of the repressed, the notion of the uncanny elucidates politics too, that ideological juncture of the "will to interpret and the fear of what will be revealed" (Engle 113).

Transfixed by what he reads, almost setting himself afire with an unsnuffed candle, oblivious to the crowded room, Oliver suddenly interrupts the company's sociable conversation with a loud groan: "There was, by common consent, a general silence in the room, whilst every one looked at Oliver, as at a picture." He clutches the huge book with one hand and a tall china jar of West Indian sweetmeats just sent him by his uncle with the other—so spasmodically gripped that it cannot be pried from his arm. He is so engrossed in a

He was sitting at a little table intent upon his book &c p. 152.

Published Sep.r 1st 1801 by J. Johnson St. Paul's Church Yard.

FIGURE 1. Frontispiece from Maria Edgeworth's *Moral Tales for Young People*, 1801. Courtesy of the Department of Special Collections, Charles E. Young Research Library, UCLA.

different world that when kindly Dr. B., whom he reveres, tries to get his notice, Oliver impatiently shoves him away, snapping rudely, "Be quiet! I must finish this." It was, the text tells us, "the account of the execution of two rebel Koromantyn negroes, related in Edwards's History of the West Indies," and there's a footnote with the exact reference: "Volume II, page 57: second edition" (116).[24] The intertextual Edgeworth, who puts the facts, footnotes, and allusions she loves to work for her, gets lots of her effects from retelling in a different voice the cultural narratives available, and she always assumes her audience's lively curiosity and ability to make connections. But when inquisitive young readers' detective instincts send them straight to Edwards, they'll confront an interpretive dilemma: the graphic paradigm of the colonial encounter as patriarchal torture, the Manichean Allegory of oppressor and eclipsed Other in its grimmest form. The focalized reference is clearly a key piece in the story's puzzle, a challenge to the child reader's empathy and understanding, an even bigger challenge to the adult interpreter who must cross-read as that child and as a postimperialist critic too.

Taking JanMohamed's antithesis of imperialist oppressor versus erased native a step further, Terry Eagleton identifies the basic postcolonial critical model as, like Edgeworth's footnote, a literal scene of torture: "The flayed, crucified, disembowelled body has become a veritable emblem of this critical approach, which is always more fascinated by the victims of oppressive power than by those who successfully oppose it" (7).[25] Eagleton's blanket indictment assumes that the historical interpreter is torturing evidence, that the bodies are produced by the critic's own perverse agenda of what counts as context, not that they are encrypted in a text itself—much less in a child's book we've been conditioned to think innocuous. But clearly, Edgeworth's *Moral Tales for Young People* (like her French models) purvey cultural "moeurs," not sanitized maxims. Eagleton is nevertheless on target in challenging interpretive scenarios that reduce literary history to punitive powers confronting victimized Others. In thus denying resources for resistance and hope to the blacks, Indians, peasants, or adolescents whose vulnerability it depicts, postcolonial practice, Eagleton implies, reproduces the punitive power it critiques.

In complex children's literature where the compensatory and the dystopian meet, however, torturing evidence can figure otherwise, not just dramatizing brutal power relations as inescapable but galvanizing young protagonists and readers into imagining a different commonalty. Here's what causes Oliver's groan and what the curious young investigator would find upon following up Edgeworth's reference to Bryan Edwards's very popular and influential *History, Civil and Commercial, of the British Colonies in the West Indies*, a multivolume work repeatedly reissued and expanded way into the nineteenth century. (Oliver is reading the folio edition of 1794.) Edwards produced one of the most widely read travel narratives of the Revolutionary era, an index of popularity indeed, for voyages and ethnographic explorations enjoyed phenomenal success, most typically functioning as utopias or dystopias for a shaken European culture seeking to envision alternative communities. Edwards's description of the exemplary punishment inflicted on the ringleaders of Tacky's 1760 rebellion by the Jamaican planters is based on firsthand information. According to Edwards, his relative and benefactor was instrumental in trying to stem the insurrection that broke out among newly enslaved Koromantyn or Gold Coast natives, the Koromantyns being proverbial for bodily fortitude and ferocious disposition, with a magnanimous indifference to death that rivaled Aphra Behn's famed Noble Savage, Oroonoko, who calmly smokes on while he is dismembered and burned. Edwards attributes the revolt not to specific instances of ill treatment, the instigators being newcomers, but to the bare fact of captivity. The rebels are said to have butchered numerous settlers and drunk their blood mixed with rum; because "a general inclination to revolt appear[ed] among all the Koromantyn Negroes in the island, it was thought necessary to make a few terrible examples of some of the most guilty" when they were caught. One was condemned to fire and two more to suspension alive in irons until they perished. Hanging in chains on a gibbet, they "diverted themselves all day long in discourse with their countrymen"—it took one a week to die; the other lasted to the ninth morning. "The wretch that was burnt was made to sit on the ground," Edwards continues, "and his body being chained to an iron stake, the fire was applied to his feet. He uttered not a groan, and saw his legs reduced to ashes with the utmost firmness and composure; after which, one of his arms . . . getting loose, he snatched a brand from the fire that was consuming him, and flung it in the face of the executioner" (2: 78–79).[26]

As Elaine Scarry points out in *The Body in Pain*, institutionalized structures of torture convert the victims' real pain into the perpetrators' "fiction of power" (chap. 1). Since "successful" narratives must dramatize the sufferer's body yet erase his voice, confirming the torturer's agency through his disclaimer of identification with the pain he inflicts, Oliver's groan and the Koromantyns' intransigence work to deny totalizing interpretive systems even as they disclose Edwards's colonialist stance. "I mean only to state facts as I find them," Edwards may remark, but Edgeworth's citation of torture is clearly a site of instruction, a dreadful literalization of British commerce and consumption tellingly delivered in the words of the masculine colonizer himself (2: 75). Revealing the sordid violence and repression, the brutal economic exploitation upon which the Creole plantocracy is founded, the fracture in Edgeworth's text brings the patriarchal empire and the Law of the Father onto the good aunt's hearth. But the unstable meanings of domestic comfort and dirty secrets which transform Freud's *heimlich* into the disturbing revelation of what should have stayed concealed do more than align English firesides and private locales with the incendiary public politics of Oliver's mother country, Jamaica. Suturing scenarios of protection and violation, the innovatory and unsettling narrative structure of "The Good Aunt" reconstitutes the domestic sphere as the contestatory site of a multidimensional social identity and the reading child as a decentered subject-in-process whose homecoming entails painful border crossings.

Both ideologically and formally, the threatening gap is part of the message, for it stimulates readers to active engagement with cultural as well as textual difficulties. Oliver's responsive reading models an intersubjective drama of social understanding (and hence potential change) as well as self-reflexivity, moving the audience along with the protagonist to another plane of interpretation.[27] Breaching the generic contract and defying the audience's comfortable expectations, the little Creole's fictional slippage from morally determined comic action into real-life horror story paradoxically inscribes the involved external reader into the tale, both as a way of referring and applying the textual lessons to life and as a route to the recognition of interpersonal difference. Dramatically encoded in the visual and verbal representations of little Oliver's reverie, interactive and intertextual reading links us all through shared feelings and a hermeneutics of identity, even as it gives voice to the discourse of the Other ordinarily silenced by hegemonic culture.[28] In fiction as in real life, subject positions produce identity through an ongoing process that can enable as well as repressively mold. As the Scottish philosopher Dugald Stewart (an Edgeworth family favorite and friend) describes the ideational social uses of "fictitious histories," "Imagination is the great spring of human activity, and the principal source of human improvement" (1: 529–30).

If Freud's uncanny elucidates the return of the Jamaican repressed, the butchered revenant who haunts the child's text and won't stay dead, postmodern models of subjectivity and narratology identify the multiple functions of Edgeworth's embedded microtext. As the literary homology of emotional interrelatedness, intertextuality formalizes the dialogic interplay between people—between self and Other—and between the personal and the political that the story thematizes. As theorists of referential dynamics note, quotations habitually "accumulate in art when the boundaries between it and other forms of social consciousness become vague" and increase during cultural crises and sociopolitical revolutions (Morawski 704). Because proliferating quotations and allusions link the private activity of reading with the larger contexts within which this reading takes place, a referential aesthetic furthers claims for reading as a border crossing that transgresses those boundaries most critical discourses establish between child and adult, between self and Other, and between the domestic and the public spheres. If intertextuality has sometimes been thought of as an imperialistic mode, it can be alternatively deployed as decolonization. Interreferential scenes of writing and reading like those I've discussed offer an inclusive model of culture and subcultures which foregrounds the significance of daily life and domestic space in reproducing and subverting relations of power. Counting the reading child and the educational story in redefines the private sphere as equally political to the conventionally public domain, as equally determined by and contestatory of structures of power. Oliver's embedded dialogue with his homeland's history not only rewrites his own positionality, but it solicits the child reader, along with the juvenile protagonists, to rewrite the future of the social world which permitted that history as well. Significantly, the syncretic community which provides the tale's Utopian closure assembles not in the good aunt's home but in a civic space where children and women are active participants. Much as Oliver's reading interlude situates narrative form and political interrogation as cognate, flattering the juvenile interpreter outside the tale into coextension with the protagonist, so the crowded final scenes of

"The Good Aunt" persuasively miniaturize a Habermasian public sphere, an embodiment of an enlightened new mental space that challenges generational and gendered apartheid by its representational inclusiveness.

The finale underlines what the dystopic reading episode footnotes: the ambiguous relationship of England and Jamaica materialized in the sweetmeat jar and, more important, Oliver's role as interpretive sleuth and mediatory presence. Similarly packed with talk, action, political implication, and emblematic props, the interrelated scenes function as alternative conclusions for the colonialism the tale problematizes. Everybody gets to speak, including Cuba and the rough-and-ready sailor who delivers both the coachman's lost packet and the good aunt's hijacked cargo ship, but it's Oliver who most warmly solicits the reader's engagement with his detective skills and his peace-making prowess: "After all, quarrelling, and bearing malice, are very disagreeable things." The lively embodiment of gratitude and forgiveness, the little boy who "like[s] to hear about best friends" moves the tale from tragic exclamation—"I must finish this!"—to comic explanation—"how all this came about" (122, 96, 117, 131). Paradoxically, Oliver's reading scene both produces and questions the tale's cheerful resolution, as his china jar from home metamorphoses, generating in turn sugary luxuries, illegal lottery tickets secreted by the thieving Holloway, and the antique gold toothpick case which the quick-sighted child singles out among Mr. Carat's prizes.[29] Part of the good aunt's missing jewels, the case is the other half of Cuba's keepsake thimble, given to the mulatto woman long ago by her "best friend," the child Frances Howard. Hence it's the clue whereby Oliver recovers the mature good aunt's missing fortune from the naval hijackers and their fence, Carat. It's tempting to think of the jar and the seamlessly joined gadget as different (and differently gendered) images of England's and Jamaica's colonial interdependence: the economic commerce of sugar, slavery, and exploitation versus the harmonious emotional commerce of imagined community, the sense of fellow feeling that's the basis of society.[30] The allegorical props similarly invite association with the competing worldviews which ironize the conclusion: the threateningly aleatory versus the transitive relationship with reality guaranteed by enlightened comedy. What the good characters give and get, the denouement emphasizes, is "not accident" (140). But the dazzling coincidences and contrivances that wind up the tale are so outrageously overdetermined and high-spirited, the author's tongue so teasingly in her cheek, that even a young reader would recognize the barrage of story conventions, from the reconciliation of long-lost family to the recovery of long-lost fortunes, as sleight of hand. At the same time that the causal plot offers a rationale and a reward for moral exertion, a belief that one shapes one's own fate, the fortuitous happy ending bestowed by authorial beneficence thus conveys the insularity of a comic world environed by the larger colonial world of misery that Oliver's reading signals.

Edgeworth's pervasive intertextuality functions politically, urbanely eliding the boundaries between the domestic and national spheres, between the private world of a child's tale and the public world of men's politics. It trivializes her technique of layered referentiality if we decide that Edwards's repulsively gory details are embedded in a footnote because the author is chary of wounding the sensibilities of young readers or of scaring off potential parental buyers. It makes the whole story illegible if we explain away puzzles and incongruities, as Romantic critics of historical juvenile genres so often do, by deciding that the author is most likely just a benighted imperialist herself, keen to hide the dirt from little boys whom she's indoctrinating into managing the British empire. Nor is Edgeworth's citational aesthetic the fetish of a utilitarian obsessed with facts, although her Enlightened philosophical and literary background is usually conflated anachronistically with the reductive utilitarianism of a later generation, as caricatured in Mr. Gradgrind of Dickens's *Hard Times*. Romantic lovers of faerie who resented the intrusion of the factual into the fictional dismissed Edgeworth as a bluestocking pedant insistent on labeling sources. I argue instead for her factual footnotes not just as the grounding but as the catalyst of a Utopian fiction, a potent thematizing of textuality's political power. Obviously the parent texts footnoted and cited summon the filial tale into being. Edgeworth's most basic narrative strategy is recasting cultural master narratives: reimagining men's plots from a feminine and juvenile point of view and appropriating patriarchal language to say something else. References like those to Gibbon, Day, Darwin, and Edwards are also, quite literally, the instrument by which the fictional model of a reformed syncretic community can be made to come true. It's appropriate that a story about participatory relationships, about counting almost everyone in, focalizes the participatory response of readers: a following up of footnotes that makes connections and takes the fictional message back into the world.[31] Edge-worth's citations and narrative fractures provoke her readers' active involvement in the production of a social text which recognizes the *unheimlich* site of threat and explanatory breakdown as also a place for discovery and hope.

And, in this story of a youngster's coping with his difficult place in a world he didn't make, it is ironic and fitting that telltale secrets both horrific and healing most often come to light through the medium of little Oliver, simultaneously the victim of a colonialist cultural heritage he feelingly deplores, a legacy for which he enacts reparation, and of the masculinist father culture which bred those degenerate sons. As a woman and Irish colonial, Edgeworth evades easy binaries of them and us, the depraved settlers versus the virtuous homeland. With remarkably evenhanded justice, she traces the sins Oliver mourns back to the hierarchical, the parochial, and the decadent in British cultural institutions. Not only, as A. P. Stanley writes of Rugby, is "School a Little World" with "boyhood an exact type of manhood—school a faithful mirror of public life" (100), but fictions about schooling are also telltale cultural texts, as inherently political as they are often intertextual. As so often happens in school stories, the educational institution and the way it operates function as a synecdoche for the larger culture within which it is embedded and which, in producing the nation's future rulers, it is continually reproducing. With tact and economy, "The Good Aunt" shows how masculinist educational practices construct colonizers who legitimate their domination of others by torture, by a violence inscribed upon the victim's body which the juridical punishment then literally erases—the meat picked off the skeleton by carrion, the flesh and bones crumbling to ashes in consuming fire. But the physical violations and psychic triumphs that Oliver groans over have already been prefigured in the barbarities earlier inflicted on his own body and mind as fag victim of a tyrannical ruling order—and in the resistance and regeneration emblematized in Howard's successful defense of the young Creole against Holloway. The Augustus Holloways, Lord Rawsons, Mr. Supines, and Mr. Carats who debase English culture and commerce are everywhere, and they're resilient, the narrative demonstrates, but they're not the whole of the story.

Like many of Edgeworth's juvenile protagonists, young Charles Howard first goes it alone, successfully aiding Oliver physically and regenerating him mentally; then his efforts are validated by generous adult support—the good tutor Mr. Russell, the good schoolmaster Dr. B. But the story's propitious origins and its predictive conclusions belong to the good aunts. Frances Howard inside the narrative, whose wise domestic education enables young Howard to transform the masculinist ethos of the public school, is the surrogate for the authorial good aunt outside the fiction, Maria Edgeworth herself, whose revisionary school story imagines and epitomizes a larger change in a wider world. As the tale's vividly dramatized pedagogy exemplifies, learning is a relational matter under the aunt's tutelage, grounded in and generating love, friendship, and gratitude. Howard himself suffers greatly when his aunt has to send him into an instructional environment ordered by male savagery, but he takes what he's learned at home and eventually converts even the masculinist Holloway. Initially aligned through their mutual figuration as feminized victims, Howard and Oliver reproduce in their relationship the aunt's earlier loving pedagogy, and they extend that care to the story's most visible Other, the mulatto emigrant Cuba, who's rescued and restored through children's everyday magic. Patriarchal traditions flog boys into learning and dismember recalcitrant slaves; the curative narrative of "The Good Aunt" rearticulates and reincarnates those lacerated and dispersed bodies. Having given up her Jamaican estates through conscience, the good aunt models a colonial paradigm of interrelationship which, like her revisionary pedagogy, displaces savagery with salvaging. Female authoriality in her tale thus constitutes the act of writing as an act of mothering (or, rather, aunting) which displaces bad fathers and exposes corrupt paternal inheritances both institutional and textual, both domestic and imperial. Through its allusive and interlocking narratives of taking care and reciprocity, the narrative produces and embodies a reformed and reconciliatory community whose members are at once responsible individual agents and interdependent friends. Augustus Holloway and his ambitious alderman father are ultimately rehabilitated and included when they exchange their toadying to "manly" aristocrats for tutelage from the notionally feminine Charles Howard and his primary caretaker and first educator, Frances Howard.[32]

Edgeworth's novelette catches the ambiguities and complexities built into the child's text that takes the child *as* text, that sees the child protagonist in the text and the child reader in the world not as passive object of adult propaganda but as locus of revisionary possibility and communal change. When we contextualize stories from

the past, noting their worldly referentiality and their literary intertextuality and not just their extractable morals, we can see how deceptively simple tales for young readers are multiply coded. We can
recognize how they both represent and interrogate their culture; how
in shaping the social identity of juvenile protagonists and readers
they teach the young to transform the culture they seemingly accept;
and how in thus undermining the grounds of their own representation they both illustrate the oppositional paradigm of recent theory
and challenge it. In granting agency and interventionary capacity
to the liminal figures of the children and the manumitted Cuba,
the children's author also in some measure achieves it herself. If
no writer can altogether step free of the frames of reference and discursive positions a culture offers, the ambivalent intercolonialism
intrinsic to the juvenile author confers the enfranchisement of oc-
cupying variable sites. What postmodern theory appropriates as its
deconstructive discovery—the so-called death of the unified subject
—children's literature has always produced as possibility: the multiple positionalities which cross-writing produces and cross-reading
identifies.

Self-consciously thematizing schooling, textuality, and the formation of subjectivity, cross-written teaching tales like "The Good
Aunt" instruct grown-up postmodern critics as well as their original
child and adult readers. The Enlightenment master narrative of improvement sought to domesticate the aleatory and to disperse the
shadows of chance, but as recent critics of the postmodern anti-
Enlightenment critique note, the so-called *grands récits* of rationalism and progress, as nuanced and negotiated by lived experience,
were never the simple stories to which late-twentieth-century phi-
losophies would reduce them: "postmodern thought has not un-
covered anything that the Age of Enlightenment, in its more lucid
moments, did not already know" (Racevskis 77). Like all master
narratives, genealogies construct history by leaving things out, making "sense in the present by making sense selectively out of the
past" (Clifford, "On *Orientalism*" 267). Thus the "Romantic" legacy
for twentieth-century children's literary studies might be appraised
more usably as *also* an Enlightened or Revolutionary legacy, as *also* a
gendered legacy. In arguing that Revolutionary texts produced under the sign of the child are peculiarly liminal, peculiarly relational,
peculiarly political works, generated by, written about, structured to
produce cultural mediation and negotiation, I also argue for the im-

portance of little history, for the interrogation of universalizing master narratives—whether Romantic or Marxist—by the many alternative local stories which resourcefully blur boundaries between the public and private spheres, the political and the personal, the adult and the child, the grown-up canon and juvenile literary studies. I conclude by situating a revisioned and de-Romanticized children's literature as border crossing, as the ideal investigatory site for all postmodern methodologies which blur disciplinary and generic boundaries or investigate the interplay of history, literature, language, and subjectivity. The varied current methodologies seeking to reconstitute literary studies (and culture itself) through seeing all the arts and their contexts as part of a continuum, rather than singling out elite adult texts as the exclusive objects of study, can learn from Revolutionary *petits récits* that demonstrate the permeability of boundaries between literature and history, that intervene in material reality rather than aestheticizing it. As Ashis Nandy relevantly observes of the child under colonialism, "Children, too, bring up their elders," if those elders overcome their "fear of the liminality between the adult and the child" ("Reconstructing" 73–74).

My analysis suggests that the conventional Romantic Imaginary does not organize the juvenile literary scene in any coherent and meaningful way, does not, in fact, allow us to comprehend what's been in front of us or to align historical cultures and crises with contemporary theoretical understandings and postcolonial literatures. When we shed the interpretive traditions of children's literary studies to which we're habituated, we discover a past simultaneously familiar (*heimlich*) and uncanny (*unheimlich*), "that class of the frightening," as Freud puts it, which "leads back to what is known of old and long familiar" (220). I've extended Freud's notion of the uncanny to politicize and historicize the telltale secrets of a specific real text and its resonance for the fictional child reader who engages it and the author who produces him, for the readers of his story, and for us now. More globally, I've located children's literature (like the criticism addressing it) as a generic site for the uncanny, as epitomizing in its cross-writing of genders, genres, generations, and sociopsychic themes those "moments of breakdown that occur when an interpretive scheme encounters a particular object or events that it cannot satisfactorily interpret" (Engle 110). When we update Romantic schemata with contemporary revisionism, we discover child figures symbolically negotiating cultural differences who are more relevant to the cross-cultural dilemmas we currently face than the dead maidens, infant philosophers, and solitary wanderers who people Romantic poetry. Perhaps postmodern defamiliarizations of yesterday's as well as today's texts—old wine in new bottles—will prove sufficient to console us for the loss of a Romantic paradigm that limits our past understandings, stifles our present research, and clouds our thinking about the future. Defying the laws of conventional science, homeopathic remedies cure through infinitesimal doses of substances that would in larger amounts cause the symptoms from which the patients suffer. If Romanticism's nostalgic worship of childhood innocence induces cultural malaise, perhaps a touch of Utopian cultural studies can effect a salutary theoretical and curricular revisionism.[33]

NOTES

1. It's a surprise to find that the French commonplace in my title has a knowable if obscure author (Alphonse Karr). But because exploring uncanny secrets within the commonplaces of the literary discourse on childhood is this essay's project, it's weirdly apropos. Homeopathy—the notion that drugs producing the same symptoms as the disease being treated will cure if taken in fantastically diluted dosages—currently figures among alternative medicine's returning repressed. Once scorned as quackery, it's now being featured in mainstream journals like *Consumer Reports* (see "Homeopathy: Much Ado about Nothing?"). How homeopathy relates to Romanticism, as well as to the sequence of explanatory models the subtitle postulates, emerges in the course of the essay. It's worth observing here, however, that the Greek roots for curative medicine and poisonous witchcraft are homologous. I'd like to thank the John Simon Guggenheim Memorial Foundation for the Fellowship which enabled my research: the extensive scholarly notes for my project are deleted to fit the generalist audience for this volume.

2. Benjamin's "illumination" usefully describes this essay's project: "To articulate the past historically . . . means to seize hold of a memory as it flashes up at a moment of danger. . . . Historicism gives the 'eternal' image of the past; historical materialism supplies a unique experience with the past" (255, 262).

3. The Smiths' *Addresses* were in their eighteenth large printing by 1833, as the preface to the 1888 reprint records. Setting aside the widespread dismissive attitudes toward childhood that she inadvertently underlines, Garlitz's selective quotations in "The Baby's Debut" lead her to the mistaken conclusion that reader response to Wordsworth's "cult of the child" quickly moved from early-nineteenth-century parody to a celebratory "climax" by midcentury

(93). The ripest sentimentalizations of the child seem to occur later in the century, however; the most massive exposure of the conceptual instability and chronological incoherence of "Romanticism" as we've learned to think of it remains Whalley's "England: Romantic-Romanticism."

4. See Myers and Knoepflmacher.

5. What McGavran terms the "moral indeterminacy" of Wordsworth's child-centered poems might be extended to the author's aesthetic indeterminacy in current criticism as well ("Catechist and Visionary" 67). As Paul has wittily observed, the authors in McGavran's anthology *Romanticism and Children's Literature in Nineteenth-Century England* split along radical "pink" and conventional "blue" lines ("Interrupting" 213). On competing paradigms, see also my introduction ("Here's Looking at You, Kid") for the special issue of *Nineteenth-Century Contexts, Culturing Childhood* (21.2), which also includes Alan Richardson's essay in this volume.

6. See, respectively, Bhabha, *The Location of Culture* 25; Giroux, *Border Crossings* and "Border Pedagogy"; Hicks, *Border Writing*, the introduction; and Pratt, "Arts of the Contact Zone" 40. For a provocative configuration of the postmodern, postcolonial theorist as border crosser, see JanMohamed, "Worldliness-without-World."

7. For history as "man's truth," see Crosby's introduction; Catherine Morland's comments can be found in chap. 14 of *Northanger Abbey*'s first volume (5: 108 in R. W. Chapman's edition of *The Novels of Jane Austen*).

8. In a special issue of *Race and Class* devoted to literary colonialism, the juvenile survey title exemplifies this reductivism: "Nature's Outcast Child: Black People in Children's Books," a catch phrase culled from the material sampled (Forster).

9. Readers not working with multicultural materials may be most familiar with Said's schema through Nodelman, "The Other," which provocatively and disturbingly aligns children's literature criticism and child psychology topic by topic with Said's argument. The literature on "Orientalism" is by now enormous, ongoing, and suggestive for postcolonial children's literature studies: see, for example, the work of MacKenzie and the responses to him and Said in the multiply authored "Forum: MacKenzie on Said and Imperialism."

10. If, as Mackenzie points out, the recurrent Orientalist use of "native" as a racial category is a demeaning "resurrection of imperial usage," neither can "the quest for an authentic other" be "fulfilled by children" who are "a piece of our selves" ("Occidentalism" 343; Jordanova, "Children in History" 6).

11. As thematic in literary accounts and educational histories as the ritualized violence, brutality, and rebellion endemic to public schools are the fag's gendering as female, the flourishing underground romantic attachments,

and the familial disruption entailed by institutionalized life: see Chandos; Gathorne-Hardy; Honey; and Quigly esp. 7. Particularly valuable are Thomas's analysis of the school as "a model of political life, a practical lesson in the exercise of authority" (4); and Mack's magisterial study: memoirs, journalism, and educational histories more usefully contextualize Edgeworth's school stories than do literary histories. Except where otherwise indicated, references to "The Good Aunt" in the text refer to the Garland reprint of the 1801 second edition.

12. Unlike many authors who use the mocking classical names (Venus, Pompey) which were also contemporaneously popular for black characters and persons, Edgeworth prefers the African names used for the day of birth; Cuba is the feminine form of Wednesday, a fitting choice in view of her mediatory function in the story. Edgeworth could have found the Akan day names in several travel books she read, including Long, *The History of Jamaica* 2: 427.

13. Gibbon's autobiography exists in multiple versions, only one of which (the Oxford edition) would have been available to Edgeworth. Gibbon remarks that no man's life shows a "more remarkable change" than from home to "the rude familiarity of his equals, the insolent tyranny of his seniors, and the rod, perhaps, of a cruel and capricious pedagogue." Like Frances Howard, Catherine Porten conversed with the boy "like friends of an equal age," but the delicately nuanced relationship between teacher and pupil in the story owes little to Gibbon, who was spoiled at Westminster and quite unaware of his aunt's impending ruin, and much to Edgeworth's own life, as in the child's becoming his aunt's business assistant (Gibbon 24–26; "Good Aunt" 23).

14. Richard Lovell Edgeworth's best friend and his daughter's sometime teacher, Day is an emotionally fraught figure for Maria Edgeworth—at once the good and bad uncle—because of his embargo on her public authorship. Had he not died early, she might never have published, and she recurrently ironizes the educational legacy she recycles.

15. The trope of slavery is pervasive among early-nineteenth-century critics of fagging: Lewis calls the practice "a rule which legalizes tyranny," so that the weaker always become "the slaves of the stronger boys" (74–75); and Southey remarks, "There is nothing to be said in defence of the system which might not be applied in defence of the slave-trade, or the Turkish despotism" (142). Even memoirists who feelingly recount the miseries of fags couldn't resist later temptation: "we too soon fell into the ways of pashas" (Brinsley-Richards 285). Chandos notes that Westminster juniors were "unofficially called 'slaves'" (89n) and vividly details the school's ritualized torture, burning, and poisoning in chap. 4 ("Trial by Ordeal") and chap. 5 ("Fags and

Their Masters"). Under the pseudonym of "Zeta," Froude so revealingly narrated a boy's corruption by Westminster bullying—"the life was as hard, and the treatment as barbarous, as that of the negroes in Virginia"—that his father suppressed *Shadows of the Clouds* (27). Westminster historians usually concerned to refurbish old school ties also recount lurid anecdotes of flogging, fighting, tyranny, and insubordination, as well as the torments of cold, rats, and hunger.

16. Sometimes liberals like Charlotte Smith manage to have it both ways: her "Little West Indian" in *Rambles Farther* (1796) occasions a mother-daughter dialogue which both indicts slavery and celebrates English "civilization and . . . commerce" (19). It's easy to see why Day's primitivist (and masculinist) utopias, interchangeably stocked with spartan Noble Savages of every country and hue, should strike a responsive chord in idealistic youngsters like Leigh Hunt, who never forgot how John Newbery's "mercenary and time-serving ethics was first blown over" by Day's "fresh country breeze" (*Autobiography* 51). Interestingly, writers with actual West Indian connections, whether beloved as in Hunt's case or detested as in Charlotte Smith's, confirm the traits modern readers tend to think of as merely literary conventions. "Creole" just signifies native to the West Indies, white and black people born there, as well as indigenous flora and fauna; it is not a euphemism for racial mixing.

17. Although Clark's 1996 study does not treat this tale, it deserves mention for its emphasis on gender and its inclusion of some early examples of the school genre.

18. Pickering, for example, recognizes class as an issue in the fight, but Howard's victory is more complex than an allegorical triumph of the middle class: Oliver isn't lower class, and, as his name indicates, Holloway isn't an Augustan ruler but a bourgeois choosing a hollow way (130–32). In her chapter on "The Manly Boy 1800–1914," Avery remarks that the fight shows "the difference between the moralist's conception of manliness and the Georgian public schoolboy's" (170), but Mack's comprehensive survey of the critiques mounted by former Georgian public schoolboys suggests otherwise, as do realistic moral tales written by nineteenth-century men who were far keener on the institution than most of their forebears. See, for example, Murray, "'Collagers v[ersus] Oppidans': A Reminiscence of Eton Life," in which the hero shows the despairing dunce that (like Oliver) he too can learn and make something of himself.

19. In contrast, Alderman Holloway has already prostituted his "young statesman," expecting that the earl of Marryborough will deliver a pocket borough in return for the merchant's cash: the friendship of Augustus and Lord Raw-

son thus ironizes those "fortunate connexions, which some parents consider as the peculiar advantage of a public school" (42). For the Whig antislavery discourse of liberty, generosity of spirit, and enlarged sympathy with which Charles Howard is aligned, see Kriegel. It's noteworthy that "The Good Aunt" was published in the year Sypher calls "admittedly the darkest in abolition history," shortly after many thousands of British soldiers and civilians perished in West Indian rebellions (21).

20. Only access to the "liminality between the adult and the child which many of us carry within ourselves," Nandy suggests, can transform the "shared culture" of colonialism to the liminal "communitas" and "coactivity" which characterize the anthropologist's integrative social drama ("Reconstructing Childhood" 73, and *Intimate Enemy* 2, 11; Turner, "Social Dramas and Ritual Metaphors," chap. 1). Patterson's classic analysis of slavery as "institutionalized marginality, the liminal state of social death" and of the enslaved as internal outsider, forever deprived of the claims of community, also develops the notion of the slave as revenant, one who can cross boundaries "between community and chaos, life and death, the sacred and the secular" which others cannot (*Slavery and Social Death* 46, 44, 51).

21. Jamaican travels invariably report on the likeness of "manners and barbarous dialect" produced through daily proximity of the races (especially among children), the local expression for which was to "exhibit much of the *Quashiba*" (Stewart, *Account* 160). The narrative never refers to Oliver except by the single name, thus further aligning him with Cuba, who has no surname, as was usual with slaves. For the stereotypical slave characterization that Cuba controverts, see Patterson, "An Analysis of 'Quashee'" (the masculine of Quashiba or Quasheba) in *The Sociology of Slavery* (174–81). Patterson's rich discussion of the release from slavery as a "classic instance of the anthropology of gift exchange" has implications beyond Frances Howard's release of Cuba; the ongoing repayment of gifts of life, love, and literacy constitutes the entire story's motive force, involving virtually all the characters. In Edgeworth's tales (and personal writing life), as in many cultures' dialectical progressions of giving, all members of the community must be involved eventually: it's the chain of exchanges which establishes a moral communal order (211; see chap. 8, "Manumission: Its Meanings and Modes" in *Slavery and Social Death*). For the mulatto woman's positive positioning as the key "narrative device of mediation" in black women's texts as well, see Carby (89).

22. Earlier in the tale, Holloway flees in terror from Cuba's look lest she "*blow him*," thus revealing his guilt to Charles Howard (74–75). Edgeworth's tale,

like much recent ethnographic work on the native who gazes back, complicates Mulvey's classic construction of the white European male's controlling look as normative (reprinted and qualified in *Visual and Other Pleasures*, chaps. 3, 4). Brooks's analysis of melodrama as the genre which clarifies "the cosmic moral sense of everyday gestures," thus democratizing moral knowledge through emblematic representations clear and legible to all, is also applicable to Edgeworth's genre of the moral or philosophical conte (14; for mutes as signifiers of virtue, see chap. 3).

23. I adapt the term "political uncanny" from Engle's fine essay. Because the development of Oliver and Cuba has already interrogated "original genius" and "hereditary temper," even a young reader would reject these specious cultural arguments for the treatment of the black insurgents in Oliver's reading; interestingly, the good aunt firmly opposes such notions, while the male schoolmaster argues warmly in their favor (116). Edgeworth's allusion to Warton's popular Romantic ode underlines the imaginative identification and empathic response that the reading scene is designed to evoke.

24. In the first edition of "The Good Aunt," the reading scene (4: 151–58) is depicted at the moment when the good aunt and Dr. B. steal behind the distracted boy to discover why he groans. Although Oliver is so young that the Jamaican sweetmeat jar is as big as he, his enormous shadow broods ominously in the background; the artist was probably pragmatically depicting the unsnuffed candle's glare, but the eerie effect also implies the tainted legacy of his homeland that the innocent boy is discovering. Like the tableaux of melodrama which conclusively resolve the meaning of scenes and acts, Edgeworth's verbal and the unknown artist's visual representations of Oliver's reading arrange and freeze the characters' attitudes and gestures to provide a "visual summary of the emotional situation," but unlike that of the typical theatrical tableau, the signification of Edgeworth's episode is not obvious and unambiguous (Brooks 48).

25. In "The Historian as Body-Snatcher," a *TLS* review of Stephen J. Greenblatt's *Learning to Curse* as exemplar of American New Historical critical practice, Eagleton draws attention to its formulaic anecdotal structure: first, the critic finds an exemplum of appalling human barbarity and then arranges whatever historical practices he wants to talk about alongside it, so that he can "contextualize" by reading one out of the other and vice versa.

26. Although nowadays Edwards is sometimes linked with virulent Negrophobics such as Edward Long, his informative *History* ranges from sentimental liberalism to punitive pragmatism; its incoherences warn postcolonial critics against reconstructing a monovocal "colonialist discourse" which erases

the dissonances that Edgeworth's story positively exploits. Edgeworth apparently couldn't exorcize the victims' fate from her mind; she returned to Edwards's Jamaican rebellion narrative and gave it a happy ending a few years later in "The Grateful Negro" (*Popular Tales*).

27. If the reading of Oliver's reading I develop seems like too much to ask of a young audience, we might recall that Adam Smith's *Theory of Moral Sentiments* originated as a pedagogic manual for adolescents: with its self-judging "impartial spectator" (82–85) and its social ethic of sympathy, this favorite of Edgeworth's is very much to the point.

28. Much recent work outside children's literary studies furthers my case for the empathic child figure as a locus of revisionary possibility. See, for example, Nandy, *The Intimate Enemy* and "Reconstructing Childhood"; Khare; and Hamilton. Khare's argument that love is as potent as power politics and that it provides the only bridge across the self/Other divide inherent in cultural representation learnedly theorizes what most writers and readers of children's literature empirically practice. Nandy expands the conventional homology between childhood and the colonized to include "liminality" as well as repression, the transformative "threshold" state of becoming, as developed in anthropological practice. As Turner remarks in his analysis of this "subjunctive mood" of sociocultural action, "The hard saying 'except ye become as a little child' assumes new meaning" ("Social Dramas and Stories" 164–65).

29. Because of their sugary stickiness, smell, and status as expensive gift, Oliver's Jamaican sweetmeats are undoubtedly candied ginger, an authorial choice that foregrounds the linkage of slave-produced sugar and the child's homeland. More complexly, Oliver hoards his family's gift only so he can give the candies away, and, as Edgeworth with her interest in political economy would have noted, the sweetmeats' status as an exorbitantly taxed import underlines the Jamaican planters' subordinate colonial status as well as their slaveholding. Because preserved ginger was "liable to so high a duty as a succade," Long observes, it made no profit and was sent only for gifts (*History of Jamaica* 3: 702).

30. Because they're grooved to screw together into one unit, the thimble and toothpick case embody syncretic community; the Jamaican jar's association with men's gambling, lotteries, and commercial speculation goes beyond its involvement with the mercenary schemes of Mr. Carat and young Holloway. The Creole passion for extravagance and gambling, Edwards suggests, derives from the chancy venture of sugar planting: "a West-Indian property is a species of lottery" (2: 18).

31. As Ray relevantly notes, the dialogical dimension of narrative "necessarily

looks to an Other for its endorsement or ratification," the engaged interpreter within and without the text who rescripts history's buried truths (12).

32. Only unregenerate exploiters are expelled from the magic circle which closes the book: Lord Rawson, the worthless aristocrat; Mr. Supine, the irresponsible tutor; and Mr. Carat, the Jewish receiver of stolen goods. In a later novel focalizing Jewish identity (*Harrington*, 1817), Edgeworth critiqued her own earlier tales for unthinkingly perpetuating literary stereotypes.

33. For an incisive analysis of Romanticism's dangerous legacy, see Warner's chap. 3, "Little Angels, Little Devils: Keeping Childhood Innocent." Homeopathic medicine was, fittingly, pioneered by the German practitioner Samuel Hahnemann in the Revolutionary 1790s. Discovering that the drug which cures malaria gave the healthy the symptoms of the disease, Hahnemann devised remedies which frequently worked, although they contained only microscopic amounts of the original curative substance. Recent studies often corroborate Hahnemann's "cures," but no one knows how. Perhaps the minute amounts stimulate the body's own immune system to heal itself, perhaps it's a placebo effect, but the highly diluted "medicines" work best when they're carefully tailored to the individual case, therapeutically contextualized, so to speak.

WORKS CITED

Austen, Jane. *Northanger Abbey*. Vol. 5. *The Novels of Jane Austen*. Ed. R. W. Chapman. 5 vols. 3rd ed. 1933. London: Oxford, 1959. (rpt. from 1818 ed., which also includes *Persuasion*.)

Avery, Gillian. *Childhood's Pattern: A Study of the Heroes and Heroines of Children's Fiction, 1770–1950*. London: Hodder and Stoughton, 1975.

Benjamin, Walter. "Theses on the Philosophy of History." *Illuminations*. Ed. Hannah Arendt. Trans. Harry Zohn. New York: Schocken, 1968. 253–64.

Berger, John, with Jean Mohr and Nicholas Philibert. *Another Way of Telling*. New York: Vintage International, 1995.

Bhabha, Homi K. *The Location of Culture*. London: Routledge, 1994.

Brinsley-Richards, James. *Seven Years at Eton 1857–1864*. London: Richard Bentley, 1883.

Brooks, Peter. *The Melodramatic Imagination: Balzac, Henry James, Melodrama, and the Mode of Excess*. New Haven: Yale UP, 1976.

Carby, Hazel V. *Reconstructing Womanhood: The Emergence of the Afro-American Woman Novelist*. New York: Oxford UP, 1987.

Chandos, John. *Boys Together: English Public Schools 1800–1864*. New Haven: Yale UP, 1984.

Clark, Beverly Lyon. *Regendering the School Story: Sassy Sissies and Tattling Tomboys*. New York: Garland, 1996.

Clifford, James. "Introduction: Partial Truths." *Writing Culture: The Poetics and Politics of Ethnography*. Ed. James Clifford and George E. Marcus. Berkeley: U of California P, 1986. 1–26.

———. "On *Orientalism*." *The Predicament of Culture: Twentieth-Century Ethnography, Literature, and Art*. Cambridge: Harvard UP, 1988. 255–76.

Crosby, Christina. *The Ends of History: Victorians and "The Woman Question."* New York: Routledge, 1991.

Darwin, Erasmus. *The Botanic Garden, a Poem: In Two Parts*. 1789–91. 4th ed. 2 vols. London: J. Johnson, 1799.

Day, Thomas. *The History of Sandford and Merton*. Intro. by Isaac Kramnick. 1783, 1786, 1789. 3 vols. Classics of Children's Literature 1621–1932. New York: Garland, 1977.

Eagleton, Terry. "The Historian as Body-Snatcher." Rev. of *Learning to Curse*, by Stephen J. Greenblatt. *TLS*, January 18, 1991, 7.

Edgeworth, Maria. "The Good Aunt." *Moral Tales for Young People*. 5 vols. London: J. Johnson, 1801. 4: 1–190.

———. "The Good Aunt." *Moral Tales for Young People*. 3 vols. New York: Garland, 1974. 2: 1–144.

———. "The Grateful Negro." *Popular Tales*. 3 vols. London: J. Johnson, 1804. 3: 191–240.

Edwards, Bryan. *The History, Civil and Commercial, of the British West Indies, with a Continuation to the Present Time*. 1819. 5th ed. 5 vols. New York: AMS, 1966.

Engle, Lars. "The Political Uncanny: The Novels of Nadine Gordimer." *Yale Journal of Criticism* 2.2 (Spring 1989): 101–27.

Forster, Imogen. "Nature's Outcast Child: Black People in Children's Books." *Literature: Colonial Lines of Descent. Race and Class: A Journal for Black and Third World Liberation* 31.1 (July–September 1989): 79–86.

"Forum: MacKenzie on Said and Imperialism." *Nineteenth-Century Contexts* 19.1 (1995): 63–100.

Freud, Sigmund. "The 'Uncanny.'" *The Standard Edition of the Complete Psychological Works of Sigmund Freud*. Ed. James Strachey et al. 1955. London: Hogarth P, 1978. 17: 219–52.

Garlitz, Barbara. "The Baby's Debut: Contemporary Reaction to Wordsworth's Poetry of Childhood." *Boston University Studies in English* 4.2 (Summer 1960): 85–94.

———. "The Immortality Ode: Its Cultural Progeny." *SEL: Studies in English Literature 1500–1900* 6.4 (Autumn 1966): 639–49.

Gathorne-Hardy, Jonathan. *The Old School Tie: The Phenomenon of the English Public School*. New York: Viking P, 1978.

Gibbon, Edward. *Autobiography of Edward Gibbon as Originally Edited by Lord Sheffield*. Intro. by J. B. Bury. 1796. 1907; Oxford: Oxford UP, 1978.

Giroux, Henry A. *Border Crossings: Cultural Workers and the Politics of Education*. New York: Routledge, 1992.

———. "Border Pedagogy in the Age of Postmodernism." *Postmodern Education: Politics, Culture, and Social Criticism*. Minneapolis: U of Minnesota P, 1991. 114–35.

Hamilton, Karl F. *"I Am You": The Hermeneutics of Empathy in Western Literature, Theology, and Art*. Princeton: Princeton UP, 1988.

Hicks, D. Emily. *Border Writing: The Multidimensional Text*. Intro. by Neil Larsen. Theory and History of Literature 20. Minneapolis: U of Minnesota P, 1991.

Hofland, Mrs. [Barbara]. *The Barbadoes Girl: A Tale for Young People*. 1816. New York: William Burgess, 1831.

"Homeopathy: Much Ado about Nothing?" *Consumer Reports* (March 1994): 201–7.

Honey, J[ohn] R[aymond] de S[ymons]. *Tom Brown's Universe: The Development of the English Public School in the Nineteenth Century*. New York: Quadrangle/New York Times Book Co., 1977.

Hunt, Leigh. *The Autobiography of Leigh Hunt*. Ed. J. E. Morpurgo. London: Cresset P, 1949.

JanMohamed, Abdul R. "The Economy of Manichean Allegory: The Function of Racial Difference in Colonialist Literature." In *"Race," Writing, and Difference*. Ed. Henry Louis Gates, Jr. Chicago: U of Chicago P, 1986. 78–106.

———. "Worldliness-without-World, Homelessness-as-Home: Toward a Definition of the Specular Border Intellectual." *Edward Said: A Critical Reader*. Ed. Michael Sprinker. Oxford: Blackwell, 1992. 96–120.

Jeffrey, Francis. Rev. of *Rejected Addresses* (November 1812). *Contributions to the* Edinburgh Review. 4 vols. London: Longman, Brown, Green and Longmans, 1844. 4: 470–86.

Jordanova, Ludmilla. "Children in History: Concepts of Nature and Society." *Children, Parents, and Politics*. Ed. Geoffrey Scarre. Cambridge: Cambridge UP, 1989. 3–24.

Khare, R. S. "The Other's Double—The Anthropologist's Bracketed Self: Notes on Cultural Representation and Privileged Discourse." *New Literary History* 23.1 (Winter 1992): 1–23.

Kriegel, Abraham D. "A Convergence of Ethics: Saints and Whigs in British Antislavery." *Journal of British Studies* 26.4 (October 1987): 423–50.

[Lewis, George Cornewall]. "Public Schools of England: Westminster and Eton." *Edinburgh Review* 53.105 (March 1831): 64–82.

Long, Edward. *The History of Jamaica; or, A General Survey of the Antient and Modern State of That Island.* 3 vols. London: Lowndes, 1774.

Lyotard, Jean-François. *The Postmodern Condition: A Report on Knowledge.* 1979. Trans. Geoff Bennington and Brian Massumi. Theory and History of Literature 10. 1984; Minneapolis: U of Minnesota P, 1989.

Mack, Edward C. *Public Schools and British Opinion 1780–1860: The Relationship between Contemporary Ideas and the Evolution of an English Institution.* New York: Columbia UP, 1939.

MacKenzie, John M. "Edward Said and the Historians." *Special Issue: Colonialisms. Nineteenth-Century Contexts* 18.1 (1994): 9–25.

———. "Occidentalism: Counterpoint and Counter-polemic." *Journal of Historical Geography* 19.3 (July 1993): 339–44.

———. *Orientalism: History, Theory, and the Arts.* Manchester and New York: Manchester UP, 1995.

Marrs, Edwin W., Jr., ed. *The Letters of Charles and Mary Anne Lamb.* vol. 2 1801–9. Ithaca: Cornell UP, 1976.

McGavran, James Holt, Jr. "Catechist and Visionary: Watts and Wordsworth in 'We Are Seven' and the 'Anecdote for Fathers.'" *Romanticism and Children's Literature in Nineteenth-Century England.* Ed. James Holt McGavran, Jr. Athens: U of Georgia P, 1991. 54–71.

Mohanty, Satya P. "Kipling's Children and the Colour Line." *Literature: Colonial Lines of Descent. Race and Class: A Journal for Black and Third World Liberation* 31.1 (July–September 1989): 21–40.

Morawski, Stefan. "The Basic Functions of Quotation." *Sign, Language, Culture.* Ed. A. J. Greimas et al. The Hague: Mouton, 1970. 690–705.

Mulvey, Laura. *Visual and Other Pleasures.* Bloomington: Indiana UP, 1989.

[Murray, Grenville]. "'Collagers v[ersus] Oppidans': A Reminiscence of Eton Life." *Cornhill Magazine* 24.144 (December 1871): 688–717.

Myers, Mitzi. "Here's Looking at You, Kid: or, Is Culturing Childhood Colonizing Casablanca?" Intro. to *Special Issue: Culturing Childhood. Nineteenth-Century Contexts.* Ed. Mitzi Myers. 21.2 (1999). 157–67.

Myers, Mitzi, and U. C. Knoepflmacher. "Cross-Writing and the Reconceptualizing of Children's Literary Studies." *Children's Literature* 25: Theme volume on *Cross-Writing.* Ed. Mitzi Myers and U. C. Knoepflmacher. New Haven: Yale UP, 1997. vii–xvii.

Nandy, Ashis. *The Intimate Enemy: Loss and Recovery of Self under Colonialism.* Delhi: Oxford UP, 1983.

————. "Reconstructing Childhood: A Critique of the Ideology of Adulthood." *Traditions, Tyranny, and Utopias: Essays in the Politics of Awareness*. Delhi: Oxford UP, 1987. 56–76.

Nodelman, Perry. "The Other: Orientalism, Colonialism, and Children's Literature." *Children's Literature Association Quarterly* 17.1 (Spring 1992): 29–35.

Patterson, Orlando. *Slavery and Social Death: A Comparative Study*. Cambridge: Harvard UP, 1982.

————. *The Sociology of Slavery: An Analysis of the Origins, Development, and Structure of Negro Slave Society in Jamaica*. Rutherford, NJ: Fairleigh Dickinson UP, 1969.

Paul, Lissa. "Interrupting the Critical Line from Rationalism to Romanticism." (Rev. of *Romanticism and Children's Literature in Nineteenth-Century England*, ed. James Holt McGavran, Jr.) *Children's Literature*. Ed. Francelia Butler, R. H. W. Dillard, and Elizabeth Lennox Keyser. New Haven: Yale UP, 1994. 22: 210–14.

[Peacock, Lucy]. "The Young Negro: A Drama in Three Acts." *The Juvenile Magazine; or, An Instructive and Entertaining Miscellany for Youth of Both Sexes* (July 1788): 403–20; (August 1788): 466–75; (September 1788): 520–36. London: J. Marshall.

Pickering, Samuel F., Jr. *Moral Instruction and Fiction for Children, 1749–1820*. Athens: U of Georgia P, 1993.

Pratt, Mary Louise. "Arts of the Contact Zone." *Profession* 91. New York: Modern Language Association, 1991. 33–40.

Quigly, Isabel. *The Heirs of Tom Brown: The English School Story*. London: Chatto and Windus, 1982.

Racevskis, Karlis. *Postmodernism and the Search for Enlightenment*. Charlottesville: UP of Virginia, 1993.

Ray, William. *Story and History: Narrative Authority and Social Identity in the Eighteenth-Century French and English Novel*. Cambridge, MA: Basil Blackwell, 1990.

Said, Edward W. *Culture and Imperialism*. New York: Knopf, 1993.

————. *Orientalism*. 1978. New York: Vintage Books/Random House, 1979.

————. "Representing the Colonized: Anthropology's Interlocutors." *Critical Inquiry* 15.2 (Winter 1989): 205–25.

Scarre, Geoffrey. Introduction. *Children, Parents, and Politics*. Ed. Geoffrey Scarre. Cambridge: Cambridge UP, 1989. ix–xiv.

Scarry, Elaine. *The Body in Pain: The Making and Unmaking of the World*. New York: Oxford UP, 1985.

Smith, Adam. *The Theory of Moral Sentiments*. Ed. D. D. Raphael and
A. L. Macfie. The Glasgow Edition. 1976; Indianapolis: Liberty Classics,
1982.

Smith, Charlotte. "Dialogue I. The Little West Indian." *Rambles Farther: A
Continuation of Rural Walks: In Dialogues Intended for the Use of Young
Persons*. 2 vols. in 1. Dublin: P. Wogan, 1796. 1–23.

[Smith, Horace, and James Smith]. *Rejected Addresses; or The New Theatrum
Poetarum*. 1812. London: Routledge, 1888.

[Southey, Robert]. "Elementary Teaching." *Quarterly Review* 39.77 (January
1829): 99–143.

[Stanley, A. P.] "School a Little World." *Rugby Magazine* 1.2 (October 1835):
95–105.

Steedman, Carolyn. "True Romances." *Patriotism: The Making and Unmaking
of British National Identity*. Vol. 1: *History and Politics*. Ed. Raphael Samuel.
London: Routledge, 1989. 26–35.

Stewart, Dugald. *Elements of the Philosophy of the Human Mind*. 6th ed.
London: Cadell and Davies; Edinburgh: Constable, 1818. Vol. 1.

Stewart, John. *An Account of Jamaica*. 1808. Black Heritage Library Collection.
Freeport, NY: Books for Libraries P, 1971.

Sypher, Wylie. *Guinea's Captive Kings: British Anti-Slavery Literature of the
Eighteenth Century*. Chapel Hill: U of North Carolina P, 1942.

Thomas, Keith. *Rule and Misrule in the Schools of Early Modern England*. The
Stenton Lecture 1975. Reading, England: U of Reading, 1976.

Tiffin, Helen. "Introduction." *Past the Last Post: Theorizing Post-Colonialism
and Post-Modernism*. Ed. Ian Adam and Helen Tiffin. Calgary: U of
Calgary P, 1990. vi–xvi.

Turner, Victor. "Social Dramas and Ritual Metaphors." *Dramas, Fields, and
Metaphors: Symbolic Action in Human Society*. Ithaca: Cornell UP, 1974.
23–59.

———. "Social Dramas and Stories about Them." *On Narrative. Critical
Inquiry* 7.1 (Autumn 1980): 140–68.

Warner, Marina. *Managing Monsters: Six Myths of Our Time*. 1994 Reith
Lectures. London: Vintage, 1994.

Whalley, George. "England: Romantic-Romanticism." *"Romantic" and Its
Cognates: The European History of a Word*. Ed. Hans Eichner. Toronto:
U of Toronto P, 1972. 157–262.

Zeta [James Anthony Froude]. *Shadows of the Clouds*. London: John Ollivier,
1847.

PART TWO

Romantic Ironies, Postmodern Texts

Dieter Petzold

TAKING GAMES SERIOUSLY: ROMANTIC IRONY IN MODERN FANTASY FOR CHILDREN OF ALL AGES

he title of this essay connects notions that, at first sight, seem hardly compatible. On reflection, we may see that Romantic ideas about the imagination, and about children, have endured and are in evidence in much of contemporary fantasy fiction, but linking irony with fantasy fiction (especially when it is for children) appears to be a different matter. Looking at the beginnings of the genre, we might admit that the new, sophisticated interest in fairy tales emerging right in the age of Rationalism (vide Basile, Perrault, the French *contes de fées*) was by no means devoid of irony. But surely in the Romantic period fantasy, and its close association with childhood, were both taken very seriously? After all, was it not the Romantics' refusal to treat children and their love of the fantastic with condescending irony that made the development of fantasy fiction as a genre possible? Only the Grimm brothers' transformation of the peasants' humble folktales into "Kinder- und Hausmärchen" (children's and household tales) made them acceptable to the dominant middle classes and endowed them with literary prestige; it was Romantics like Coleridge, Wordsworth, and Lamb who defended the child's rights to imaginative tales against the attacks of rationalist pedagogues, to be seconded a little later by Dickens, Ruskin, and countless authors and reviewers of children's books throughout the nineteenth century, and the child's ever-ready ability to fantasize became the centerpiece of the late Victorian and Edwardian neo-Romantics' cult of childhood.[1]

By and large, present-day views of fantasy still reflect this cluster of nineteenth-century ideas. It is true that J. R. R. Tolkien, who might be regarded as the father of modern fantasy (or at least the unwitting instigator of the fantasy boom of the 1970s and 1980s), objected to Andrew Lang's conventional association of fantasy fiction with childhood, but only because he felt it to be too restrictive. His claim that "enchantment" by fantasy is not a child's prerogative but an experience adult readers of fairy tales should equally aspire to is a reinstallment, not a refutation, of Romantic ideas. Taking up the old notion, dear to the Romantics, of the poet as a God-like "sub-creator,"[2] Tolkien out-Coleridges Coleridge by replacing the latter's "willing suspension of disbelief" with his more radical idea of "secondary belief," according to which the ideal readers of "fairy stories" (i.e., fantasy fiction) mentally enter the storyteller's "secondary world" and believe in it "while [they] are, as it were, inside" (Tolkien 132).

Much (though not all) of Tolkien's poetic practice is in accordance with this theory, as is that of most of Tolkien's followers, in other words, the bulk of contemporary fantasy fiction. There can be little doubt that the superficial Romanticism inherent in this literary practice is antimodernist and escapist. Readers enjoy fantasy fiction because it offers an escape both from the rationalistic drabness of modern life and from the disturbing expressions of the modern experience of life (fragmentation, disorientation, angst, etc.) in contemporary mainstream literature.

But this basically conservative use of Romantic ideas is only part of our Romantic heritage, which is in fact multifaceted and contradictory. In part, this diversity is a result of historical developments. Side by side with the Romantic glorification of the imagination and of the naive child as its purest practitioner, we find, in particular, the Romantic glorification of the author's supreme subjectivity. The two notions seem compatible enough, but they have led to diametrically opposed results. On the one side we have the idea of "secondary belief" and "enchantment," the reader's total (and childlike) submersion in the author's "secondary world" of make-believe, on the other the author's insistence on his or her sovereignty over the text. While the first attitude demands the creation of a consistent (however fantastic) universe that seems convincingly "real," the other leads to the creation of a text that is deliberately inconsistent. While in the first case the implied authors/narrators try to efface themselves in order to facilitate the reader's secondary belief, in the second they remain in evidence, explicitly or implicitly, in order to remind the reader that in telling the story they are really playing a game. Instead of concealing the rules of this game, the self-conscious authors/narrators actually foreground them. The result is a deliberate deconstruction of secondary belief: the most prominent indication of a profoundly ironic attitude toward the text.

The justness of the label "Romantic irony" for this specific form of irony may be debatable, but it is certainly widely established. While it might be argued that "Romantic irony" is a "misnomer" (Furst 238), since it was neither invented nor exclusively practiced by the writers of the Romantic period, it is equally clear that its prominence is due to a cluster of philosophical and poetical ideas which are rightly associated with Romanticism.

I shall not here attempt to define what has persuasively been declared to be undefinable (Dane 118), nor is this the place to unravel the complex implications the term *Romantic irony* has acquired in the course of its development.[3] While most scholars agree that the destruction of fictional illusion in itself does not comprise the full meaning of Romantic irony, it may still be regarded as its most prominent manifestation. From the start, the implications of Romantic irony were as much philosophical as they were poetological. At its center we find the period's (especially the German idealistic philosophers') discovery of subjectivism. Friedrich Schlegel, certainly the first and seminal theoretician of Romantic irony (although he did not use the term and is notoriously difficult and obscure), understood irony as the only adequate expression of a specific worldview—a worldview that reflects the individual's subjectivity, skepticism, and sense of alienation. "Irony is transformed [by Schlegel] into a way of seeing the world, of embracing within one's consciousness paradox and chaos" (Furst 27). As has frequently been pointed out, this reveals an essentially modern consciousness. "To study Romantic Irony is to discover how modern Romanticism could be, or, if you like, how Romantic Modernism is" (Muecke 182).

If Romantic irony provides a close link between Romanticism and modernism, the one between Romanticism and postmodernism is even closer. In particular, what has been labeled "metafictional" writing seems to be just an application, or elaboration, of the German Romantics' ideas of irony. The similarity lies not only in the frequent use of rhetorical devices that disrupt fictional illusion but equally in the underlying philosophical premises. Mellor's definition of "philosophical [Romantic] irony" as "this inevitable and all-important consciousness of the limitations of human knowledge and of human language" (11) and Furst's explanations of Romantic irony quoted earlier are strikingly echoed in Waugh's description of metafiction: modern metafiction "reflects a greater awareness within contemporary culture of the function of language in constructing and maintaining our sense of everyday 'reality.' The simple notion that language passively reflects a coherent, meaningful and 'objective' world is no longer tenable" (3). The similarity becomes even more striking when we compare Waugh's statement that "the paranoia that permeates the metafictional writing of the sixties and seventies is [now] slowly giving way to celebration, to the discovery of new forms of the fantastic, fabulatory extravaganzas, magic realism" (9) with Mellor's distinction between modernist writing and Romantic ironic writing. While the former uses irony frequently to express a sense of the absurdity of existence, or of existentialist angst, Romantic irony, according to Mellor, is less negative, displaying an "exuberant playing with the possibilities of an ever-changing world and life, [an] expanding participation in a variety of selves and modes of consciousness, [an] openness to new ideas and experiences" (188).

It is on this level that a connection can be made between Romanticism, postmodernism, and some contemporary children's books. This connection may well seem far-fetched to a person who believes that writers for children should not be ironical because children are naive readers and will therefore be confused or disturbed by irony. But modern critics have rightly pointed out that children can be quite sophisticated readers, well capable of understanding and appreciating irony (Wall 2). Still, one might argue that postmodern irony is unsuitable for children because of its radically skeptical, sometimes even nihilistic quality. It may be true that late-twentieth-century children are no strangers to the paradoxical nature of modern life (as it is portrayed in much of modern literature); but if it is equally true that children need help, guidance, and reassurance,[4] one consequence is that their books should not be totally disillusioning and negative.

But then, pervasive irony need not necessarily be nihilistic. In particular, fantasy, since it does not pretend to imitate reality, allows for a use of irony which is less a comment on the contradictory nature of the real world than a celebration of the powers of the imagination. By reminding their readers that they are participating in a game, the authors of ironic fantasy allow themselves and their readers to have their cake and eat it too: to remember that the fictional world they are enjoying is just make-believe and to realize at the same time that it is, nevertheless, profoundly meaningful. Moreover, by insisting on the importance of the reader in this game, authors of ironic fantasy for children have also managed to reconcile the Romantic belief in the naive, imaginative child with the Romantic belief in the sovereignty of the subjective (therefore ironic) author, as we shall see.

Some ambivalences remain, however. The history of children's literature is not devoid of texts that make oblique comments on the complexities of reality by playing with the conventions and trappings of fairy tale and fantasy—in other words, fantasy texts that employ Romantic irony. However, there have always been readers who found such books somewhat disturbing, and there is a widespread feeling that these are not really children's books since they are appreciated by adults at least as much as by children. Cases in point are the *Märchen* by the German Romantic writers Clemens Brentano (e.g., "Das Märchen von Gockel und Hinkel," 1815) and E. T. A. Hoffmann (especially *Nussknacker und Mausekönig*, 1816), Charles Kingsley's *The Water-Babies* (1863), Lewis Carroll's *Alice* books (1865–71), and J. M. Barrie's *Peter Pan* (1904). Yet, whether in spite or because of these ambivalences, these texts have been popular in their times (in part extremely so), both among adults and children, and they have endured. It is likely that the same will be said of the more recent examples of fantasy fiction which I am going to discuss: fantasy stories that so consistently play self-conscious games—in other words, employ Romantic irony so pervasively—that they might well be called metafantasies. This term is, of course, a neologism formed after the somewhat better established term *metafiction*. It was apparently coined by R. E. Foust in an article on Peter Beagle's fantasy novel *The Last Unicorn*. What the label implies is, in fact, that this novel is informed by its consistent use of Romantic irony.

First published in 1968, *The Last Unicorn* rapidly became very popular among young people and has since been made, according to Zahorski, "assigned reading in hundreds, perhaps thousands, of high school and college literature courses" (38). An animated film version has doubtlessly also contributed to the popularity of the story among the young. It is true, however, that it was not written specifically for children and belongs, therefore, to the limbo world of "books for all ages" rather than to children's literature in a strict sense.

Beagle's sustained ironic stance is expressed in his style, which wavers permanently between the precious and the mundane, and in his highly self-conscious, playful use of the traditions and conventions of myth and fantasy.[5] The eponymous unicorn, a female, lives "in a lilac wood, . . . all alone" (Beagle 3). When she learns that she is the last of her kind, she sets out to see if this is true or if she can find other unicorns. A butterfly tells her that there were indeed others, but they were driven away by a Red Bull. Subsequently she is captured by a witch called Mommy Fortuna, who exhibits her in her traveling show along with other fabulous beasts, most of which, however, are fakes, transformed only by Mommy's meager magic. An equally inept but kind magician with the unpromising name of Schmendrick frees her; they join forces, only to be made prisoners by a certain Captain Cully, an outlaw whose ambition is to become, like Robin Hood, the object of ballads. To confound them, Schmendrick conjures up the real Robin Hood, and they manage to flee in the ensuing confusion.

They reach the castle of a certain King Haggard, who is responsible for the disappearance of the unicorns: in his desire to possess and permanently preserve the beauty of the unicorns, he has imprisoned them in the sea. Their liberation involves a great many complex moves which include the temporary transformation of the immortal unicorn into a human girl (the Lady Amalthea) and the exploits of a young prince who grows from a lazy, ridiculously romantic good-for-nothing into a real hero who dies fighting the formidable Red Bull. In the end King Haggard's castle collapses, Prince Lír is revived, and the unicorns are released, but the prince's love for the Lady Amalthea remains unrequited since she is retransformed into a unicorn.

Innumerable allusions, many of them parodistic, underscore the deliberate conventionality of the quest story. By creating links both with other works of literature and with the outside reality, they successfully prevent the readers from developing secondary belief. There is, for example, the Carrollian butterfly whose nonsensical speech is wholly made up of quotations: proverbs and sayings, snippets of poetry, pop songs, plays, and novels. There is Captain Cully, who mistakes Schmendrick for the famous American collector of ballads, Professor Child, and who, in his ambition to be a legendary hero, makes ballads about himself (which are parodies of genuine Child ballads). Characters are sometimes aware of their own nature as fictions, as in the following part of a dialogue between Schmendrick and his sidekick, Molly: "Haven't you ever been in a fairy tale before? . . . The hero has to make a prophesy come true, and the villain is the one who has to stop him—though in another kind of story, it's more often the other way around. And a hero has to be in trouble from the moment of his birth, or he's not a real hero. It's a great relief to find out about Prince Lír. I've been waiting for this tale to turn up a leading man" (Beagle 96).

As in all true cases of Romantic irony, the function of such anti-illusionary devices is not purely negative. While they serve as a reminder of the essential intertextuality of fantasy fiction, they do not downgrade fantasy as "mere" fiction. On the contrary, Beagle seems to insist on the importance, even the superiority, of the world of the imagination over "mere" reality. When Captain Cully, disturbed by the sudden appearance of his idol Robin Hood, nervously resorts to the rationalist view that "Robin Hood is a myth, . . . a classic example of the heroic folk-figure synthesized out of need," Molly counters, "Nay, Cully, you have it backward. . . . There's no such a person as you, or me, or any of us. Robin and Marian are real, and we are the legend!" (Beagle 67, 68).

The motifs out of which this fantasy—any fantasy—is constructed may be familiar, well worn, and easily made fun of, yet what they stand for remains relevant. Beagle's Platonic world comprises several grades of reality: Schmendrick and his companions are more real than the butterfly who consists exclusively of empty verbal shells, but they are, in turn, less real than Robin Hood. The most real of all, it seems, is the immortal Unicorn, as the continuation of dialogue between Schmendrick and Molly (mentioned above) suggests: "The unicorn was there as a star is suddenly there, moving a little way ahead of them, a sail in the dark. Molly said, 'If Lír is the hero, what is she?' 'That's different. Haggard and Lír and Drinn and you and I— we are in a fairy tale, and must go where it goes. But she is real. She is real'" (Beagle 68).

The Unicorn is more real than Schmendrick and the rest because she represents the very idea of Beauty. Although it is not an allegory pure and simple, the novel, on one level, is about beauty in general and the beauty of literary fantasy in particular.[6] It is also about the dangers of our loss of access to the ideal: we are today, like King Haggard, obtuse, possessive, and unable to cherish life's true joys precisely because we cannot accept their impermanence.[7]

Much the same message can be extracted from my second example, *Die unendliche Geschichte* by the German author Michael Ende. First published in 1979, the book proved an immediate and overwhelming success in Germany, quickly equaling, in part even surpassing, Ende's earlier fantasy stories for children and adults. An English version, made by the renowned translator Ralph Manheim, appeared in 1983 under the title *The Neverending Story*.[8]

Even more than in *The Last Unicorn*, the Romantic irony in *The Neverending Story* is predominantly structural rather than stylistic. We need to look at the story line, therefore, in order to see to what extent Ende's novel can be regarded as a metafantasy. What strikes the reader first is the physical appearance of the book: parts of the story are printed in red, others in green. These colors correspond to two levels within the narrative. One, the "realistic" level, is about Bastian, a rather fat little boy of about ten or twelve who, because of his awkwardness, is an outsider at school and who is equally lonesome at home since his mother died and his father abandoned himself to his grief. Fleeing from his taunting classmates, he enters a used book shop, where a strange-looking volume attracts his attention. This book has the same title and the same appearance as the book the reader is holding in his hands. Bastian steals the book, finds a hiding place, and begins to read. At this point the letters change from red to green, and we are, as it were, with Bastian, reading a story that at first sight looks like any fantasy story. It is soon interrupted, however, by red printing telling us about Bastian's reactions to what he is reading.

His strong emotional response is caused by an exciting, at times also funny, tale about the land of Fantastica and its many different inhabitants. Many of these seem faintly familiar because they are taken from classical mythology, fables, fairy tales, and legends. There are giants, gnomes, will-o'-the-wisps, witches, vampires, and ghosts; there is a centaur named Cairon and a flying horse called Pegasus. As we read we encounter motifs taken from the *Odyssey* and passages or figures reminiscent of stories by Lindgren, Tolkien, C. S. Lewis, Hoffmann, and Novalis. In short, there are innumerable literary allusions which make it clear that Fantastica is indeed the product of ages of storytelling and that any story, and this one in particular, is really a web of intertextual relations.[9]

The creatures of Fantastica are alarmed because large chunks of their land have simply vanished recently. This mystery seems somehow to be connected with the illness of Fantastica's ruler, the Childlike Empress. A boy hero named Atreyu is sent on a quest to find a remedy, but it turns out that he cannot fulfill his mission, for what is really needed is a person from the outside world who is able to give the Childlike Empress a new name. Fantastica, it appears, depends for its very existence on the inhabitants of the outside (real) world taking an interest in it, believing in it, as it were. The naming of the Childlike Empress has therefore a symbolic significance: it is the reader who, by dint of his or her creative imagination, gives life to the world of fantasy.

At first sight Ende seems inconsistent here, for is he not pleading for a naive belief in the reality of the secondary fantasy world while at the same time pointing out that it is only a construction of the mind? But what he is exploring in this book, quite consciously, is exactly this paradox, which, as we have seen, can be traced back to Romantic thought: the writer is the supreme manipulator, yet his imagination is not just idle fancy but serves to reveal, through poetic images, some higher, ideal reality. The game that he plays is amusing and serious at the same time, and he requires a partner in his game who is both appreciative of the fun and willing to abandon himself to the game.

Bastian is such an ideal reader of fantasy. Being endowed with imaginative powers that match the author's, he finds the naming of the Childlike Empress an easy task. From then on he is literally drawn into the story he is reading, becoming eventually one of the inhabitants of Fantastica. Thus the part of the book that deals with Bastian—which we had up to now regarded as realistic—turns out to be fantastic after all, since things begin to happen that we know to be impossible. The effect may well be confusion as we read what Bastian is reading, which is how Atreyu, the admired hero of the story, becomes aware of Bastian when looking into a magic mirror.

> What [Atreyu] saw was something quite unexpected, which wasn't the least bit terrifying, but which baffled him completely. He saw a fat little boy with a pale face—a boy his own age—and this little boy was sitting on a pile of mats, reading a book.
>
> *Bastian gave a start when he realized what he had just read. Why, that was him! The description was right in every detail. The book*

trembled in his hands. This was going too far. How could there be
something in a book that applied only to this particular moment and
only to him? (Ende 90–91)[10]

Even more confusing is the actual transition, which occurs many
pages later, at the very center of the book. The Childlike Empress enters a magic egg and finds there a volume entitled *The Neverending
Story* which looks exactly like the book Bastian—and the reader—
are holding. Bastian's thoughts, we learn, are "in a whirl," and so
may well be the reader's, for now even stranger things happen. The
Childlike Empress discovers that the book is held by an old man,
who seems to be writing in the book, but

> his stylus glided slowly over the empty page and the letters and
> words appeared as though of their own accord.
>
> The Childlike Empress read what was being written, and it was
> exactly what was happening at that same moment: "The Childlike
> Empress read what was being written . . ."
>
> "You write down everything that happens," she said.
>
> "Everything that I write down happens," was the answer, spo-
> ken in the deep, dark voice that had come to her like an echo of
> her own voice. (Ende 171)

When the Childlike Empress asks him to read the beginning of the
book, the story literally starts all over again, and Bastian realizes,
"Why, this was all about him! And it was the Neverending Story. He,
Bastian, was a character in the book which until now he had thought
he was reading. And heaven only knew who else might be reading it
at the exact same time, also supposing himself to be just a reader"
(Ende 175). At this point the story is in danger of becoming truly
never-ending, for the natural consequence of this setup is that it
moves in a circle. Bastian, however, manages to break the circle by
giving the Childlike Empress a new name. As a result, he now finds
himself completely inside the story, a true inhabitant of Fantastica.

Bastian's renaming of the Childlike Empress ends the quest in that
it stops the disintegration of Fantastica, but it is also a creative act
that marks the beginning of a long series of imaginative creations
and thus of a new story. The second part of Ende's book is essentially
a maturation story, for Bastian has to learn how to handle his new-
found freedom and virtual omnipotence. The price he has to pay for
his unlimited magical creativity is the loss, step by step, of his mem-

ory. While he is acquiring a new, more glamorous identity, he is in danger of losing himself in his own fantasy world. Only after he has learned self-discipline and responsibility is he able to return from the world of his fantasies to the real world and to bring his father the "Water of Life" which will cure him of his self-centered, paralyzing melancholy.

Ende's Romantic irony results in a constant challenge to the reader's conventional distinction between reality and make-believe that is only occasionally funny. More frequently, the reader will probably find Ende's deft juggling with levels of reality baffling if not downright disturbing. The disruptions of a conventional storyline cannot be laughed away because the author himself is taking his game very seriously. Like Beagle, Ende tells a story in a playful spirit to convey a serious, and very Romantic, message about the importance of the imagination and of storytelling.

It may not come as a surprise to find that when the master of magic realism, Salman Rushdie, wrote his first book of pure fantasy, he actually produced a piece of metafantasy. What is surprising, however, is how similar Rushdie's *Haroun and the Sea of Stories*, first published in 1990, is to Ende's *Unendliche Geschichte*. Like Ende's book, this is a fantasy story ostensibly written for children but to be enjoyed equally (if not more) by adults; this too is a quest story with a boy hero, and this too employs two levels, mixing elements of everyday reality with fantastic ingredients derived from various literary sources. Here, too, the quest has a cosmic as well as a personal significance. Above all, this too is a story about storytelling.

This is indicated in the very first sentence, which sets the story "in the country of Alifbay" in "a city so ruinously sad that it had forgotten its name" (Rushdie 15). To a speaker of Hindustani, or a user of the glossary of names that Rushdie has thoughtfully appended to his story, the meaning of this name, Alifbay, is just as obvious as Ende's Fantastica: it comes from the Hindustani word for "Alphabet." The use of telling names like these (and there are many more) suggests an allegorical reading; but just like Beagle's and Ende's stories, *Haroun and the Sea of Stories* is far more complex than a straightforward allegory, offering multiple meanings rather than a simple one-on-one relationship between signifier and signified.

Even though it is obviously a fantasy story, *Haroun and the Sea of Stories* contains many elements of reality which it presents predominantly in a satirical mood. Haroun's and his father's hair-raising bus ride to the Valley of K and their stay with that oily arch-politician, "Snooty" Buttoo, are cases in point. What seems to be a Bunyan-esque allegorical journey to the Moody Land with its Mist of Misery (Rushdie 47) is really a description of a trip to the Dal Lake in Kashmir, and the similarity between their host's name and that of Pakistan's former head of state is hardly a coincidence.

At the same time we are reminded that this story (like any story) is an artifact made of words. The bus travels from the Town of G over the Pass of H and through the Tunnel of I to the Valley of K; later in the story creatures named Butt and Iff take Haroun to the moon Kahani (which in Hindustani means "story").

But Rushdie is concerned less with language itself than with supralinguistic literary units like motif and plot. Most importantly, he is concerned with the uses, and abuses, of storytelling. Kahani, the place where all the stories come from, is mostly covered by the Ocean of the Streams of Story;[11] it is increasingly being polluted through the machinations of the people of Chup (Hindustani for "quiet"), who resent the dominance of the land of Gup (Hindustani for "gossip" or "nonsense"). The meaning of this parable of storytelling is not as straightforward as it may seem at first sight. For instance, the idea of the pollution of the Streams of Story appears rather ambiguous on closer inspection. Its consequences are brought home to Haroun in a dreamlike sequence:

> He found himself standing in a landscape that looked exactly like a giant chessboard. On every black square there was a monster: there were two-tongued snakes and lions with three rows of teeth, and four-headed dogs and five-headed demon kings and so on. He was, so to speak, looking out through the eyes of the young hero of the story. It was like being in the passenger seat of an automobile; all he had to do was watch, while the hero dispatched one monster after another and advanced up the chessboard towards the white stone tower at the end. At the top of the tower was (what else but) a single window, out of which there gazed (who else but) a captive princess. What Haroun was experiencing, though he didn't know it, was Princess Rescue Story Number S/1001/ZHT/420/41(r)xi; and because the princess in this particular story had recently had a haircut and therefore had no long tresses to let down (unlike the heroine of Princess Rescue Story G/1001/RIM/

777/ M(w)i, better known as "Rapunzel"), Haroun as the hero was required to climb up the outside of the tower by clinging to the cracks between the stones with his bare hands and feet.

He was halfway up the tower when he noticed one of his hands beginning to change, becoming hairy, losing its human shape. Then his arms burst out of his shirt, and they too had grown hairy, and impossibly long, and had joints in the wrong places. He looked down and saw the same thing happening to his legs. When new limbs began to push themselves out from his sides, he understood that he was somehow turning into a monster. (Rushdie 73–74)

Excessive intertextual promiscuousness, it seems, has led to a confusion of genres: we move from Lewis Carroll's chessboard world to Arabian Nights–like monsters to the Grimms' *Household Tales* to a metamorphosis reminiscent both of Kafka and of modern horror movies. There seems to be a satirical intention present, but it is not clearly focused. On the one hand, Rushdie ridicules the predictability of conventional folktales and the pedantic cataloging of motifs used by folklorists; on the other hand, he seems to resent changes in stories, at least if they are radical enough to subvert the genre. Moreover, it could be argued, Rushdie's book is itself just such a heady mixture of styles and genres.

All the same, Rushdie's irony does not lead into total negativity. His book does have a moral message, even though it is more complex than might be expected of a fantasy story. It is true that the two diametrically opposed peoples on Kahani, associated as they are with light and darkness, suggest, in well-established fantasy manner, a clear separation of good and evil. But Rushdie gradually makes the reader see that both parties, the garrulous Gupwallas and the taciturn Chupwallas, have their good and their bad sides. The real evil stems from the artificial separation of the two, for which the much more pleasant-seeming inhabitants of Gup are responsible. They have used their technological superiority very unfairly to their own advantage, thus depriving the Chupwallas of their share of sunshine and inadvertently shutting themselves off from the moderating influence of their more serious-minded cousins.

Thus the story can be read as a satirical comment on imperialism and racism, especially since its Oriental setting encourages us to see it in a postcolonial context. The didactic message, then, is a plea for fairness, toleration, and open-mindedness, directed in particular at a Western audience who at first is invited to identify with the jolly, pleasant inhabitants of Gup, only to find out that these people are downright silly at times and—what is worse—have allowed themselves to be guided by a totally amoral technological power elite.

This sociopolitical meaning, however, forms just the frame for the book's more immediate concern, which is the nature, and importance, of storytelling in our time. Khattam-Shud, the instigator of the Chupwallahs' attempt to corrupt and destroy stories, combines two contradictory attitudes toward literature. On the one hand, there is a disdain of "mere" fiction as something irrelevant. It seems likely that this attitude is widespread, for even Haroun falls prey to the narrow-minded utilitarianism expressed in the fatal question, "What's the use of stories that aren't even true?" (Rushdie 22). (His quest is a kind of atonement for this fall from readerly innocence and filial solidarity.) On the other hand, there is the despotic Cult-master's fear of stories, which betrays a secret belief in their potency: "Inside every single story, inside every Stream in the Ocean, there lies a world, a story-world, that I cannot Rule [sic] at all" (Rushdie 161). Ende makes a similar point when he has Gmork the Werewolf explain that the "Manipulators" of this world, who know that "the power to manipulate beliefs is the only thing that counts" (133), fear stories about Fantastica because these cannot be manipulated. Khattam-Shud may turn out to be a "skinny, scrawny, measly, weaselly, snivelling clerical type" (Rushdie 153), but while he rules he is a dangerous ayatollah-like despot who needs to be taken seriously. His power derives from the fact that he and his corruption of story-telling are really symptoms of a more general corruption of culture. This in turn is caused by the writers' loss of contact with the people and its traditions and by their self-prostitution to party politics and popular entertainment. Rashid's employment in political election-eering campaigns illustrates this loss of artistic innocence.

Rushdie's remedy is at the same time conservative and liberal: he pleads for a return to the unpolluted sources of culture and for open-mindedness and versatility. This ambiguity is reflected in Haroun's helpers. On the one side there is the Floating Gardener, who is a conservationist, and on the other side there are the genie Iff and the robot-bird Butt. "If" is a conjunction that signals conjecture, imagination, and desire ("What if . . . ," "If only . . ."); "but" denotes contradiction, the refusal to accept the status quo and the seemingly obvious. By championing versatility and contradiction, Rushdie places himself in a Romantic tradition. According to Mellor, turning contradiction into an asset is the hallmark of Romantic irony, which "embraces a mental habit of tolerance and a discourse of ambiguity. Romantic irony is thus opposed to the 'gross dichotomizing' or rigid thinking in polarities that has become the prevailing imaginative structure of modern times" (188).

While Rushdie elaborates the sociopolitical importance of storytelling to a much larger extent than Ende, he does not neglect the personal level of meaning which is central to *Die unendliche Geschichte*. Both books have heroes who seem, at first sight, unlikely to succeed. But even though Haroun's attention span does not exceed eleven minutes, his love of stories and the power of his imagination are so great that, like Bastian, he can enter the realm of stories. In both cases, name giving is the essential test. Bastian must find a new name for the Childlike Empress; and the Water Genie Iff gets Haroun on his trip by encouraging him to "pick" (imagine and name) a bird, which is possible because "to give a thing a name, a label, a handle; to rescue it from anonymity, to pluck it out of the Place of Namelessness, in short to identify it—well, that's a way of bringing the said thing into being" (Rushdie 63). Once more, the child is father (i.e., protector) of the man: both Bastian and Haroun rescue their fathers from their own negativity and despondency. The Romantic image of the child as savior and healer prevails.[12]

Whether children can appreciate all these intricacies and understand these messages need not concern us overmuch. The old truism that individual readers will read in individual ways and that no reader can exhaust the potential of meaning inherent in a work of fiction applies to young readers as much as to old ones. What is certain is that the books discussed here have been read and loved not only by adults but equally by young readers. In fact, it seems that Beagle and Ende have heralded quite a pervasive shift of taste, away from Tolkienesque high fantasy seriousness to much more lighthearted— and ambiguous—forms of enjoying a sense of wonder, as witnessed by the phenomenal success of such writers as Douglas Adams (in the field of science fiction) and Terry Pratchett since the late 1980s.[13] At first sight, Adams's and Pratchett's exuberant burlesques may seem more superficially funny than the books discussed in this essay, but they display, at closer scrutiny, a quite radical sense of cosmic despair (which may, incidentally, account for the fact that these writers have become cult authors among college students rather than among children). In a stricter sense than Adams or Pratchett, Beagle, Ende, and even Rushdie are Romantics in that they are centrally concerned with imagination. They are, at the same time, moderns because they react to contemporary rationalism, skepticism, utilitarianism, and despotism, which they see as endangering human imagination in general and storytelling in particular. But, unlike many metafictional texts, their stories are essentially optimistic, expressing the hope that these dangers can be overcome. This optimism may well be one reason for their success. Another reason is undoubtedly that these stories can be enjoyed simply as gripping yarns. Neither Beagle's deliberate confusions of reality levels nor Ende's complex Chinese-box structures nor Rushdie's exuberant wordplay and wide-ranging satirical irony impair the stories' excitement and wonder. Metafantasy, it seems, cannot do without either.

NOTES

1. For evidence to support these claims, see the studies of Zipes and Watson and my own *Englische Kunstmärchen* and "A Race Apart."

2. For the history of this idea, see Abrams esp. 272–85 ("The Poem as Heterocosm").

3. There are numerous investigations of Romantic irony. I am particularly indebted to those by Mellor, Furst, and Dane.

4. Cf. Alan Richardson's chapter in this volume, where the author argues convincingly that the idea that children are vulnerable and need protection is an important progressive achievement of Romanticism.

5. Like all interesting irony, Beagle's does run the risk of being missed. Manlove's dismissal of the book as "anaemic fantasy" and his further caustic remarks (148–54) seem to be the result of his failure to see Beagle's consistently ironic stance.

6. There is no contradiction in the fact that, on another level, the Unicorn appears to be a Christ symbol, most clearly in Schmendrick's dream near the end of the novel (212–16).

7. For a fuller discussion of Beagle's Neoplatonism and of many other aspects of *The Last Unicorn*, see Zahorski (38–57).

8. Not being concerned here with stylistic niceties, I hope to be excused for quoting from the English version in this essay.

9. Cf. Ludwig for a detailed presentation of Ende's use of literary sources.

10. In the book, the first part of this quotation is printed in green, the second in red. I have used italics here and in the following quotations to indicate the difference.

11. This name is in fact the English title of a collection of Sanscrit verse narratives, the *Katha-sarit-sagara*, by the eleventh-century Kashmiri Brahmin Somadeva (Aklujkar 2). Rushdie's allusion to this book is deliberate (Haroun finds it in Mr. Buttoo's library); but, as Aklujkar points out, the metaphor is quite common in Indian literature. Nor need a Western audience find the idea of a virtually inexhaustible store of stories totally strange: it suggests itself readily to anyone familiar with folklore studies. Tolkien, for instance, uses similar metaphors in his essay "On Fairy Stories." He speaks of the "Tree of Tales" (120), a metaphor that stresses the organic growth of the immense complex of folktales and motifs, and, a little later, of the "Cauldron of Story" (127), which metaphor neatly encapsulates the infinite variability of stories made out of a limited number of motifs.

12. In an article published after the completion of this essay, Judith Plotz stresses Rushdie's romanticism even more emphatically, drawing parallels between Rushdie and Blake, Coleridge, Shelley, Schiller, and Goethe, identifying "Rushdie's depiction of imaginative creativity" as a "Romantic tactic" and pointing out that *"Haroun . . .* makes the Romantic connection among art, play, and psychological and political well-being" (103).

13. This is not to deny that Tolkien often displays a wonderful sense of humor. Pervasive irony, however, is rare in his work, except in *Farmer Giles of Ham*.

WORKS CITED

Abrams, M. H. *The Mirror and the Lamp: Romantic Theory and the Critical Tradition.* New York: Oxford UP, 1953.

Aklujkar, Vidyut. *"Haroun and the Sea of Stories*: Metamorphosis of an Old Metaphor." *Commonwealth Novel in English* 6.1 (Spring 1993): 1–14.

Beagle, Peter S. *The Last Unicorn.* New York: Viking, 1968.

Dane, Joseph A. *The Critical Mythology of Irony.* Athens: U of Georgia P, 1991.

Ende, Michael. *Die unendliche Geschichte.* Stuttgart: Thienemanns, 1979.

———. *The Neverending Story.* Trans. Ralph Manheim. New York: Doubleday, 1983.

Foust, R. E. "Fabulous Paradigm: Fantasy, Meta-Fantasy, and Peter S. Beagle's *The Last Unicorn.*" *Extrapolation* 21 (1980): 5–20.

Furst, Lilian R. *Fictions of Romantic Irony.* Cambridge: Harvard UP, 1984.

Ludwig, Claudia. *Was du ererbt von deinen Vätern hast . . . Michael Endes Phantásien—Symbolik und literarische Quellen.* Frankfurt: Lang, 1988.

Manlove, C. N. *The Impulse of Fantasy Literature*. London: Macmillan, 1983.

McGavran, James Holt, Jr., ed. *Romanticism and Children's Literature in Nineteenth-Century England*. Athens: U of Georgia P, 1991.

Mellor, Anne K. *English Romantic Irony*. Cambridge: Harvard UP, 1980.

Muecke, Douglas C. *The Compass of Irony*. London: Methuen, 1969.

Petzold, Dieter. *Das englische Kunstmärchen im neunzehnten Jahrhundert*. Tübingen: Niemeyer, 1981.

———. "A Race Apart: Children in Late Victorian and Edwardian Children's Books." *Children's Literature Association Quarterly* 17 (1992): 33–36.

Plotz, Judith. "*Haroun* and the Politics of Children's Literature." *Children's Literature Association Quarterly* 20 (1995): 100–104.

Rushdie, Salman. *Haroun and the Sea of Stories*. London: Granta, 1991.

Tolkien, J. R. R. "On Fairy Stories." *The Monsters and the Critics and Other Essays*. Ed. Christopher Tolkien. London: Allen and Unwin, 1983. 109–61.

Wall, Barbara. *The Narrator's Voice: The Dilemma of Children's Fiction*. Basinstoke: Macmillan, 1991.

Watson, Jeanie. " 'The Raven: A Christmas Poem': Coleridge and the Fairy Tales Controversy." *Romanticism and Children's Literature in Nineteenth-Century England*. Ed. James Holt McGavran, Jr. Athens: U of Georgia P, 1991. 14–33.

Waugh, Patricia. *Metafiction: The Theory and Practice of Self-Conscious Fiction*. London: Methuen, 1984.

Zahorski, Kenneth J. *Peter Beagle*. Starmont Reader's Guide 44. Mercer Island, WA: Starmont House, 1988.

Zipes, Jack. *The Brothers Grimm: From Enchanted Forests to the Modern World*. New York: Routledge, 1988.

Richard Flynn

"INFANT SIGHT": ROMANTICISM, CHILDHOOD, AND POSTMODERN POETRY

he idea of the child and the *ideal* of the child have, since their simultaneous invention, been inseparable—in Schiller's words, the child is "a lively *representation* of the ideal," a representation we adults construct "from the limitation of our condition" (51, my emphasis). Our tendency to view childhood as an idea or ideal makes it difficult for us to see childhood as lived experience. In art, childhood is a representation or a construct that the adult recaptures or recalls, and hence it is mediated both through the artistic process and through an experiential state, adulthood, that is temporally and emotionally distanced from the original experience. Since the Romantic poets, particularly Blake and Wordsworth, recognized its metaphoric potential, childhood as a subject for poetry has increasingly preoccupied post-Romantic poets. For postmodern poets (historically speaking, poets working since World War II) the subject has taken on even greater importance, both as a counterreaction to an academic version of modernism that was anti-Romantic and aesthetically conservative and as a field for wrestling with the difficulties of subjectivity introduced by the Romantics but made more complex in a postindustrial society. For postmodern poets, "the recourse to childhood" may be, as Mark Edmundson argues, a "major mode of resistance to oppressive social forms" (750), but at the same time it may also be regressive—perhaps an ultimately nostalgic response to the "depthlessness" that Fredric Jameson argues characterizes postmodernity.

Defining postmodern poetry itself is complicated by multiple competing discourses. Anxious about a critical discourse they perceive as paying insufficient attention to the human person, many mainstream poets exhibit what Edmundson describes as "instinctive hostility" to a critical theory advanced by "conceptual disciplines" that themselves "become authoritarian, intoxicated with the universal presumptions of theory [whose] practitioners forget that poetry (childhood, power, and play) exists" (760–61). In his provocative essay, "Vital Intimations: Wordsworth, Coleridge, and the Promise of Criticism," Edmundson traces the contemporary crisis in both poetry and criticism to the split between Coleridge and Wordsworth when Coleridge denounced the passage in the "Immortality" ode that calls the child the "best philosopher" as "mental bombast." Contending that "academic literary criticism has followed the spirit that Coleridge evinces in this judgment when it should have been listening just as hard, if not harder, to Wordsworth" (739–40), he laments that the idea of childhood as a meaningful construct has "become all but untenable within the provinces of [contemporary] high culture. . . . The child as ideal is something that, in the wake of Freud, one must leave high culture to find" (750–51) in, say, the novels of Stephen King. The gulf between philosophy and poetry, Edmundson argues, has "enervated literary culture in part because the critics are not talking to — or defending — the poets anymore: they've gone hand and glove with the other people in the school of arts and sciences" (759). Though Edmundson's essay is a spirited defense of poetry, it is doubtful that the gulf between criticism and poetry is primarily traceable to the rise of literary theory. Certainly, throughout the twentieth century, both mainstream writers and experimental writers have concerned themselves with negotiating the perceived gap between theory and practice.

Although later I shall discuss some more experimental writing, especially that of Lyn Hejinian, I begin with a literary-historical account of how certain "mainstream" postmodernist poets—Randall Jarrell, Robert Lowell, and Elizabeth Bishop—formulated their relationship to childhood in reaction to their New Critical literary mentors. Beginning in the 1950s, these poets found the need to reject the aesthetically conservative stances of their modernist mentors— Ransom and Tate for Lowell and Jarrell, and Marianne Moore for Bishop. Bristling against the classicism and decorum demanded by these mentors and distrusting the hostility toward Romanticism in the New Criticism, these poets sought, in Jarrell's words, to "write the kind of poetry that replaces modernism" ("Note" 51). If Jarrell could argue (then heretically) that "'modern' poetry is, essentially, an extension of romanticism," then the "best modern criticism [was] extremely anti-romantic" ("Note" 48). As we know now, this criticism was to help rewrite the history of modernist poetry in such a way as to deemphasize the more radical elements of modernist experimentation (downplaying the achievements of writers like Stein and Williams) and to emphasize the unity, impersonality, and autonomy of the lyric poem.

If the New Critics' agrarian conservatism, along with their disdain for Romanticism, could not long exercise its hegemony over a generation of poets raised on Darwin, Marx, and Freud, that generation nevertheless wrote its early work under the pressure of the New Criticism's influential aesthetics. But the politically and aesthetically conservative stances of Eliot in his criticism, and even more so those of southern modernists like Ransom, Tate, and Brooks, were felt ambivalently. Younger poets publishing their early work in the 1930s and 1940s began to emerge from the long shadow cast by the more reactionary manifestations of the rise of Eliot's version of modernist poetics and the New Criticism. Despite their feeling that the New Critical orthodoxy was intimidating and Procrustean, young poets like Jarrell and Lowell owed their early success to the mentoring of the older generation they were trying to reject. By the end of the 1940s, as "modern" poetry gained respectability and the academy began to canonize the self-contained, detached, ironic lyric to invent the "mainstream" of American poetry, younger generations of poets were finding that mainstream oppressive, nearly paralyzing to their creative efforts. Turning toward the anti-Eliotic example of William Carlos Williams, they began to revise their poetic practices in order to write themselves out of an enervated version of modernism.[1]

In their criticism, the younger poets' rebellion against New Critical mentors took the form of subtle digs in the middle of generally admiring critiques of their poetry. In his essay on "John Ransom's Poetry" (1948), Jarrell identified "the rhetorical machinery" of his mentor's poems: "He is perpetually insisting, by his detached, mock-pedantic, wittily complicated tone, that he is not feeling much at all, not half so much as he really should be feeling—and this rhetoric becomes over-mannered, too-protective, when there is not much emotion for him to pretend not to be feeling, and he keeps on out of habit" (*Poetry and the Age* 98). Though he is charitable to Mr. Ransom's "self-protective rhetoric" because Ransom "was writing in an age in which the most natural feeling of tenderness, happiness, or sorrow was likely to be called sentimental," one senses the roots of Jarrell's aversion to the habitual, detached, wittily complicated aesthetic of his age. Ransom's "classical, or at worst, semi-classical treatment of romantic subjects," he writes, is a stance in which "the poet himself is an existence away from the Innocent Doves he mourns for" (*Poetry and the Age* 99).

Ransom's "Bells for John Whiteside's Daughter" illustrates the conservative-modernist depiction of childhood, which the first generation of postmodernists was struggling to reject:[2]

There was such speed in her little body,
And such lightness in her footfall,
It is no wonder her brown study
Astonishes us all.

Her wars were bruited in our high window.
We looked among orchard trees and beyond,
Where she took arms against her shadow,
Or harried unto the pond

The lazy geese, like a snow cloud
Dripping their snow on the green grass,
Tricking and stopping, sleepy and proud,
Who cried in goose, Alas,

For the tireless heart within the little
Lady with a rod that made them rise
From their noon apple-dreams and scuttle
Goose-fashion under the skies!

But now go the bells, and we are ready,
In one house we are sternly stopped
To say we are vexed at her brown study,
Lying so primly propped.
        (*Selected Poems* 7)

This deliberately impersonal elegy pays a great deal of attention to the child's body, both as remembered from life and "looked" at as a corpse, reminding us somewhat of the Victorian fascination with infant deaths. The child here is an object of erotic fixation for the "royal we" speaker of the poem. In life, as in death, she occasions a libidinous vexation on the part of the adults, something to be "looked" at, in life as the eroticized "little / Lady with a rod," in death as a study in coyly erotic primness—a sexualized innocence, now fixed by "our" gaze into a minor work of art. The sentimentally fetishized "little body" of John Whiteside's daughter (the title indicating that the child is at best a piece of property) which contained "such speed" no longer eludes the lookers. But the final attainment of the child as erotic object is made possible only by her status as a corpse. Particularly for the agrarian wing of modernists, this reification of the child is characteristic of their attempts to reconcile the anti-Romantic stance of their criticism with their often "Romantic" subjects. If Robert Lowell, in 1948, admired Ransom's ability to write "of the death of a child, a child's hen, or a childish coquette, without cynicism, sentimentality or trifling," he nevertheless notes that "these are the hardest of poems; their admirers must have something of the sensibility of Alexander Pope" (*Collected Prose* 19).[3]

As Lynn Keller notes in her excellent book, *Remaking It New*, "by the late 1940s a narrowed modernist orthodoxy had evolved. . . . This later modernism—dominated by Eliot, upheld by Ransom and Tate—followed at that time by young poets like Wilbur, Lowell, Rich, Merwin, Simpson—advocated not free verse, collage, and open forms, but allusive, well-wrought, impersonal structures shaped by the balanced tensions of paradox and ambiguity" (260). Thus, in his introduction to *Mid-Century American Poets* (1950), John Ciardi could argue that "pre-eminently this is a generation not of Bohemian extravagance but of self-conscious sanity in an urbane and cultivated poetry that is the antithesis of the Bohemian spirit" (xxix). Although "all of them have paid homage to Mr. Eliot's poetry and criticism . . . ," Ciardi continues, "they all insist on their own freedom to accept or reject according to their own view":

[Midcentury poetry] is never, then, a poetry of movements and manifestoes. It is more nearly a blend of the classical and metaphysical, a poetry of individual appraisal, tentative, self-questioning, introspective, socially involved, and always reserving for itself the right to meet experience in its humanistic environment—the uncoerced awareness of the individual man, which in art must be subjected always to principles of craftsmanship. (xxx)

Ciardi's description of the freedom of the poet in 1950 (before the advent of "confessional" poetry) may help us see the advent of confessional poetry in context. This kind of valorization of the "sanity," "urbanity," and "cultivation" often resulted in a poetry of forced maturity—written by the individual yet representative "man" or "craftsman."

The elevation of the "principles of craftsmanship" over emotionally and politically committed poetic discourse, along with the academic elevation of classical and metaphysical poetry over Romantic and Victorian "subjectivity," resulted in an arid and academic verse by poets that Randall Jarrell argued in 1962 came "out of Richard Wilbur's overcoat":

> The work of these academic, tea-party, creative-writing-class poets rather tamely satisfies the rules or standards of technique implicit in what they consider the "best modern practice," so that they are very close to one another, very craftsman-like, never take chances, and produce (extraordinarily) a pretty or correctly beautiful poem and (ordinarily) magazine verse. Their poems are without personal force—come out of poems, not out of life; are, at bottom, social behavior calculated to satisfy a small group of academic readers, editors, and foundation executives. (*Third Book* 329)

Jarrell's injunction to the poets of the midcentury to "take chances" and to write poems with "personal force" that come "out of life" shows that, like other members of his generation, he distrusted the New Critics' devaluation of Romantic poetry. If, from our vantage point, the personal autobiographical lyric seems commonplace, even exhausted, its rise during the late fifties was a felt necessity, a reaction to the exhausted impersonal, ironic, and detached lyric artifacts of magazine verse. Writing to Elizabeth Bishop in 1956, Jarrell complained, "The world of the younger poets, at present, certainly is the world of Richard Wilbur and safer pale mirror-images of Richard Wilbur—who'd have thought the era of the poet in the Grey Flannel Suit was coming?" (*Letters* 413).

In the 1990s it is sometimes difficult for us to understand these poets' radical break from the province of irony.[4] But in the 1950s the sense that modernist "impersonality" equaled corporate mentality—that craft was a form of "social behavior"—explains how the "emotional intensity" of the confessional, as Charles Altieri points out, seemed for poets like Lowell "one of the few valid ways to resist the aesthetic and cultural pressures imposed upon writers by their immediate heritage" (39). Jarrell characterized the Eisenhower years as "years when Fred Waring was in the White House," and Lowell in "Inauguration Day: January 1953" wrote:

Our wheels no longer move.
Look, the fixed stars, all just alike
as land-lack atoms, split apart,
and the Republic summons Ike,
the mausoleum in her heart.
   (*Life Studies* 7)

Compelled by the exigencies of an antipoetic cultural climate, the poets of the fifties found themselves concentrating on prose fiction, autobiography, biography, and memoir—Lowell's aborted autobiography; Bishop's brilliant autobiographical stories about childhood, "In the Village" and "Gwendolyn"; Berryman's biography of Stephen Crane (and his poetic auto/biographical "Homage to Mistress Bradstreet"); and Jarrell's novel and cultural criticism. Indeed, Jarrell might have been speaking for most of his close contemporaries when he complained that "a wicked fairy has turned me into a prose writer."

The autobiographical impulse and the postmodern turn toward childhood represented an attempt to understand and rewrite the personal and the familial into a potentially transformative resistance to a bankrupt and hostile political and cultural climate. Rather than representing a retreat from public issues into a narrowly personal obsession with domestic concerns, the focus on childhood and family history represented a revolutionary, or at least a rebellious, critique of the status quo. In historical context, then, the advent of confessional and Beat poetry about family began a neo-Romantic strain of postmodernism that challenged conservative-modernist notions of the "representative man" and the impersonality of the poet and the poem. This is not to say that these poets merely resurrected Wordsworth's revolution in poetic diction and subject matter delineated in the 1800 Preface to *Lyrical Ballads*, though the conversational, prosaic tone of their poems and their increasing concern with "ordinary" subject matter bears some family resemblance to Wordsworth's youthful poetic project. If the so-called confessional school of poetry was to represent a new orthodoxy by the end of the sixties, the radical subjectivity and deliberately prosaic effects of confessional verse represented a significant departure from the hermetic lyrics of the academic mainstream in what Lowell called "the tranquilized fifties."

As poet Robert Hass usefully reminds us in his essay "Families and Prisons," "before the appearance of Robert Lowell's *Life Studies* and Allen Ginsberg's *Kaddish*, it's hard to think of serious work in poetry that touches on the subject [of family], even though it has, in the last thirty years, become fundamental, as commonplace and omni-present a subject as erotic love was in the sixteenth century" (553). Hass points out that writing about the family is distinct from writing about other relationships because of the "presence . . . of the idea of the child" ("Families and Prisons" 554). "The subject of the child," he argues, "enters literature with romanticism," and "its appearance is connected to most of the propositions of romanticism —subjectivity, radical freedom, radical inwardness, sincerity, visionary innocence, transparency of language, realism as a mode of representation . . . romantic political thought . . . [which] braided together our feelings about the abuse of power and the abuse of children" ("Families and Prisons" 556). With Freud's discovery of the unconscious and the increasing influence of psychoanalysis, postmodern poets experienced a conflict between their sense that the child's perspective was fundamental to their poetic and cultural project and their sense that this perspective eluded representation.

Lowell's *Life Studies* (1959) was perhaps the most visible sign of the first generation of "mainstream" postmodernists' rejection of Eliot's famous doctrine of the impersonality of the poet in "Tradition and the Individual Talent." For Elizabeth Bishop, Lowell's autobiographical turn promised a qualified hope "towards changing, or at least unsettling, minds made up against us . . . in the middle of our worst century so far" (*Life Studies* dust jacket). Significantly, Bishop connects what she admires about Lowell's new vision with her own recollection of the power of the child's vision (reminiscent, as we shall see, of Bishop's own theory of infant sight articulated in her poem "Over 2,000 Illustrations and a Complete Concordance" and much of her late poetry): "As a child, I used to look at my grandfather's Bible under a powerful reading-glass. The letters assembled beneath the lens were like a Lowell poem, as big as life and as alive, and rainbow-edged. It seemed to illuminate as it magnified; it could also be used as a burning-glass" (*Life Studies* dust jacket).

The poem of Lowell's that Bishop most admired, "My Last Afternoon with Uncle Devereaux Winslow" (1957), is far from Ransom's detached "study"; a *life* study, it blends adult- and childlike diction appropriate to its central concern with the child. The child's "Olympian models" (literally the mannequins of Roger Peet's Boy's Store) are also Olympians in Kenneth Grahame's sense, with their "Mother and Father's / watery martini pipe dreams at Sunday Dinner" or Grandfather's Edwardian "decor / . . . manly, comfortable / overbearing, disproportioned" (Lowell, *Life Studies* 59–60). These stiff, lifeless models have rendered the five-and-a-half-year-old boy in "formal pearl gray shorts" into "a stuffed toucan / with a bibulous, multicolored beak" (Lowell, *Life Studies* 61). The child picks at the anchor on his confining and infantilizing "sailor blouse washed white as a spinnaker" and wishes for a "fluff of west wind puffing / my blouse, kiting me over our seven chimneys, / troubling the waters" (Lowell, *Life Studies* 62). As the superficial trappings of the "Social Register" and upper-class "family gossip" recede and the speaker takes a last look at his uncle's tattered "student posters," he reaches a crisis occasioned by his new awareness of his uncle's mortality. The child's recognition that his uncle is "dying of the incurable Hodgkin's disease" at age twenty-nine occasions his terrifying transformation from child to premature adult among childish "actual" adults.

The deft and deceptively simple epiphany of this crisis lies in the speaker's recognition of his child-self at the moment of its disappearance. The emotional center of the poem resides in its reversal of adult and child roles, in which Lowell subtly manipulates "adultlike" and "childlike" diction. Lowell's stance toward childhood suffering is in direct contrast to Ransom's study of the child as a lifeless object:

> My Uncle was dying at twenty-nine.
> "You are behaving like children,"
> said my Grandfather,
> when my Uncle and Aunt left their three baby daughters,
> and sailed for Europe on a last honeymoon . . .
> I cowered in terror.
> I wasn't a child at all—
> unseen and all-seeing, I was Agrippina
> in the Golden House of Nero.
>   (Lowell, *Life Studies* 63)

Here Lowell skillfully manipulates conflicting levels of diction; the flat, prosaic statement of the first eight and a half lines of the passage is ironically undercut by the allusion to Nero's mother, who foresaw her own assassination, ordered by her son, a move the rest of the poem has prepared us for. But unlike Ransom's brand of irony, the very ostentatiousness of the classical allusion privileges emotion over detachment. The seeming simplicity of lines like "I cowered in terror. / I wasn't a child at all" announces Lowell's breakthrough in poetic diction. By contrast, the inflated reference to Agrippina calls attention to its own grandiosity as it too-neatly reinforces the theme of adult/child role reversal. The tension between the late modernist aesthetic and the new directness Lowell was learning from Williams shows its seams here, but the speaker's struggles to find a voice for the child-self in the context of his family history is a rehearsal for even more accomplished poems like "For the Union Dead," in which the perceptions of the child are played against the adult's more jaded historical awareness.

Less obviously confessional than his friend Lowell, Randall Jarrell was even more insistent on the value of childhood as his primary mode of poetic and cultural resistance, writing both his autobiographical poetry about childhood in *The Lost World* as well as his late now-classic children's books.[5] In his poems about childhood the trappings of a bygone popular culture (Hollywood in the twenties) could provide "arms" for the child's battles against the encroaching cynicism of adulthood. Jarrell's "last and best book," as Lowell called it, was so seemingly stripped of modernist irony and artifice that it *was* misunderstood. Indeed, it was virulently attacked and labeled as sentimental by a number of critics, who in deploring what Irvin Ehrenpreis called "odd childhood experiences sentimentally recalled . . . [in] Mr. Jarrell's miscellaneous lines" (167) ignored even the formal virtuosity of Jarrell's terza rima. Early reactions to these poems resembled the bewilderment of Jarrell's speaker in "The One Who Was Different": "I feel like the first men who read Wordsworth / It's so simple I can't understand it" (*The Lost World* 45). Almost thirty-five years later, however, most critics of Jarrell's work agree that in *The Lost World* Jarrell was finally beginning to make himself into the postmodernist poet he had wished to become since the late thirties. "Children's arms" and, indeed, the playfulness of the terza rima helped Jarrell both celebrate and criticize the world of popular culture that had disturbed and fascinated him. The child's ability to experience fear and to "go on in breathless joy" simultaneously seemed a means for negotiating the quotidian.

If Jarrell's woman at the supermarket who speaks the poem "Next Day" (1963) fails to transform the detergents "Cheer," "Joy," and "All" into their emotional equivalents, perhaps, he believes, recovering the child's perspective can. Thus, commercial symbols (bill-boards, movie sets, real estate offices) in "The Lost World" (1963) are potentially transformed by the child's utopian reading of 1926 Holly-wood as a "blue wonderland" (*Complete Poems* 292). But in "Think-ing of the Lost World" (336–38), in which the 1960s adult revisits the Los Angeles of his youth, the speaker's attempt to trade the adult's emptiness (brought on by his apprehensiveness about aging) for the emptiness of a remembered, spectral child ("A shape in tennis shoes and khaki riding pants") is ambiguous at best. The speaker wishes (almost desperately) that the child may serve as a symbol of poten-tial, as a redemptive figure to the aging adult, but since the useful-ness of the child's perspective for the poet depends on a rejection of such nostalgia, the speaker comes up empty:

> I reach out to it
> Empty-handed, my hand comes back empty,
> And yet my emptiness is traded for its emptiness
> I have found that Lost World in the Lost and Found
> Columns whose gray illegible advertisements
> My soul has memorized world after world:
> LOST — NOTHING. STRAYED FROM NOWHERE. NO REWARD.
> I hold in my own hands, in happiness,
> Nothing: the nothing for which there's no reward.
> (*Complete Poems* 338)

Among the characteristic techniques of postmodern poetry Lynn Keller has identified are the use of "cliches, banal expressions, and dully discursive manners non-ironically, implying that mundane language, however slack, at least has the advantage of keeping art close to the ordinary present, the now in which human interactions, and connections, occur" (12). Like the Romantics, the mainstream poets of the "middle generation" found themselves caught between competing needs: to keep language close to the ordinary present and to affirm their belief in language's transcendental function.

James Longenbach has recently argued for "mapping the story of recent American poetry on [Elizabeth] Bishop's career rather than Lowell's" (484), and certainly Bishop's influence is felt more strongly today as she emerges as the major figure among her contemporaries. Even her friends Jarrell and Lowell seem to have understood that Bishop's postmodernism had become far more advanced than theirs. Bishop's greater influence on succeeding generations stems from her focus on process and her reluctance to accept fixed interpretations, characteristics which Keller shows typify the postmodern: "focusing on the process of epistemology rather than on achieved knowledge, [contemporary poets] portray the mind engaging itself in the world and attending to events, without imposing fixed interpretations on that experience" (12). Describing the convergence of the Amazon and Tapajos Rivers in her late poem "Santarem" (1978), Elizabeth Bishop says:

> Even if one were tempted
> to literary interpretations
> such as: life/death, right/wrong, male/female
> —such notions would have resolved, dissolved, straight off
> in that watery, dazzling dialectic.
> (*Complete Poems* 185)

In addition to the mentioned binaries, we might appropriately add adult/child, since the attempt to resolve, dissolve that split dialectically is one of the major focuses of her late career.[6] Bishop's postmodernism seems to me to be directly tied to her frequent representation of the child's-eye view.

Bishop's postmodern poetics—employed increasingly in her late work—grows out of the need for the poet to look with what, in "Over 2,000 Illustrations and a Complete Concordance" (1948), she calls "infant sight." In this poem, Bishop's speaker tries to come to terms with the geographic and emotional dislocations by using paratactic strategies to represent and articulate a child's-eye perspective. This perspective is rooted in a rejection of traditional biblical parataxis that focuses on a linear narrative of begetting, enabling the speaker to view even the nativity scene as "a family with pets." At the beginning of the poem, the speaker looks at an elaborate engraved Bible, reminiscing about her world travels. Wistfully, she longs for travels that are "serious, engravable," like the pictures in the Bible. At first, these pictures seem comfortably "tired / and a touch familiar." Quickly, however, they become stereotypical depictions of the "foreign" ("Often the squatting Arab, / or groups of Arabs, plotting, probably, / against our Christian Empire") and become "vast and obvious, the human figure / far gone in history or theology." The observer recognizes in the grimly imperial, narrow vision of the Bible images that "resolve themselves" too easily, and her

. . . eye drops, weighted, through the lines
the burin made, the lines that move apart
like ripples above sand,
dispersing storms, God's spreading fingerprint,
and painfully, finally, that ignite
in watery prismatic white-and-blue.
  (Bishop, *Complete Poems* 57)

Leaving the narrowness of the Bible's engravings, the speaker enters first the "Narrows" of her own Nova Scotia childhood with its "touching bleat of goats." But as it was for the child Elizabeth,[7] this touching pastoral is ephemeral, and the speaker falls into a disjunctive and increasingly horrifying series of adult geographical dislocations in the rest of the second verse-paragraph.

Moving in a dizzying and apparently random geographical sequence from the Vatican to Mexico, French Morocco, Ireland, England, and, finally, a scene in and around Marrakesh, the speaker/traveler is confronted with the dismaying twin vision of sexuality and death occasioned initially by suspiciously childlike prostitutes. It is at this point that the first-person singular pronoun enters the poem, reminding us of the moment in Bishop's late poem "In the Waiting Room" ("you are an *I*, / you are an *Elizabeth*, / you are one of *them*. / *Why* should you be one, too?" [*Complete Poems* 160]):

And in the brothels of Marrakesh
the little pockmarked prostitutes
balanced their tea-trays on their heads
and did their belly-dances; flung themselves
naked and giggling against our knees,
asking for cigarettes. It was somewhere near there
I saw what frightened me most of all:
a holy grave, not looking particularly holy . . .
  (*Complete Poems* 58)

Commenting on the disjointed account of the adult's travels, whose primary grammatical connection is three "ands," the final verse paragraph becomes a pivotal articulation of the ways in which Bishop will use "infant sight" in her later poems. We return to the Bible, now, perhaps with Bishop's understanding of the way we can use the glass through which we read it both for illumination and as a "burning-glass":

Everything only connected by "and" and "and."
Open the book. (The gilt rubs off the edges
of the pages and pollinates the fingertips.)
Open the heavy book. Why couldn't we have seen
this old Nativity while we were at it?
—the dark ajar, the rocks breaking with light,
an undisturbed, unbreathing flame,
colorless, sparkless, freely fed on straw,
and, lulled within, a family with pets,
—and looked and looked our infant sight away.
 (*Complete Poems* 58–59)

"'Infant sight,'" as John Ashbery noted, is "both our torment and our salvation" (*Complete* 204).

Since Wordsworth, the paradox of looking with infant sight in order to look it away rests on another paradox of language. The first poetic spirit of the infant that Wordsworth describes in Book II of *The Prelude* as the spirit to which the adult poet must attune her- or himself to make poetry is itself inarticulate.[8] David Kalstone has noted that Bishop originally wrote "silent sight," cognizant that the Latin root meaning of "infant" is speechless (130). The deep sources of childhood aren't really, as Frost would have it, our waters and our watering place where we can "drink and be whole again beyond confusion"; rather, as for Bishop's speaker in "At the Fishhouses," "a believer in total immersion," they invite the reader to dip a hand into the sea of contingent experience, to experience a fiery "transmutation" in the waters of childhood:

If you tasted it, it would first taste bitter,
then briny, then surely burn your tongue.
It is like what we imagine knowledge to be:
dark, salt, clear, moving, utterly free,
drawn from the cold hard mouth
of the world, derived from the rocky breasts
forever, flowing and drawn, and since
our knowledge is historical, flowing, and flown.
 (*Complete Poems* 66)

The impulse of the speaker to derive knowledge "from the rocky breasts / forever" as an infant is untenable from the perspective of the adult. The utter freedom of "what we *imagine* knowledge to be" conflicts with our attempts to put such knowledge into language. The child's entry into narrative involves a negotiation between seemingly freer paratactic or anaphoric structures and the subordinating structures of the temporal and the narrative. *Because* knowledge becomes historical it also becomes elusive. Yet Bishop is generally more successful than her beloved friend Lowell in negotiating and eluding the potentially reifying manifestations of "those blessed structures plot and rhyme" in order to "make something imagined, not recalled" (Lowell, *Day by Day* 127). As Victoria Harrison has noted, what "Bishop offers us" is a "relational subjectivity at once flexible and connective" (17).

Bishop's child's-eye perspective seeks to "resolve, dissolve" the more limited perspective of the adult. Preferring the "more delicate" colors of the mapmaker to those of the historian ("The Map" [1935], *Complete Poems* 3), Bishop's speaker identifies with the "crisis of historicity" which Fredric Jameson argues characterizes the postmodern. Noting that the binary positions employed in our arguments about postmodernism "are in reality moralizing [political positions]" masquerading as "an aesthetic debate" (62), Jameson, in a now-famous formulation, says, "The point is that we are *within* the culture of postmodernism to the point where its facile repudiation is as impossible as any equally facile celebration of it is complacent and corrupt" (62). Jameson calls upon the critic to provide us with a "cognitive mapping" whereby we may negotiate the complexities of living within this culture. But Jameson's own sense of literary history—what he calls his "own cultural periodization of the stages of realism, modernism, and postmodernism" (36)—is limited by his unwillingness to take Romanticism into account. He dismisses as "largely academic . . . another series of debates . . . in which the very continuity of modernism as it is here reaffirmed is itself called into question by some vaster sense of the profound continuity of romanticism, from the late eighteenth century on, of which both the modern and the postmodern will be seen as mere organic stages" (Jameson 59).

What Jameson's loaded dismissal of the importance of Romanticism overlooks is that artists' continuing concern with the propositions of Romanticism such as those delineated by Hass no longer seem predicated on "continuity" or "organicism," if they ever were. If, in a larger sense, the modern and the postmodern derive a legacy from Romanticism, it is one of contradiction rather than continuity.

Radical subjectivity, freedom, and inwardness, for instance, are in many ways incompatible with sincerity, visionary innocence, and transparency of language; and it is in the contradictory field of the conflicting propositions of Romanticism that modern poetry (that is, poetry since Blake and Wordsworth) enacts and reenacts its struggle for power. Furthermore, as Hass intimates, the idea of the child becomes the locus upon which such power struggles are enacted. In any event, an account of postmodernism that dismisses Romanticism (and the invention of the construct "childhood") as "largely academic" ignores one of the fundamental problems of human subjectivity with which postmodernism continues to grapple. In Jameson's case, this dismissal has led to misreadings of poems like Bob Perelman's "China," because he ignores the poet's deliberate appropriation and subversion of Romantic ideas of childhood that are fundamental to understanding the poems.

Jameson's proposed "third term," which he calls "'realism' . . . for want of something better" as a way to remove us from "the dualisms of the modern/postmodern," in no sense suggests the cartographic metaphor he so usefully proposes. And it seems to me rather narrowly deconstructive rather than dazzlingly dialectical. As opposed to the poet's cartographic methods (which are emotional, phenomenological, and epistemological rather than narrowly cognitive), Jameson's "cognitive mapping" proposes to use the "dualism . . . against itself," to adopt postmodern strategies in order to dismantle postmodernism. As his readings of van Gogh and Warhol and his misreading of Bob Perelman's "China" demonstrate, the postmodern, for Jameson, is characterized by "a waning of affect," "depthlessness," and, for "language-oriented" poets like Perelman, the adoption of "schizophrenic fragmentation as [the] fundamental aesthetic" (10, 12, 28). Recognizing the Archimedean bind of being "within" postmodernism, Jameson adopts a moralizing position of his own in which (his protestations to the contrary) his limited version of modernism is privileged over postmodernism, and Romanticism is erased from consideration except as a straw figure in his argument.[9]

Perelman himself, in the latest of a series of responses to Jameson's "mini-discussion of language writing" ("Parataxis" 314), convincingly counters Jameson's charge that "China" and other language writing is characterized by "schizophrenia in the form of a rubble of distinct and unrelated signifiers" (Jameson 26, quoted in Perelman, "Parataxis" 314).[10] In the context of his own poetry (particularly volumes such as *Face Value* and *Virtual Reality*), Perelman's complex signification is apparent to anyone who reads his work in context. Far from engaging in a "facile celebration" of postmodernism or adopting a "waning of affect" or promoting "schizophrenia" as a "fundamental aesthetic," Perelman's work is, as Marjorie Perloff points out, "poetry as social text, a lyric at once deeply personal and yet directed outward, as a form of political critique" (quoted in Perelman, *Virtual Reality* jacket blurb).

On the surface, it seems almost comic to link the experimental writing of Perelman and the other writers loosely associated with language writing and the New Sentence to mainstream poets from Bishop's generation, since the language writers define their work explicitly in opposition to that mainstream.[11] Many of these writers, however, Perelman, Michael Palmer, Lyn Hejinian, Susan Howe, and Charles Bernstein in particular, have built on similar techniques in their representations of childhood. Poems such as Perelman's "A Literal Translation of Virgil's Fourth Eclogue," Howe's *Pythagorean Silence*, and Palmer's "childhood" poems in *First Figure* concern themselves with the complexities of the child's construction of language, and language's construction of the child, in fruitful ways. As in Bishop's work, the gap between the idealization of childhood in memory and childhood as lived, experienced, and culturally constructed plays a major role. Perhaps the differences between Bishop's use of infant sight and Hejinian's in *My Life* are not as great as they seem.

Among its many concerns, a prominent feature of Hejinian's *My Life* (1978, 1986) is its exploration of family mythology. In the second edition, the poem is written in forty-five sections of forty-five sentences each, one for each year of Hejinian's life at the time she was writing the poem. (The first edition contained thirty-seven sections of thirty-seven sentences.) Her description of the child's relationship to language in her famous essay/talk "The Rejection of Closure" illuminates the method of *My Life*:

> We discover the limits of language early, as children. . . . Children objectify language when they render it their plaything, in jokes, puns, and riddles, or in glossolaliac chants and rhymes. They dis-

cover that words are not equal to the world, that a shift, analogous to parallax in photography, occurs between things (events, ideas, objects) and the words for them—a displacement that leaves a gap. (278)

The length of *My Life* and its richly interactive structure preclude a full reading here.[12] Hejinian's insight that "a person is a bit of space that has gotten itself in moments" (*My Life* 114), along with her use of language as a plaything, exploiting and calling attention to the multiplicity of its tropes (repetition, analogy, allusion, paranomasia, metaphor, parataxis, and metonymy), both disrupt and enrich temporality, subjectivity, and narrative. A demanding text, a performative text, its attitude toward childhood eschews reductive nostalgia —as Hejinian puns, "You cannot linger 'on the lamb'" (*My Life* 11). Using ambiguous sentences and ambiguous figures as its method, the poem recognizes that there were (and are) "more storytellers than there were stories, so that everyone in the family had a version of history and it was impossible to get close to the original, or to know 'what really happened'" (Hejinian, *My Life* 21). By virtue of Hejinian's insistence on "generative" rather than "manipulative" form ("Rejection" passim, *My Life* 289), childhood becomes, in a sense, *re*generative; "depth" and "affect" don't need to be "recovered" because they are never "lost":

> One is growing up repeatedly. But every night I was afraid that my parents were packing to leave us, so I kept an eye on them. The fenceposts were long lozenges covered with moss—ink is darker and wetter than moss—and sunk into soil patchy with acrid powdery grass among which grew poison oak and rattlesnake weed. On my mother's side, a matriarchy. I wanted to be a brave child, a girl with guts. (*My Life* 25)

Hejinian's recognition that "I am a stranger to the little girl I was, and more—more strange" doesn't change the fact that "one sits in a cloven space" (*My Life* 75). Traversing the postmodern forest of childhood with its poison oak and rattlesnake weed takes guts. But to reach the mother's side of the fence ("a matriarchy") gives a false sense of closure. Rejecting closure but not form, Hejinian's poem says, "Form then, be expressive. As for we who 'love to be astonished,' consciousness is durable in poetry. My heart takes occupancy" (*My Life* 98).

In a striking essay titled "The Person and Description" (delivered as part of Carla Harryman's lecture series on "The Poetics of Everyday Life"), Hejinian asserts that "subjectivity is not an entity, but a dynamic." Her disruption of the temporal and narrative structures of life stories is part of a project in which she seeks to "break down . . . the epistemological nightmare of the solipsistic self . . . [so that] the essentialist yearning after truth and origin is discarded in favor of the experience of experience" (Hejinian, "The Person" 167). Here, Hejinian's position resembles that of the Romantic ironist, which Anne Mellor (drawing on the play theory of Winnicott) describes as demanding "exuberant playing with the possibilities of an ever-changing world and life . . . participation in a variety of selves and modes of consciousness . . . openness to new ideas and experiences . . . a mental habit of tolerance and a discourse of ambiguity" (188). But the utopian and transcendental manifestations that Mellor celebrates here are colored by a postmodern worldview. In a 1996 interview, Hejinian dismisses "the romantic version of the poet [as] not very exciting anymore. . . . It seems extremely limited and solipsistic": "It would be stupid and limiting to enshrine myself as some unitary voicing of the world as if I were a representative person, which I'm not; *nobody* is living in such a complex culture as this" ("A Local Strangeness" 135).

Hejinian's dissatisfaction is with "the romantic, unitary voice" and its hidden "claims for objectivity" ("A Local Strangeness" 135). Her call for a radical subjectivity attempts to "open up enormous possibilities for diffusion and multiplicity of points of view" ("A Local Strangeness" 135). But the recognition that "the 'personal' is already a plural condition" also "raises several issues which can be regarded as boundary problems, problems which are artistic and literary in one sense but which are played out in social and economic life, which responds to the rigidity of boundaries (between, for example, public and private, history and daily life, male and female) and to their breakdown" (Hejinian, "The Person" 170, 169). Such boundary problems are also particularly troublesome for women: "Being an object of description but without the authority to describe, a woman may feel herself to be bounded by her own appearance, a representation of her apparent person, not certain whether she is she or only a quotation" (Hejinian, "The Person" 170).

Similarly, as Marjorie Perloff has noted, Hejinian portrays "the child's world" as a "mass of contradictions" in which the language and "'lessons' given by the well-meaning adults defy all logic" (224). For Bishop's almost-seven-year-old Elizabeth in "In the Waiting Room," these contradictions cause her to experience her body and the world as places she is not quite "inside" or "outside." The unsettling and simultaneous discovery of Elizabeth's subjectivity and her connection with the world of adults occasions a boundary crisis:

> Why should I be my aunt,
> or me, or anyone?
> What similarities—
> boots, hands, the family voice
> I felt in my throat, or even
> the *National Geographic*
> and those awful hanging breasts—
> held us all together
> or made us all just one?
> (*Complete Poems* 160–61)

Hejinian's elaboration on her statement that "the 'personal' is already a plural condition" could serve as a gloss on this passage from Bishop: "Perhaps one feels that it is located somewhere within, somewhere inside the body—in the stomach? the chest? the genitals? the throat? The head? One can look for it and already one is not oneself, one is several, incomplete, and subject to dispersal" (Hejinian, "The Person" 170).

Resistant to the more utopian manifestations of Romantic subjectivity and equally resistant to conservative-modernist claims to objectivity, postmodern poets like Bishop and Hejinian turn to the astonishment of language in all its contingency. The simultaneous formal and free play of signifiers that Hejinian discovers in her "autobiographical" writing may serve to lighten the shades of the prison house of language even as we recognize that "ink is darker than moss." At their best, postmodern poetries struggle to liberate childhoods from their "bourgeois memorabilia," to make "them useful by a simple shift," and to recognize through the "symmetrical letters of the alphabet" that "a child is a real person, very lively" (Hejinian, *My Life* 22, 79). Poets like Bishop and Hejinian hope to simultaneously "resolve" and "dissolve" the adult/child binary dialectically. In this dialectic, Edmundson's gap between Wordsworth and Coleridge (and between poetry and criticism, play and work) seems a false dichotomy. The figure of the child in postmodern poetry becomes the "best philosopher" with a difference, showing us, in Hejinian's words, that "both subjectivity and objectivity are outdated filling systems" (*My Life* 99).

NOTES

I wish to acknowledge the Faculty Research Committee at Georgia Southern University for a faculty summer research award which helped enable me to write this essay.

1. Of course, the terms *postmodernism*, *modernism*, and *Romanticism* are notoriously slippery. The conservative, Eliotic version of modernism enshrined in the academy for so long is obviously undergoing massive revision by contemporary critics.

2. Jarrell listed "Bells for John Whiteside's Daughter" as one of Ransom's best poems, so it is clear that he admired it. And in Jarrell's early poems there are a number of dead children, but his attitude toward them is never so objectifying.

3. Ransom's poem also neatly illustrates that despite the contempt for the literature of the nineteenth century expressed in much of his criticism, the tension between the simultaneous idealization and demonization of the figure of the child, often located in the eroticizing of that figure, shows how influential that literature was.

4. At this point, it seems useful to distinguish the New Critics' definition of irony from "Romantic irony." The province of irony from which these poets were trying to escape was one in which the lyric poem was a verbal artifact divorced from extratextual contexts. For Cleanth Brooks, as Joseph Dane points out, "irony" is both Brooks's "word for what is interesting in poetry" (152)—a result of fruitful tension between the poem and its "verbal or thematic" context (though decidedly not its historical or social context)—and a quality which certain "great poetry" transcends because it fuses "the irrelevant and discordant" into a "stability of context in which the internal pressures balance and support each other" (Brooks 732–33; see discussion in Dane 149–58). Ironically, Brooks's essay "Irony as a Principle of Structure" first appeared in book form in Zabel's *Literary Opinion in America* alongside Randall Jarrell's essay "The End of the Line," in which Jarrell elaborates on his argument that modernist poetry, though "generally considered to be a violent break with romanticism . . . is actually . . . an extension of romanticism" (742–43). This irony is further compounded by Brooks's explication of Jarrell's poem "Eighth Air Force" as an exemplum of the best modernist ironic

practice. For a discussion of Romantic irony, see Dieter Petzold's essay "Taking Games Seriously: Romantic Irony in Modern Fantasy for 'Children of All Ages'" in this volume, as well as Dane and Mellor.

5. I have analyzed Jarrell's uses of childhood at length in *Randall Jarrell and the Lost World of Childhood* and refer the reader to that book for an extended analysis of his work about childhood.

6. Bishop's marginal status as orphan, lesbian, expatriate—her "eye of the outsider," as Adrienne Rich calls it—makes her especially suspicious of the exclusionary binaries that characterize "literary interpretation."

7. Bishop's difficult childhood certainly contributed to her concern with childhood in her work. Her father died when she was an infant, and her mother was permanently committed to an asylum when Bishop was five. Uprooted from a relatively secure life with her maternal grandparents in Great Village, Nova Scotia, most of Bishop's childhood was spent unhappily with her father's relatives in Worcester, Massachusetts. These childhood deprivations are the source of her brilliant autobiographical stories, "In the Village" and "Gwendolyn," as well as some of her finest poetry. See Millier, *Elizabeth Bishop*.

8. In her recent book, *Elizabeth Bishop: Restraints of Language*, Doreski discusses Bishop's debt to Wordsworth's poetry as well as her divergence from it. Doreski notes the Wordsworthian paradox implicit in the concept of "infant sight": "Bishop suggests that inspiration stems from originary speechless witnessing, but concurs with Wordsworth that such preliterate, sensuous states must be relinquished in order to record such visions" (7). However, her subsequent reading of Bishop's poem about the "child-artist," "Sestina" (Doreski 9–11), and her other perceptive readings of Bishop's works about childhood suggest that their power derives from Bishop's attempts at linguistic representation of the child's-eye perspective that differ from Wordsworth's famous "spots of time" in that they foreground the child's refusal to "be engulfed by [grief and loss]. She prefers to frankly embrace it, drawing upon it as she begins the life-long process of constructing her world" (Doreski 10). See also Travisano's germinal discussion of "infant sight" in *Elizabeth Bishop* (114–22).

9. As Jameson's famous misreading of Perelman's poems suggests, Jameson's version of modernism tends to exclude "poetry" altogether. One gets the impression that his considerable critical powers are not the kind suited to the study of verse.

10. For a revised and expanded version of Perelman's argument, see his book *The Marginalization of Poetry*, particularly chap. 4.

11. One admittedly tenuous argument for connecting these writers with Bishop is her influence on John Ashbery, a champion of both Bishop and Perelman's work. A useful and accessible introduction to some of these writers is Renfield, *Language Poetry*. I am personally indebted, as well, to my wife, Professor Patricia Pace, of Georgia Southern University, whose 1986 dissertation on language writing, as well as her challenges to my more mainstream tastes, have contributed greatly to my ability to understand and enjoy this writing. Pace's article "Language Poetry" is a cogent and accessible explanation of some of this group's concerns.

12. Some extended readings of *My Life* that I have found illuminating include those by Clark, Dworkin, and Jarraway.

WORKS CITED

Altieri, Charles. *Self and Sensibility in Contemporary American Poetry*. Cambridge: Cambridge UP, 1984.

Ashbery, John. *The Complete Poems* (review). *Elizabeth Bishop and Her Art*. Ed. Lloyd Schwartz and Sybil P. Estess. Ann Arbor: U of Michigan P, 1983. 201–5. Rpt. of "Throughout Is a Quality of Thingness." *New York Times Book Review*, June 1, 1969, 8, 25.

Bishop, Elizabeth. *The Collected Prose*. Ed. Robert Giroux. New York: Farrar, 1984.

———. *The Complete Poems: 1927–1979*. New York: Farrar, 1983.

Brooks, Cleanth. "Irony as a Principle of Structure." *Literary Opinion in America*. Ed. Morton Dauwen Zabel. Rev. ed. New York: Harper, 1951. 729–41.

Ciardi, John, ed. *Mid-Century American Poets*. New York: Twayne, 1950.

Clark, Hilary. "The Mnemonics of Autobiography: Lyn Hejinian's *My Life*." *Biography* 14 (1991): 315–35.

Dane, Joseph A. *The Critical Mythology of Irony*. Athens: U of Georgia P, 1991.

Doreski, C. K. *Elizabeth Bishop: The Restraints of Language*. New York: Oxford, 1993.

Dworkin, Craig Douglas. "Penelope Reworking the Twill: Patchwork Writing and Lyn Hejinian's *My Life*." *Contemporary Literature* 36 (1995): 58–81.

Edmundson, Mark. "Vital Intimations: Wordsworth, Coleridge, and the Promise of Criticism." *South Atlantic Quarterly* 91 (1992): 739–64.

Ehrenpreis, Irvin. "Poetry without Despair." *Virginia Quarterly Review* 42 (1996): 165–67.

Flynn, Richard. *Randall Jarrell and the Lost World of Childhood*. Athens: U of Georgia P, 1990.

Harrison, Victoria. *Elizabeth Bishop: Poetics of Intimacy*. Cambridge: Cambridge UP, 1993.

Hass, Robert. "Families and Prisons." *Michigan Quarterly Review* 30 (1991): 553–72.

Hejinian, Lyn. "A Local Strangeness: An Interview with Lyn Hejinian." Conducted by Larry McCaffery and Brian McHale. *Some Other Frequency: Interviews with Innovative American Authors*. By Larry McCaffery. Philadelphia: U of Pennsylvania P, 1996.

———. *My Life*. Los Angeles: Sun and Moon, 1991.

———. "The Person and Description." *Poetics Journal* 9 (1991): 166–70.

———. "The Rejection of Closure." *Writing/Talks*. Ed. Bob Perelman. Carbondale: Southern Illinois UP, 1985.

Howe, Susan. *Pythagorean Silence*. New York: Montemora, 1983. Rpt. in *The Europe of Trusts*. By Susan Howe. Los Angeles: Sun and Moon, 1990.

Jameson, Fredric. *Postmodernism, or The Cultural Logic of Late Capitalism*. Durham: Duke UP, 1991.

Jarraway, David R. "*My Life* through the Eighties: The Exemplary L-A-N-G-U-A-G-E of Lyn Hejinian." *Contemporary Literature* 33 (1992): 319–35.

Jarrell, Randall. *The Complete Poems*. New York: Farrar, 1969.

———. "The End of the Line." *The Nation*, February 21, 1942, 222–28. Rpt. in revised form in *Literary Opinion in America*. Ed. Morton Dauwen Zabel. Rev. ed. New York: Harper, 1951. 742–48.

———. "A Note on Poetry." Preface to "The Rage for the Lost Penny." *Five Young American Poets*. Norfolk, CT: New Directions, 1940. Rpt. in *Kipling, Auden & Co.: Essays and Reviews, 1935–1964*. By Randall Jarrell. New York: Farrar, 1980.

———. *Poetry and the Age*. New York: Knopf, 1953.

———. *Randall Jarrell's Letters: An Autobiographical and Literary Selection*. Ed. Mary Jarrell. Boston: Houghton, 1985.

———. *The Third Book of Criticism*. New York: Farrar, 1969.

Kalstone, David. *Becoming a Poet: Elizabeth Bishop with Marianne Moore and Robert Lowell*. Ed. with a preface by Robert Hemenway. Afterword by James Merrill. New York: Farrar, 1989.

Keller, Lynn. *Remaking It New: Contemporary American Poetry and the Modernist Tradition*. Cambridge: Cambridge UP, 1987.

Longenbach, James. "Elizabeth Bishop and the Story of Postmodernism." *Southern Review* 28 (1992): 469–84.

Lowell, Robert. *Collected Prose*. Ed. and introduced by Robert Giroux. New York: Farrar, 1987.

————. *Day by Day*. New York: Farrar, 1978.

————. *Life Studies*. New York: Farrar, 1959.

Mellor, Anne K. *English Romantic Irony*. Cambridge: Harvard UP, 1980.

Millier, Brett C. *Elizabeth Bishop: Life and the Memory of It*. Berkeley: U of California P, 1993.

Pace, Patricia. "Language Poetry: The Radical Writing Project." *Literature in Performance* 7 (1987): 23–33.

Palmer, Michael. *First Figure*. San Francisco: North Point, 1984.

Perelman, Bob. *Face Value*. New York: Roof Books, 1988.

————. "Parataxis and Narrative: The New Sentence in Theory and Practice." *American Literature* 65 (1993): 313–24.

————. *Virtual Reality*. New York: Roof Books, 1993.

————, ed. *Writing/Talks*. Carbondale: Southern Illinois UP, 1985.

Perloff, Marjorie. *The Dance of the Intellect: Studies in the Poetry of the Pound Tradition*. Cambridge: Cambridge UP, 1985.

Ransom, John Crowe. *Selected Poems*. 3rd ed., rev. and enlarged. New York: Ecco, 1978.

Renfield, Linda. *Language Poetry: Writing as Rescue*. Baton Rouge: Louisiana State UP, 1992.

Rich, Adrienne. "The Eye of the Outsider: Elizabeth Bishop's *Complete Poems, 1927–1979*." *Blood, Bread, and Poetry: Selected Prose, 1979–1985*. New York: Norton, 1986. 124–35.

Schiller, Friedrich von. *Naive and Sentimental Poetry and On the Sublime*. Trans. Julias A. Elias. New York: Frederick Ungar, 1966.

Travisano, Thomas. *Elizabeth Bishop: Her Artistic Development*. Charlottesville: UP of Virginia, 1988.

Wordsworth, William. *Poetical Works*. London: Oxford, 1969.

Zabel, Morton Dauwen, ed. *Literary Opinion in America*. Rev. ed. New York: Harper, 1951.

James Holt McGavran

WORDSWORTH, LOST BOYS, AND
ROMANTIC HOM(E)OPHOBIA

his essay originates in my concern with the plight of homeless children in America today as it intersects with my work as a critic working in British Romanticism and gender studies. After noting what some psychologists, social workers, and educators have said about the gap between boys' and girls' experiences of homelessness, I turn to some fictions of homelessness written by contemporary writers for children and adolescents to see how they have dealt with this gap. What I find in these texts is disconcerting: first, a general adherence to rigidly stereotyped gender roles for both boys and girls; second, an antimale bias hiding under a veneer of sympathy for homeless boys; and third, a failure to provide a space, a home in the text, where young male heroes—and, to be sure, young male readers—could come to see and know themselves. One reason such exclusions occur, I will argue, lies in a largely unconscious homophobia originating in long-felt but poorly understood and rarely discussed tensions which continue to destabilize American manhood and to vitiate the efforts of those who try to write honestly about it.

Homelessness as a concept, of course, has a history as old and complex as Western thought itself. To the degree that Americans today are still influenced by Judeo-Christian tradition, and regardless of whether the freedom our ancestors sought here was religious, cultural, or economic, we all exist in a spiritual diaspora, removed in time and space and sin from our banished garden home; slavery and its aftermath have created for African Americans another, more brutally materialistic condition of diaspora. In the classical tradition, the two Homeric epics provide directly conflicting commentaries on the issue, the *Iliad* glorifying the male impulse to band together, leave home, and fight to the death, and the *Odyssey* glorifying the desire of one clever man to return home to his wife and son. Our cultural experience of these tensions, however, is more immediately influenced by the history of Western Europe in the late eighteenth century, when the popular demand for liberty, equality, and fraternity coincided with the beginnings of an industrial market economy to produce divisions of class, race, generation, nation, and gender whose strictures and effects we are still confronting today.

Recent studies of children's literature have historicized the development of the influential Romantic figure of the child, documenting associationist, organic, transcendental, Augustinian, and feminist versions of childhood (Richardson 123; Myers 133) and deconstructing the dichotomy between imaginative and moralistic children's books that until recently has hung stultifyingly over study of this period (see also McGavran, "Introduction"). I wish to refocus these concerns to concentrate on the conflict between the ideology of the nuclear bourgeois family, which emerged in the late eighteenth century but is still alive and well today, and the Romantic vision of boyhood which that same ideology paradoxically brought into being. The concept of the highly structured but nurturing, protected but isolated home, dominated by the rich, proud, controlling capitalist father and supported by the domestic labors of the subservient, nurturing mother, clashed with, even as it helped to produce, an alluring but "bad" image of simultaneously idealized yet aberrant boyhood.[1] This highly conflicted image offers boys an escape from the entrapping powers and responsibilities of patriarchy, but, tainted— however unconsciously—by its negative correlation with the concept of the nuclear family and by its positive association with loves that dare not speak their name, it can find no secure dwelling place in either the mind or the home of the bourgeois gentleman.

Brave critics like Jacqueline Rose (xiii–xiv, 3) and, before her, Leslie Fiedler (3–6) have noted the paradox that our patriarchal, homophobic society retains a special but rarely voiced affection for texts like *Peter Pan* and *Huckleberry Finn* that give simultaneous narrative space—what I am calling a textual home—to the conflicting demands of homeless boyhood, with its autoerotic and homoerotic tendencies, and of "normal," patriarchally controlled domesticity. This conflict, I will show, is discreetly but deeply inscribed in the poetry of the most influential poetic voice of canonical male Romanticism, the once-homeless orphan William Wordsworth; thus I will read Wordsworth not as a higher, purer antithesis to Barrie and Twain but simply as their precursor and as one to whom children's writers today should pay more attention for both the psychological complexity and the high moral seriousness of his vision of adolescent male development.

Wayne Booth has written, "The moral question is really whether an author has an obligation to write well in the sense of making his moral orderings clear, and if so, clear to whom" (*Rhetoric* 386). Surely authorial silence on a subject so conflicted is not moral, whether that silence is kept out of fear of being caught speaking about a topic that some consider unspeakably immoral or out of an obsession that a story have a "happy ending" (Booth, *Company* 132), even if that ending violates common sense and is life-threatening to its own main characters. So I am also suggesting that unless our society is willing to break the silence surrounding adolescent male development and its social and sexual ambivalences, we will continue to lose boys to drugs, gangs, AIDS, and other more overt forms of teen suicide.

A gender gap does indeed confront late-twentieth-century educational, psychological, and social work professionals who work with homeless children (North and Smith). Whether from biological reasons—relative physical weakness and greater vulnerability through rape and/or pregnancy and motherhood—or from social pressures creating a perceived need, homeless girls and young women generally welcome offers of shelter from social services personnel and work to establish a sense of community, usually with other women (Calsyn and Morse; Kaplan). But mutual fears and suspicions often problematize young males' relationships with these same caregivers (Calsyn and Morse; Susser), who see the boys, accurately enough, as more violent and disruptive, more prone to harbor or develop antisocial or criminal behaviors. For their part boys often resist the caseworkers' siren songs, struggling to escape from and/or remain free of what they experience as constraining societal and cultural structures, even though the institutions of patriarchal capitalism continue to privilege males over females; and boys run higher risk of involvement in crime and sexual, including homosexual, behavior and HIV infection (Garrison; Bond; Burt and Cohen). What is driving boys to turn away from the very sources of their growth and potential empowerment in a male-dominated society? Again, as with the girls, we may imagine both biological and socially constructed pressures, facts, and images of manhood, but the life-and-death danger is far greater for the boys.

This gender-based behavioral difference not only repeats but entrenches itself in recent fictions for children and adolescents that deal with homelessness. As Rose has argued of children's fiction generally (33–34), the pattern is glaringly simple: girls generally follow the route of Barrie's Wendy Darling from home to adventure and then back toward domestication, but boys often become latter-day Peter Pans, adorably but hopelessly alienated from themselves and their worlds. Katherine Paterson's *Great Gilly Hopkins* (1978), Cynthia Voigt's Dicey in *Homecoming* (1981), and Kaye Gibbons's *Ellen Foster* (1987), all haunted by memories or fantasies of their loved, lost mothers, undergo feminized odysseys of various fostering and unfostering experiences before they find homes and supportive females —Gilly and Dicey down South with their maternal grandmothers and Ellen, who is already down South, with her "new mama" (Gibbons 139) in a loving, politically correct foster home where she can invite her black friend, Starletta, to visit. In these fictions about pubescent girls, society *is* the family, or the foster family, and interpersonal relationships; these girls will grow to womanhood in homes where they will be nurtured by older women. With the partial exception of *Homecoming*, where Dicey is challenged by institutional forces ranging from the federal highway system to the Roman Catholic Church, the larger structures of American society exist only peripherally in these fictions, and the question of the girls' potential for future participation within these structures is not addressed. The main point seems to be that as their narratives end, Gilly, Dicey (and her siblings), and Ellen are safe in homes where they can grow through interaction with other females to become strong, although it would seem very conventional, women.

Very different concerns occupy, and very different fates await, the young Manhattan males up North and up against the capitalist system in three fictions about lost boys: Virginia Hamilton's *The Planet of Junior Brown* (1971), Felice Holman's *Slake's Limbo* (1974), and Maurice Sendak's *We Are All in the Dumps with Jack and Guy* (1993). American capitalism and its institutions play prominent roles in these texts; however, these forces are shown not to empower but rather to be extremely hostile toward individual male identity and to be virtually genocidal in their attitudes toward marginalized groups. Homeless from the start, the boys in these texts turn away from all personal and institutional sources of help in the manner observed by the professional caregivers noted above; and their authors never offer them either a way back to the mainstream nor a viable existence apart from it. In *Planet*, young African-American males feel alienated, even violated, by the school system that is their only ticket to escape ghetto life; in *Dumps*, the system is shown to threaten not only children of color but Jews as well, since the bakery ovens in Sendak's illustrations resemble Nazi crematoria. And *everything* threatens the solitary Aremis Slake, who is apparently a white Gentile: school, gangs of other boys, finally even the subway system where he hides.

Family influences are given much less space in these fictions about boys, and they are entirely negative. Of the boys in these stories, only Junior Brown has—or at least is said to have—a father, but he never appears, and other potential male mentors turn out to be either useless (the turbaned man and Willis Joe Whinny for Slake, Doom Moloch for Buddy Clark) or dangerous (Mr. Pool for both Buddy and Junior). Memories of home and women's care are oppressive, either in their smothering closeness (Junior) or their overt hostility (Buddy, Slake), or else they are simply nonexistent (Jack and Guy). Although all depend upon American institutions and the goods and services they provide, not one of these characters ever considers himself parasitical, nor is working within the system to change the system even an option. Instead, in *Planet* and *Dumps*, for the duration of the narratives, boys maintain utopian urban homeless communities that have no chance whatsoever of long-term survival (granted, there are girls in *Dumps*, but they have no voice, no power), and Slake seems even more totally lost, a loner pathetically yet deliberately beyond the reach of the individuals—the waitress, the fat cleaning lady, the social worker—and organizations that he nevertheless needs and uses for survival.

Increasing the disturbing effect of the boy-heroes' self-destructive alienation is the fact that their authors clearly approve of them—indeed, they seem to dote on them—for developing antisocial identities and/or communities just as much as the writers about girls approve of and admire *their* heroes for the home-and-family choices they make. Holman seems delighted at the end of her tale that her paranoid, nearsighted hero, Slake, armed with a new pair of glasses from New York's social services, has escaped his molelike limbo in the subway only to retreat like a crazed bird to the roofs of apartment buildings. Throughout the novel, Holman maintains a double narrative focus, alternating between Slake and Willis Joe Whinny, a depressed subway motorman who saves Slake's life when the boy collapses ill on the tracks in front of Willis Joe's train. But bizarrely, though the encounter leaves Willis Joe with a more positive self-image, Slake never is allowed to meet his lifesaver, who could perhaps save his mind as well, and he never is brought to consider the possibility of going back to face and deal with the ground-level realities of school, home, or other children. Holman leaves Slake with these final words, which are apparently meant to be ennobling: "Right now Slake had something he had to do. He turned and started up the stairs and out of the subway. Slake did not know exactly where he was going, but the general direction was up" (117)—to a rooftop as distanced from everyday realities as the limbo of the subway. And yet this book was recommended for holiday buying in the year of its publication by a *New York Times* reviewer who found it "moving in its concern and admiration for the stubborn human will to survive" (Berkvist 8), and at least one critic has praised *Slake's Limbo* for its inscription, within its urban landscape, of pastoral, mythic patterns of death and rebirth (Kuznets 156). Physically, Slake does indeed descend into the subway and rise to the rooftops, but Holman allows the boy none of the psychic awareness of the Jungian critic.

The general direction at the end of *Planet*, by contrast, is completely down, not only figuratively but quite literally as well. But Hamilton seems as pleased as Holman is with Slake that her hero, Buddy, has succeeded in lowering his mentally disturbed and dangerously obese friend Junior into a basement hideout in an abandoned West Side tenement, entombing the fat boy far from the psychiatric and other medical help he desperately needs. Buddy's evil mentor in this mad endeavor is Mr. Pool, a dismissed high school science teacher who has become the school janitor. Mr. Pool of all people should know, and teach the children, that the only way "up" is through education and taking one's adult place in the system; instead he glamorizes his situation by seeing it as an antiracist, anti-establishment protest, encouraging the boys to follow him and drop out. Hamilton, speaking through Buddy, tries to dignify this by calling it "to live for one another" (217), but Junior's alienation makes even such soft-core self-help rhetoric inaccessible to him, the two friends thus have no meaningful dialogue about either social or sexual maturing, and the whole scene practically reeks of decay, madness, and death.

Race is an important complicating factor here, of course. Many black students do feel alienated and threatened by the white-dominated educational system, but one wonders whether Hamilton, who like her characters is black, really finds the capitalistic mainstream to be so unmitigatedly vile that living off of scavenged food in a cold, dark basement in Hell's Kitchen should be portrayed as being better for black teens than going to school and getting a life. To give them credit, early reviewers of *Planet* were clearly disturbed by this, since there was wide disagreement as to whether, and to what degree, the book was realistic, fantastic, or even surrealistic (Townsend 274; Garden; Egoff 50–52; for a later evaluation similar to mine, see Rees 172–73). Still, for whatever reason, they back off from serious criticisms of the book and instead grant Hamilton powers beyond their humble abilities to understand or evaluate; indeed, one goes so far as to say that Hamilton "overcomes the bonds of sordid reality" and that "her imagination . . . is a liberating force" (Heins 81).

Writing *Planet* in 1971, Hamilton herself was perhaps betrayed by the as-yet-incomplete narrative of the Black Power movement and the protests against the Vietnam war, and Holman too may have been so caught up in the persuasive, or at least pervasive, antiestablishment rhetoric of those times that she neglected to give Slake any space for serious confrontation of his problems. But Sendak, creating his visually stunning picture book about twenty years later, seems to agree completely with Hamilton and Holman about both the American mainstream and the ideal fate for homeless boys. He implies in *Dumps* that *all* domiciled working adults are heartless Donald Trump–style tycoons and/or bloodthirsty crematorium rats but then shows that—fortunately!—a great white cat stepping out of the moon will save homeless children from their distress. With this *deus ex luna*—indeed totally loony—help, Jack and Guy save the black baby from the kidnapping Nazi rats only to return him to their picturesque but hopeless homeless community of meaningfully imprinted old newspapers and cardboard boxes. Unless we really have come to believe that houses are no longer better or safer than streets, we have to question—as Sendak apparently does not—the conclusion of the nursery rhyme: "We'll bring him up as other folk do." Jack and Guy simply have no chance whatsoever of accomplishing that.

What kinds of gender-specific messages are these writers sending children, and why? Girls, head South; come home where it's warm; give in to the patriarchal system that shelters you but simultaneously grips your bodies and minds in a vise of domesticity; find meaning in home, family, and what the feminist psychoanalyst Nancy Chodorow has defined as the reproduction of mothering. Boys, stay out in the Yankee cold; don't talk to each other, don't think about who you are; rebel, whether singly or in male-bonded groups; fight or die or—worse—fight *and* die so you can remain forever enshrined as our homeless antiestablishment heroes: glamorous and disturbing but totally (and safely) futile like cute little poor little mixed-up little dead little Sal Mineo in *Rebel without a Cause*. To be fair, Gibbons mercifully breaks this pattern at least partially since her first-person narrative affords Ellen Foster room for introspection, nor is Gibbons afraid to give textual space to explore the interracial friendship of Ellen and Starletta, a relationship that could conceivably grow to challenge both patriarchy and racism. No equally serious space is given by Hamilton or Sendak to Buddy's relationship with Junior or Jack's with Guy, and Holman's Slake doesn't even have a best human friend—just a rat who visits him in the subway.

All of the writers but Sendak are female, and women have relatively greater power in the interconnected worlds of education and children's book writing and publishing than in the society at large (see Anne Lundin's essay in this volume). One hopes there is not a reverse gender discrimination at work here: surely only a few very narrow-minded feminists could take comfort from this dichotomy of smart, safe girls building woman-controlled family communities within the patriarchy and stupid, stubborn, at-risk boys, so blinded by egotism that they don't even realize which side their bread is buttered on. What bothers me is the blindness with which these writers' strangely sexless yet strenuously gendered texts afford a dangerous *imprimatur* for the horrific linked phenomena of epidemic single motherhood, on the one hand, and gangs and murders, on the other, that are paradoxically killing off committed heterosexual relationships—and adolescent boys—in our cities and towns. Must these ritual sacrifices continue?

The figure of the desired, fetishized, but socially and psychically alienated and therefore doomed boy is, as I have said, far older than the current wave of concern for homeless children.[2] But in children's fiction, as Rose has brilliantly argued, there has been little development beyond the late-eighteenth-century moment when, under the influence of Locke and Rousseau, the modern child—and modern writing and publishing for children—were born (8). Instead there has been a cultural paralysis and repetition-compulsion based partly on class differences, partly on the economic pressures driving the children's book market for the last two hundred years, but mostly on desire for the child, which is really desire for oneself, that is, for the lost boy within the adult bourgeois male (Rose 8, 10). Yet in spite of Locke's and Rousseau's emphasis on material realities and experiential learning, and in spite of Freud's writings on the polymorphous perversity of childhood, "children's fiction has never completely severed its links with a philosophy which sets up the child as a pure point of origin in relation to language, sexuality and the state" (Rose 4, 8). The autoerotic and homoerotic aspects of this obsessive desire (Rose 3), as they clash with the idealization of boyhood, reach their full expression—which is for Rose their full psychosexual and moral impossibility—in *Peter Pan*. While Wendy, along with John and Michael, finally returns safely to their Bloomsbury nursery, Peter is left alone in Never Land, alienated from all the other characters, having refused the demands of patriarchal, heterosexual domestication (that is, Mr. Darling and Wendy), on the one hand, and those of the swishy-sadistic Captain Hook, on the other. Rose notes that in most productions of *Peter Pan* the same actor plays Darling and Hook (35) but that audiences seem anesthetized against the implications of this doublecasting for the crossover complexities of the adult masculine role and its relation to boyhood and home; perhaps it is the fact that Peter is regularly played by a woman that keeps them comfortably numb.

In fact, Barrie's text is not as "impossible" as Rose implies: at least the opposing viewpoints of adulthood and childhood, home and homelessness, normalcy and deviation are all represented, and Barrie makes very clear that not just Peter's domicile or sexual orientation but his very existence and identity are at stake. It is precisely this fully orchestrated tension that Holman, Hamilton, and Sendak egregiously fail to provide *their* lost boys. Except for Junior Brown, these boys, like Peter, have no home to leave *or* return to, and Junior's home, presided over by his ailing, whining, passive-aggressive mother, is not really a haven, nor, in any case, is the disturbed boy able to understand or discuss the issue clearly. Like Peter too, these boys experience exciting, strange, even fantastic events but are not permitted to experience the "awfully big adventure" (Barrie 162) of life itself. Unlike Peter, however, who is highly aware of himself in all his camped-up worries and raptures, they are given very little self-knowledge; their creators must have simply wished to avoid dealing directly with the messy, disconcerting realities of pubescent boys' sexual development, experimentations, and fantasies—and no one could claim that Barrie ignores these realities. As with Barrie, these later authors love their boys both because of and in spite of the paralysis they have imposed upon them, but even more paralyzed themselves, Holman, Hamilton, and Sendak adore not as Darling-Hooks but as ineffectual Wendy Darlings who "know" but have neither the will nor the ability to intervene.

"No one is as gay as he," Barrie gushes about Peter in his final stage direction (162); nevertheless, supporting and extending Rose's general argument both backward and forward in time, I contend that Barrie and his *Peter Pan* constitute not the decadence or perversion of an earlier, higher view of Romantic childhood but, rather, another basic expresssion of it, and that we can find the same underlying tensions in a place Rose did not look: in the texts of that avatar of clean-living canonical male Romantic propriety, William Wordsworth himself. By saying this I do not mean to imply, in the face of all the biographical evidence to the contrary, that Wordsworth ever engaged in homosexual activity, any more than one would be "outing" Samuel Clemens to say that in *Huckleberry Finn* the author gives textual space both to Huck's outsider life on the river with Jim and to Tom Sawyer's cleverness in working within the system. I do believe, however, that what Anne Mellor has called canonical male Romanticism, with its exalted sense of self, its anxieties regarding competing male writers and their works, its covert but intense worship of the child within, and its uneasy truces with bourgeois domesticity and the feminine sphere, had an important influence in the medicalization of same-sex attraction and thus in the creation of the late-nineteenth-century labels "homosexual" and "heterosexual."

Indeed, I wish to assign Wordsworth, and his influence upon Romantic boyhood, a seminal role in the dynamic of masculine identity formation first set forth by Eve Kosofsky Sedgwick in *Between Men* and further developed in her *Epistemology of the Closet*. Without making the Wordsworthian connection herself, Sedgwick argues that beginning at the turn of the nineteenth century, British patriarchy and thus all its institutions—including capitalism, colonialism, the church, and the home—were built on the rock of what she calls male homosocial desire, that is, the desire of men to study, work, fight, and play with other men—to do everything with other men, in other words, but have sexual contact with them; sexual concerns, of course, were relegated by the Victorian doctrine of separate spheres to domestic life and thus to women. Sedgwick's rock of British manliness, however, has a dark, slimy underside that she calls "homosexual panic"; this is the doubt and loathing of both self and other, caused by homophobia, that set in if ever a man feels desire for, or is accused of having desire for, another man or if a man suspects such feelings, or hears such accusations, of another man. Thus, in order to conform to the demands of this society, men must engage in as many of the culturally prescribed male bondings of patriarchy as possible and avoid at all costs the culturally proscribed horrors of sexual contact with other men (Sedgwick, *Between Men* 1–5, 89).

This binary thinking and living is simultaneously violated and reaffirmed, I suggest, by the Darling-Hook doublecasting in *Peter Pan*; moreover, it confirms my idea of Romantic boyhood as the only time in his life when a male may be free of the responsibilities of bourgeois manhood. Sedgwick's analysis is in many ways supported by Jonathan Dollimore's theory of the perverse dynamic, which also is based on a sudden turning or wandering from the approved way, a literal deviation or detour that is both thrilling to the individual and immediately suspect to himself and others, and one where culture's ordinary binaries simultaneously fracture and remain linked (*Sexual Dissidence* 121, 129). More recently, although he does not cite Dollimore, David Collings's *Wordsworthian Errancies* parallels Dollimore's argument, since Collings associates the poet's numerous textual wanderings from the safe paths of culture and society with a dangerous but vital mental, artistic, and social creativity. Collings has gone so far as to suggest that Wordsworth be considered a "flaming" deviant, "that he is far more outrageous than readers have generally recognized, that he not only champions deviance and a nearly overt homoeroticism but links them intimately with his status as a poet" (14, 13). Himself too eagerly championing the anachronistic Wordsworth he constructs, Collings does not sufficiently account for the restraining forces Sedgwick has identified and that, snuffing any putative flames, drove Wordsworth—and, I would suggest, many other young men—back onto the path of cultural and sexual normalcy if ever they were tempted to wander.

Together, I suggest, these theorists and critics help us to identify and to understand a pattern of mental, social, and textual borders and border crossings as historically inevitable, as culturally necessary for many boys to follow as Chodorow's reproduction of mothering seems to be for girls. It is worth repeating that the awareness of binaries and division I have been discussing is part of the development of the sexually "normal" masculine identity as well as that of those boys who develop same-sex preferences. Nearly everyone wanders in youth, whether politically, socially, psychically, or sexually, though it is true that some do not return from their wanderings, and an even smaller few—the great artists certainly among them— maintain the double vision, experiencing the binaries of path and wandering, home and homelessness, as both fractured and linked. I will take a closer look now at some of the earlier parts of Wordsworth's *Prelude*; further study of this pattern in Wordsworth will help me to connect Wordsworth's and Barrie's lost British boys with the lost urban Americans of Holman, Hamilton, and Sendak.

Orphaned early (he was eight when his mother died in 1778, thirteen when he lost his father), Wordsworth, who with his brothers continued to study at Hawkshead School, was not penniless and thus was not literally homeless in the current sense of the term. He did, however, become a wanderer in his young manhood, making long walking tours during his summer vacations from Cambridge and spending considerable time in France during the early years of the Revolution. Then in 1795, disillusioned by the failure of his revolutionary hopes, he willingly gave up his youthful wandering to reestablish with his sister Dorothy a model of the loving, nurturing home they had lost many years before. It was mental, verbal, and textual interaction with Dorothy and subsequently with their friend S. T. Coleridge that made Wordsworth a poet.[3] Home-adventure-return: the pattern we noted earlier in the fictions about girls is also the pattern of Wordsworth's life, which reappears in his poetry of childhood and manhood, as the man looks back on his childhood self with the sense of almost simultaneous identity and difference. Bereft and moody as an adolescent, the young Wordsworth became part of the society of boarding-school boys in Hawkshead who spent their free time restlessly roaming the hills and valleys of the English

Lakes. Here is one of his recollections, written in his late twenties, from the 1799 *Prelude*:[4]

> From week to week, from month to month, we lived
> A round of tumult. Duly were our games
> Prolonged in summer till the daylight failed:
> No chair remained before the doors, the bench
> And threshold steps were empty, fast asleep
> The labourer and the old man who had sate
> A later lingerer, yet the revelry
> Continued and the loud uproar. At last,
> When all the ground was dark and the huge clouds
> Were edged with twinkling stars, to bed we went
> With weary joints and with a beating mind.
>   (Book II: 6–16)

Following this double recognition of both the youthful breaking away from the ordinary round of daily activities and the inevitable return, the mature poet continues by directly examining the gap of time and experience between his childhood and adult selves:

> Ah, is there one who ever has been young
> And needs a monitory voice to tame
> The pride of virtue and of intellect?
> And is there one, the wisest and the best
> Of all mankind, who does not sometimes wish
> For things which cannot be, who would not give,
> If so he might, to duty and to truth
> The eagerness of infantine desire?
> A tranquillizing spirit presses now
> On my corporeal frame, so wide appears
> The vacancy between me and those days,
> Which yet have such self-presence in my heart
> That sometimes when I think of them I seem
> Two consciousnesses—conscious of myself,
> And of some other being.
>   (Book II [1799]: 17–31)

Wordsworth here feels and articulates simultaneously the self-division into "two consciousnesses"—the binary of youth and "infantine desire," on the one hand, and patriarchal "virtue and intellect," "duty and truth," on the other—and also the strange "tranquillizing spirit" which can reconcile them but "sometimes" fails to do so, even though intellectually he has accepted the fact that youth is past.

The powerful ice-skating scene in *The Prelude* starts with a bravado dismissal of the societal forces, the indoors world, to which ultimately he must yield, and to which as readers we know the adult poet *has* yielded:

> And in the frosty season, when the sun
> Was set, and visible for many a mile
> The cottage windows through the twilight blazed,
> I heeded not the summons. Clear and loud
> The village clock tolled six; I wheeled about
> Proud and exulting, like an untired horse
> That cares not for his home.
>   (Book I [1799]: 150–56)

The bright cottage windows significantly continue to issue their "summons" to study, shelter, and rest while Wordsworth recollects the games he and the other boys played on the ice. Then, in lines full of infantine desire, he writes:

> And oftentimes
> When we had given our bodies to the wind,
> And all the shadowy banks on either side
> Came sweeping through the darkness, spinning still
> The rapid line of motion, then at once
> Have I, reclining back upon my heels
> Stopped short—yet still the solitary cliffs
> Wheeled by me, even as if the earth had rolled
> With visible motion her diurnal round.
>   (Book I [1799]: 174–82)

But even as he remembers and re-creates this narcissistic, Peter Pan–like moment of joy, when the world seemed to turn adoringly around him, he lets us know that it is vanishing, that for both boy and man it *must* vanish: "Behind me did they stretch in solemn train, / Feebler and feebler, and I stood and watched / Till all was tranquil as a summer sea" (Book I [1799]: 183–85). Wordsworth—

like his reader here—stands and watches from two different perspectives—that of childhood and that of nostalgic adult recollection: the dizzy boy recovers his equilibrium after spinning on his skates, and the grown-up poet reexperiencing childhood watches it fade and both is and is not healed by the "tranquillizing spirit" of adult consciousness. Repeatedly in these recollections the boy errs, breaks away from nature's or society's permitted paths: he steals game from another's traps, eggs from a raven's nest, a rowboat left by its owner at the lakeshore (Book I [1799]: 27–129). But his pleasure mingles with guilt after each of these transgressions, and he projects his feelings into a sternly potent nature whose forces come stalking him afterward: "huge and mighty forms that do not live / Like living men moved slowly through my mind / By day, and were the trouble of my dreams" (Book I [1799]: 127–29). Collings sees this as evidence of a masochistic fantasy based on the poet's combined fear and desire for his father (136–37)—Mr. Darling, so to speak, changing into Captain Hook; certainly Wordsworth is gothicizing the landscape when he speaks of its features as "characters / Of danger or desire" (Book I [1799]: 194–95), but these lines may simply evoke the polymorphous perversity of childhood rather than any object-specific fantasy or father fixation.

Later, in his young manhood, Wordsworth is similarly both attracted and repelled by those ominous solitary male figures he meets while wandering in the landscape and whom he describes elsewhere in *The Prelude*, for example, the discharged soldier and the blind London beggar. These men on the margins, older and seemingly possessed of strange knowledge, communicate far more to the young poet than what they actually say, or than what he says about them. In the sick soldier's voice "There was a strange half-absence, and a tone / Of weakness and indifference" (Book IV [1805]: 475–76); and the poet is struck by the irony that the blind man wears on his chest "a written paper, to explain / The story of the man, and who he was" (Book VII [1805]: 614–15) that of course does not really explain anything. But simultaneously, as Wordsworth matures into manhood and the polymorphous perverse, now disciplined by homophobia, shades into the perverse dynamic, he no longer wants to hear his own desire and fear echoed back to him, so although he does tell of these encounters, he defuses them of some of their vaguely homoerotic tension. He lectures the sick soldier for lingering in the public ways when he could ask for shelter before leaving him with what he claims is a "quiet heart" (Book IV [1805]: 489–92, 504); and he precedes the description of the blind beggar with the mind-numbingly trite recognition that in the crowds of London "'The face of every one / That passes by me is a mystery'" (Book VII [1805]: 597–98).

We can see this simultaneous representation of youthful homoerotic desire and of adult homosexual panic even more acutely when, again in *The Prelude*, Wordsworth recalls with great nostalgic passion his morning walks as a boy with a beloved friend, John Fleming:

> —happy time, more dear
> For this, that one was by my side, a friend
> Then passionately loved. With heart how full
> Will he peruse these lines, this page—perhaps
> A blank to other men—for many years
> Have since flowed in between us, and, our minds
> Both silent to each other, at this time
> We live as if those hours had never been.
>   (Book II [1799]: 381–88)

Even as he remembers and speaks his passion, he makes clear that he and Fleming are no longer in touch, suggesting also that this page may remain blank to other men who read it. One senses that he half wishes himself that he had left it blank, yet he has had the courage to give a home in *The Prelude* to this more specific feeling of attraction for another youth. Finally, one needs to remember that the entire *Prelude* was usually referred to by the poet and his family as the "poem to Coleridge" because it is addressed to the much-loved friend of Wordsworth's youthful poetic heyday—although that friendship too was cooling, even as he wrote of it, from its initial intensity.

Thus along with, and frequently because of, the courage Wordsworth demonstrates in confronting their culturally forbidden aspects, there is great pain for him in experiencing these wanderings of childhood, and then there is also the double transgression of reexperiencing them as an adult while writing of his past. Sometimes the "two consciousnesses" refuse to come together for the poet—innocence and experience will not be reconciled in either mind or text. Sharing what must be one of his deepest memories of infantine desire, he writes of the Boy of Winander who "Blew mimic hootings to the silent owls, / That they might answer him" (Book V [1850]:

373–74). Sometimes they answered him directly with "jocund din," but the strongest moment of joy comes when his efforts fail him:

> when a lengthened pause
> Of silence came and baffled his best skill,
> Then sometimes, in that silence while he hung
> Listening, a gentle shock of mild surprise
> Has carried far into his heart the voice
> Of mountain torrents; or the visible scene
> Would enter unawares into his mind
> With all its solemn imagery, its rocks,
> Its woods, and that uncertain heaven, received
> Into the bosom of the steady lake.
> (Book V [1850]: 379–88)

Then, with pain as powerful as the joy, as astonishing to the reader as it must have been agonizing to Wordsworth, the poet kills the child: "This Boy was taken from his mates, and died / In childhood, ere he was full twelve years old" (Book V [1850]: 389–90). At this point Wordsworth, who as we have seen created in his text a reconciling space, a home for both boyhood and manhood, temporarily gives up, leaving the boy where Holman, Hamilton, and Sendak leave their heroes but, even so, acknowledging far more than they that a sacrifice has occurred: "A long half hour together I have stood / Mute, looking at the grave in which he lies!" (Book V [1850]: 396–97). That this represents a personal crisis is indicated by an early manuscript, which shows the poet alternating between first- and third-person pronouns (Wordsworth 492); in other words, the man commits a sort of inner suicide, killing the boy he once was by writing him out of the text. But then he rallies, reviving beyond the self-pity of thwarted desire to pronounce a saving benediction not on the one child who has died but on all the boys who have lived or will live in the future, "a race of young ones like to those / With whom I herded!" (Book V [1850]: 407–8):

> A race of real children; not too wise,
> Too learned, or too good; but wanton, fresh,
> And bandied up and down by love and hate;
> Not unresentful where self-justified;
> Fierce, moody, patient, venturous, modest, shy;
> Mad at their sports like withered leaves in winds;

Though doing wrong and suffering, and full oft
Bending beneath our life's mysterious weight
Of pain, and doubt, and fear, yet yielding not
In happiness to the happiest on earth.
    (Book V [1850]: 411–20)

Wordsworth's triumph is his reconciliation here of love with hate, of wanton freshness with wrong and suffering, of pain, doubt, and fear with happiness. This of course is what the boys' writers under review have not provided for their forlorn heroes. Hamilton, Sendak, and Holman all sympathize with their boys' attempts to re-create their lives through the learning that comes from deviation, but they fail to give their characters or readers anything even approaching a complete view of the perverse dynamic in its relation to the patriarchal norm. Slake, Buddy, and Jack and Guy are abandoned by their writers, left literally homeless yet figuratively trapped in incomplete texts with impossible, ultimately deadly "happy endings."

What should writers for children and adolescents do? How can adolescent boys' development be more fully and honestly portrayed in fiction in a society that remains as viciously homophobic as ours? I am not simply urging that more time and space be made for overtly gay characters in books for children and adolescents. Indeed, so many such books have already "come out" that "gay/lesbian children's literature" has been labeled, and thus to a degree ghettoized, as a minority subset of children's literature along with "black children's literature," "Native American children's literature," and so on. It seems unlikely that the self-appointed censors of children's books —whether members of the religious right, of teaching faculties, or of the publishing industry—will allow such a long-standing taboo to be shattered. Nor will some advocates of gay/lesbian or other minority literatures be pleased that I am advocating at least a partial deconstruction of the binaries that may have helped them to define themselves to themselves and the world. As I have shown, the "safely" heterosexual Wordsworth has been above reproach for almost two hundred years, and yet in *The Prelude* he tells the story of male desire with remarkable clarity and complexity, given the inevitable homophobia that accompanies it.

And there are more honest recent fictions, albeit adult fictions, about adolescent male development. David Guy's novel *Second*

Brother (1985) inscribes a male adolescent's coming of age, including his relationship with his best friend and shadow-self, with energy, complexity, honesty, and taste. Though Henry, the first-person narrator of his story, seems headed for a heterosexual adulthood, the book ends with an emotional elegy for his friendship with Sam: "My memory of Sam Golden is a talisman for me. I pick it up and hold it and it brings me luck. . . . When I think of how to live my life, not the things I want to do but the way I want to do them, I think of him. . . . I am glad I knew him. I am glad he lived" (Guy 264). In these lines one can almost hear echoes of Wordsworth's paean for his childhood friend Fleming. Like Wordsworth, Guy is not writing for children but for adults, but unlike the poet, Guy is writing for late-twentieth-century adults. Thus he presents several sexually explicit passages, both opposite-sex and same-sex, including one where Henry and Sam engage in mutual masturbation. However much I might believe that narrative frankness like that could and would help to bring some literally or figuratively homeless boys in from the cold, I can't make myself believe that the censors—including the children's writers themselves (West 51)—would ever open the textual space to such feelings or activities: to do so would be to violate the pure innocence of Romantic childhood, which is always being stalked by darker realities—whether sexual, economic, or political—and which, as we have seen, Wordsworth himself violated. Yet while Guy may go too far for some, these stories need to be told somehow, and told to and for children, and not to tell them constitutes an ethical failure even though the stories themselves may seem to some to contain immoral elements (Booth, *Company* 179). Another recent first-person adult novel of male development, Russell Banks's *Rule of the Bone* (1995), reverses the plight of Guy's narrator, who never literally leaves home, in that Bone chooses homelessness to escape the homosexual assaults of his stepfather; yet at the end of the novel, although he has found and then lost a loving, supportive surrogate father and has been comfortably initiated into heterosexual relations, he is still running, never "coming in" to confront his fears fully or to accept a stable adult male identity.

In "Reading Secrets," a brilliant essay on Joseph Conrad's "The Secret Sharer," James Phelan asks, "In this narrative of secrets what is the relationship between the ethical dimensions of the captain's story and the ethical dimensions of his telling?" (122). He goes on to argue that the captain, Conrad's narrator, involves his reader in a compelling but, for many, uncomfortable way with the (apparently reciprocated) homoerotic feelings he has for the runaway Leggatt and also with his refusal, based on this attraction, to help bring Leggatt to justice for the murder he has committed. By the time the captain successfully maroons Leggatt and brings his ship around in the shadow of the island, guided by the floating hat he had earlier given the homeless young man, the reader—at least a conventionally homophobic and law-abiding reader—has experienced a variety of contrasting feelings through the secrets he has been exposed to: sympathy and strong disapproval, hope that Leggatt will be discovered and hope that he will not, hope that the captain will succeed and hope that the ship will run aground. I will close by pointing out that such contrasts, such shattered yet still interconnected binaries, lie at the heart of Wordsworth's "infantine desire" and Dollimore's perverse dynamic, forming a paradoxical sort of stability in instability for both writer and reader, and probably point as clear a way as any toward the resolution we seek here, which is simultaneously, in the conceptual, institutional, and textual homes we now inhabit, never fully to be resolved.

NOTES

1. Interestingly, in this connection, at least one social work professional suggests that by idealizing the family group this ideology ironically prevents workers from doing the most they could do for at-risk children (Hartman), while another laments the extreme marginalization and demonization of homeless street children that has led to mass executions in Brazil (Bond).

2. One could of course trace back much further in time the history of men's attraction to other men, especially younger men; Crompton's *Byron and Greek Love* is a pathbreaking study in this area, and Bray's *Homosexuality in Renaissance England*, though it does not extend to the Romantic period, offers a useful and provocative historical overview which emphasizes again how paradoxically homosexuality was simultaneously excoriated and tolerated in England over several centuries in the medieval and early modern periods. Study of the ways that girls' education and development from the eighteenth century onward have been either suppressed or ignored, the degree to which girls have been both hurt by the discrimination and ironically helped by the neglect, and the recuperation of a feminine Romantic tradition, also dating from the latter eighteenth century (see Rose 84), that privileged rationality, shared identity, and community over imagination, egotistical sublimity, and antisocial revolt is central to the projects of historians of women's relationships such

as Lillian Faderman and Martha Vicinus and of Romantic feminist scholar-critics such as Anne Mellor and Mitzi Myers. Illuminating parallels might be drawn, for example, between the writings of eighteenth-century religious writer Hannah More and those of late-twentieth-century religious writer Katherine Paterson or between those of the more secular Maria Edgeworth and Cynthia Voigt, but I will not pursue them here.

3. See my article "Defusing the Discharged Soldier" for a textual analysis of the dynamics of the Wordsworth-Coleridge relationship.

4. Wordsworth's *Prelude* will hereafter be cited in the text by book (Book I or II) and year (1799, 1805, or 1850).

WORKS CITED

Banks, Russell. *Rule of the Bone*. New York: Harper, 1995.

Barrie, J. M. *Peter Pan, or The Boy Who Would Not Grow Up*. New York: Avon, 1982.

Berkvist, Robert. "Slake's Limbo" (review). *New York Times Book Review*, November 17, 1974, 8.

Bond, Lydia S. "Street Children and AIDS: Is Postponement of Sexual Involvement a Realistic Alternative to the Prevention of Sexually Transmitted Diseases?" *Environment and Urbanization* 4 (1992): 150–57.

Booth, Wayne C. *The Company We Keep: An Ethics of Fiction*. Berkeley: U of California P, 1988.

———. *The Rhetoric of Fiction*. Chicago: U of Chicago P, 1961.

Bray, Alan. *Homosexuality in Renaissance England*. London: Gay Men's Press, 1982.

Burt, Martha R., and Barbara E. Cohen. "Differences among Homeless Single Women, Women with Children, and Single Men." *Social Problems* 36 (1989): 508–24.

Calsyn, Robert J., and Gary Morse. "Homeless Men and Women: Commonalities and a Service Gender Gap." *American Journal of Community Psychology* 18 (1990): 597–608.

Chodorow, Nancy. *The Reproduction of Mothering: Psychoanalysis and the Sociology of Gender*. Berkeley: U of California P, 1978.

Collings, David. *Wordsworthian Errancies: The Poetics of Cultural Dismemberment*. Baltimore: Johns Hopkins UP, 1994.

Crompton, Louis. *Byron and Greek Love: Homophobia in Nineteenth-Century England*. Berkeley: U of California P, 1985.

Dollimore, Jonathan. *Sexual Dissidence: Augustine to Wilde, Freud to Foucault*. Oxford: Clarendon, 1991.

Egoff, Sheila A. *Thursday's Child: Trends and Patterns in Contemporary Children's Literature*. New York: American Library Association, 1981.

Faderman, Lillian. *Surpassing the Love of Men: Romantic Friendship and Love between Women from the Renaissance to the Present*. New York: Morrow, 1981.

Fiedler, Leslie. "Come Back to the Raft Ag'in, Huck Honey!" *A Fiedler Reader*. New York: Stein and Day, 1977. 3–12.

Garden, Nancy. *The Christian Science Monitor*, November 11, 1971, B5.

Garrison, Jean. "AIDS and Adolescents: Exploring the Challenge." *Journal of Adolescent Health Care* 3 (1989): 1S–69S.

Gibbons, Kaye. *Ellen Foster*. Chapel Hill, NC: Algonquin, 1987.

Guy, David. *Second Brother*. New York: New American Library, 1985.

Hamilton, Virginia. *The Planet of Junior Brown*. New York: Macmillan, 1971.

Hartman, Ann. "Children in a Careless Society." *Social Work* 35 (1990): 483–84.

Heins, Paul. "The Planet of Junior Brown" (review). *Horn Book* 48 (1972): 81.

Holman, Felice. *Slake's Limbo*. New York: Macmillan, 1974.

Kaplan, Temma. "Community and Resistance in Women's Political Cultures," *Dialectical Anthropology* 15 (1990): 259–67.

Kuznets, Lois R. "The Fresh-Air Kids, or Some Contemporary Versions of Pastoral." *Children's Literature* 11 (1983): 156–68.

McGavran, James Holt. "Defusing the Discharged Soldier: Wordsworth, Coleridge, and Homosexual Panic," *Papers in Language and Literature* 32 (1996): 147–65.

———. "Introduction." *Romanticism and Children's Literature in Nineteenth-Century England*. Ed. James Holt McGavran, Jr. Athens: U of Georgia P, 1991.

Mellor, Anne K. *Romanticism and Gender*. New York: Routledge, 1993.

Myers, Mitzi. "Little Girls Lost: Rewriting Romantic Childhood, Righting Gender and Genre." *Teaching Children's Literature: Issues, Pedagogy, Resources*. Ed. Glenn Edward Sadler. New York: Modern Language Association, 1992. 131–42.

North, Carol S., and Elizabeth M. Smith. "A Comparison of Homeless Men and Women: Different Populations, Different Needs." *Community Mental Health Journal* 29 (1993), 423–31.

Paterson, Katherine. *The Great Gilly Hopkins*. 1978. New York: Harper, 1987.

Phelan, James. *Narrative as Rhetoric: Technique, Audiences, Ethics, Ideology*. Columbus: Ohio State UP, 1996.

Rees, David. *Painted Desert, Green Shade: Essays on Contemporary Writers of Fiction for Children and Young Adults*. Boston: Horn Book, 1984.

Richardson, Alan. "Childhood and Romanticism." *Teaching Children's Literature: Issues, Pedagogy, Resources*. Ed. Glenn Edward Sadler. New York: Modern Language Association, 1992. 121–30.

Rose, Jacqueline. *The Case of Peter Pan, or The Impossibility of Children's Fiction*. 1984. Philadelphia: U of Pennsylvania P, 1992.

Sedgwick, Eve Kosofsky. *Between Men: English Literature and Male Homosocial Desire*. New York: Columbia UP, 1985.

———. *Epistemology of the Closet*. Berkeley: U of California P, 1990.

Sendak, Maurice. *We Are All in the Dumps with Jack and Guy*. New York: Harper, 1993.

Susser, Ida. "Creating Family Forms: The Exclusion of Men and Teenage Boys from Families in the New York City Shelter System." *Critique of Anthropology* 13 (1993): 267–83.

Townsend, John Rowe. *Written for Children: An Outline of English Language Children's Literature*. Rev. ed. New York: Lippincott, 1974.

Vicinus, Martha. *Independent Women: Work and Community for Single Women, 1850–1920*. Chicago: U of Chicago P, 1985.

Voigt, Cynthia. *Homecoming*. New York: Atheneum, 1981.

West, Mark I. "Teaching Banned Children's Books." *Teaching Children's Literature: Issues, Pedagogy, Resources*. Ed. Glenn Edward Sadler. New York: Modern Language Association, 1992. 51–58.

Wordsworth, William. *The Prelude: 1799, 1805, 1850*. Ed. Jonathan Wordsworth, M. H. Abrams, and Stephen Gill. New York: Norton, 1979.

PART THREE

Romanticism and the Commerce of Children's Books

Anne Lundin

SENSATIONAL DESIGNS:
THE CULTURAL WORK OF
KATE GREENAWAY

magine the actors and their actions. A framed illustration in a picture book depicts a country garden, a meadow, a picturesque farmhouse peopled with young children who are playing ritually in a Romantic rural landscape. The children bear the expressiveness of a delimited yet infinite space, of becalmed skies and flowering nature. Their bemused expressions belie the antique fancy costumes or peasant smocks in which they are dressed. The children, along with readers, stand serene in such a place, struck by the fantasy of such delicate environs, of tidy young life amid domestically cultured green spaces.[1]

The illustrations could be by any number of modern illustrators of the pastoral in children's books, where each page sings of the Romantic rhythms of innocent, fantastic childhood. Consider the work of Maurice Boutet de Monvel; Henriette Willebeek Le Mair; E. Boyd Smith; Swedish artists Carl Larsson, Elsa Beskow, Ottilia Adelborg; and the American illustrators Jessie Willcox Smith, Rachel Field, and Tasha Tudor, among others, who demonstrate a romanticized aesthetics of picture book art. The gender or nationality of the artist is not the focus, but, rather, the decorative and domesticated sense of childhood is. The commonality is a domesticated image of the child and feminized settings of home and garden. The model, the paradigm of these romanticized settings, is the style of Kate Greenaway.

Greenaway's prettified world inspired an immediate and enduring following: a company of illustrators who shared her artistic vision and reworked her motifs intertextually both in materials and points of reference. Related as well are the imitations of her style, which began immediately following the publication of her first book, *Under the Window* (1879), in the reworking of *Afternoon Tea* (1880) by Sowerby and Emmerson. The commerce of copying Greenaway has been a major industry in the products of Holly Hobby, Joan

Walsh Anglund, Laura Ashley, and, most recently, Mary Engelbreit. Greenaway's work has been debased, sentimentalized, and reinterpreted, just as has Romanticism itself in the late nineteenth and twentieth centuries. I intend to explore Greenaway's aesthetics of the picture book, a sensibility grounded in the past—from a remembered childhood to a re-created eighteenth century—which continues to shape the modern picture book landscape and popular culture. What I hope emerges is a portrait of Greenaway's constructed reputation, which is due in part to the canonical inscription of key women librarians and booksellers—notably, Anne Carroll Moore and Bertha Mahony.

The areas I will explore relate to the cultural work of Kate Greenaway as a picture book exemplar of feminine Romanticism, to her advocacy by the pioneer women of children's book publishing and librarianship in the formative years of the field, and to a survey of her intertextual appropriation in the works of late-nineteenth- and twentieth-century illustrators of children's literature. It cannot be merely a coincidence that Greenaway's work was experiencing a renaissance in public favor at the same time that newspaper columns, professional columns, and children's bookstores began to espouse her work, to promote its perpetuation in publishing, and to note contemporary re-creators of her style. The Greenaway style was a conjoined construction of a receptive sensibility.

Classics in the canon are made, not born. So Jane Tompkins's *Sensational Designs: The Cultural Work of American Fiction, 1790–1860* argues: a literary text exists only within a framework of assumptions that are historically produced. The reading and reputation of a work are affected by a series of cultural circumstances related to publishing practices, pedagogical and critical traditions, economic structures, social networks, and national needs. Whatever its intrinsic merit, a literary work succeeds or fails in terms of its reception in the immediate context, "on the degree to which it provokes the desired response" (Tompkins xviii). An author's reputation depends upon the cultural context within which the work is read and creates the values its readers "discover" there. A text that reaches an exceptionally large audience does so not by its particular uniqueness but by its common embrace of the values most widely shared. Yet literary texts may also inscribe "attempts to redefine the social order," to express solutions for cultural problems, to influence cultural discourse, the way people think and act (Tompkins xi).

This critique is part of a larger discourse that questions the canon as an institutional construction and the process of inclusion or exclusion by which social groups are represented or not represented in the exercise of power. Jane Tompkins's *Sensational Designs* is particularly valuable for the concept of "cultural work," arising from a text's historical existence and influence in the culture, and for her re-vision of sentimentality as a radical discourse of power. In discussing *Uncle Tom's Cabin*, Tompkins argues for the "sentimental women's" own sense of empowerment by the "cult of domesticity." Instead of viewing sentimentality as merely consolation and cultural denigration, Tompkins elevates sentimental rhetoric to a position of power that seeks "to reorganize society from the woman's point of view" (124). A sentimental piece of literature can be transforming and transgressive by its designs on the reader for critique, reform. A text can be conservative in its emphasis on established patterns and traditional beliefs, yet also revolutionary in extending these beliefs to an extreme of civic good and "the conduct of all human affairs" (Tompkins 145). "Cultural work" is the cultural self-expression of literature operating within a particular social context. A novel becomes an "answer" to a cultural "question" which is used to change the world of the reader and the cultural politics of a nation. Related is Michel Foucault's premise that an archive, what is preserved and what is not, itself represents an ideology. Pierre Bourdieu's *Distinction* presents a theory of taste and the politics of privileging a culture's "masterpieces." Clifford Geertz's concept of "thick description" in *The Interpretation of Cultures* heightens the need not just to describe "the meaning particular social actions have for the actors whose actions they are" but for "stating, as explicitly as we can manage, what the knowledge thus attained demonstrates about the society in which it is found, and, beyond that, about social life as such" (27). Literary practices are just one of many sites where several different discourses converge and assume meaning intertextually. Approaches toward intertextuality view imitations as supplements to the original, which function for later readers as the pre-text for the original (Clayton and Rothstein). Each imitative work is necessarily determined by the literary codes in force at the time of its writing and of its reading. Feminist critics challenge the canon by gendering Romanticism's restrictive notions of culture: art, politics, the self, and the other. Anne Mellor and Mitzi Myers, among others, have exposed the conventional view of high Romanticism: the notion that only the aesthetics of the leading male poets (six in particular) bear weight. Mellor postulates a feminine Romanticism as an ethical and familial portrayal of the self in relation to a family or community (209). To Myers, the discourse about the period and its literary production has been dominated by a peculiar masculine mythology of lyrical development, "Romanticism's claim to a mysterious, essentialized child self" (68). While male tropes of wilderness have been valorized as Romanticism in its finest spirit, women's developmental stories and imagined communities have until recently been relegated to nonliterary status as educational treatises or quotidian sketches. These related theories of cultural studies offer scholarly standpoints that illuminate the complex social, political, and material process of cultural production and demonstrate how Kate Greenaway's Romantic style and fashion in illustration are propagated.

A key to interpretation of cultural production lies in the historical studies of reader response criticism. Each generation's classics assume and foreground a set of dominant codes and values evident in the cultural politics of the age. The salient factors that shaped literary fashions and critical reputations in the late nineteenth century were embedded in the horizons of expectations of the age—the assumptions of the readership as to childhood and its literature. The horizons of expectations with respect to children's literature in the 1880s and 1890s constituted the context in which juvenile books were received. These standards are implicit in the Victorian periodicals of the day, in which reviewers and commentators of literary magazines and journals as well as the press articulated their expectations for literature and art. Drawing on Hans Robert Jauss's reception theory and on my own research into the cultural discourse on children's books in late-nineteenth-century England and America, I see the literary discourse of the period as including the following spectrum of positions: (1) treatment of children's books as a commodity; (2) elevation of children's books as works of art; (3) emphasis on illustration and pictorial effects on literature; (4) lack of rigid demarcation between adult and children's literature; (5) a growing gender division; (6) diversification of the didactic tradition; (7) continuing debate on fantasy and realism; (8) Romantic idealization of childhood and its literature; (9) attention to the historiography of children's literature; and (10) anxiety about the changing character of children's literature (Lundin 33–53).

Of these horizons, the one most persistent into the twentieth cen-

tury has been the Romantic resonance of childhood and its literature. The 1880s and 1890s were a pinnacle in the Victorian Romanticism of the child, and the periodical press was the forum for reflection and construction of this iconization. The *National Review* (1891)
described the period as "the Age of Children" (507). *Good Words*
(1904) deemed the nineteenth century as "the Children's Century"
and noted the enhanced value placed on the child as the subject of
reform movements as well as scholarly studies and fictional narratives (341). *Scribner's* (1898) explored the literary preoccupations
with the child as "a second childhood in literature," in which writers
looked back to a "golden age" for solace in uncertain times (123).
The *Illustrated London News* (1890) revealed the broad nostalgic appeal of Romantic childhood: "The pleasures of children supply the
sweetest part of parents' pleasure; and to many a kindly heart, among
good old maids and other childless persons, or the aged whose old
sons and daughters have grown up to men and women, there is
nothing so delightful, in the whole spectacle of life, as the innocent
joys of the little people, without whose presence the world, indeed,
would be horribly dull and dreary" ("Joies D'Enfants" 739).

Kate Greenaway's style—a trope of "the innocent joys of the little
people"—resonated with this charged climate. Kate Greenaway's
picture books modeled childhood for the late Victorians as a garden
idyll, with winsome children frolicking in pasturelands or village
greens surrounded by verdant images, and her influence remains in
the feminine romanticism of modern children's book illustration.
Barbara Bader, surveying the origins of the modern American picture book, appreciated Greenaway's departure from the traditional
renderings of childhood classics toward inventions of her own imagination, to creating books not only for but *about* children (4). Greenaway set the example for others to follow, a persistent strain of
feminine Romanticism in children's literature. Historicizing the appeal of Greenaway for her day helps to establish the nature of her
influence.

Romantic strands in Greenaway's work are redolent in images of
the cult of the child and a community of women, expressed through
artistic fantasies of secret gardens. The garden and its larger landscape became the metaphor for Greenaway and many of her contemporaries to express Romantic sensibilities about childhood and
its stories. Some of the recent criticism on the subject includes Mitzi
Myers in her writing on Maria Edgeworth and Anna Barbauld, Phyl-

lis Bixler on the pastoral tradition, U. C. Knoepflmacher on nature and the Victorian imagination, and Judith Plotz on the masculine Romantic view of the child-artist symbiosis. Humphrey Carpenter in his book *Secret Gardens* examines the potency of that image of the secret garden of childhood and of England for a whole frame of authors making up "the Golden Age of children's literature": Charles Kingsley, Lewis Carroll, George MacDonald, Frances Hodgson Burnett, Richard Jefferies, Kenneth Grahame, E. Nesbit, Beatrix Potter, J. M. Barrie, and A. A. Milne. He argues that around the mid-nineteenth century, children were seen as having a clear, even heightened vision of the world, and that by the second half of the century, children and childhood had become important elements in the literary imagination (Carpenter 10). Moreover, childhood had become equated with Eden, the garden, the Enchanted Place where harmony reigns. Growing up meant a loss of Paradise, a departure from the Golden Age (Carpenter 9). Thus, much writing for children became introspective and turned to escape and fantasy (Carpenter x). Kate Greenaway belongs within that visionary company as a mothered progenitor of arcadian dreams and sylvan places.

Kate Greenaway's drawings of old-fashioned girls and boys, which appeared in the 1870s, presented an idyllic childhood inhabited by children and young maidens in sophisticated rural simplicity. Greenaway's stylized children were not ostensibly contemporary but appeared old-fashioned in dress reminiscent of the late eighteenth century and redolent of village life still preserved in small pockets of the late-nineteenth-century English countryside. In actuality, Greenaway subtly drew upon the most stylish of contemporary motifs from the aesthetic movement: Queen Anne architecture, William Morris furniture and textiles, Chinese blue-and-white china, and the soft colors much in vogue, apple blossom pink and moss green. To architectural historian Mark Girouard, surveying the Queen Anne movement (1860–1900), the picture books of Walter Crane, Kate Greenaway, and Randolph Caldecott were "secret persuaders," "more convincing than any prose, of the need for artistic education, especially in the nursery" (139). While parents in the 1850s sought books for more didactic purposes, the generation of the 1870s sought books to inculcate the arts. Somehow such artistic education might offset the dehumanizing effects of industrialization and materialism on Victorian culture. Thus, these early picture books can be viewed as oppositional reading, in the sense that Janice Radway imparts to the reading of romance novels. The images offer an alternative vision, a desired state subverting reality.

Greenaway's work was particularly expressive as a feminine art form. Women artists traditionally have expressed themselves through allowable structures of the dominant culture. As Pamela Gerrish Nunn writes in *Victorian Women Artists*, a certain kind of feminine artistry was encouraged, one in which "the home and person were the only sites congenial to women's creativity" (20). While genius was suspect, women were allowed to develop talents in craft or design, which included children's book illustration. Nunn points out that by the end of the nineteenth century, the few women artists who were successful exemplified the acceptable models. The success of the three cited—Helen Allingham, Elizabeth Thompson (Lady Butler), and Kate Greenaway—indicates the sort of female artist that the late nineteenth century would accept. The persistent popularity of Allingham and Greenaway demonstrated the popular appeal of a traditionally feminine art, described as "small in scale; watercolour; addressing itself uncritically to domestic experience and incident, the appearance and behavior of children, the quaint and the picturesque; pleasing by its aesthetic charm but not arresting by its creative genius" (Nunn 220). This feminized pictorial world stood in contrast to the academy's notion of fine arts and Romantic subjects, which tended to privilege the dominant ideology of male Romanticism's lonely vision over a more relational community. John Ruskin (1819–1900) noted the subversiveness of such a vision in his Slade Lecture at Oxford University on the subject, "Fairy Land: Mrs. Allingham and Kate Greenaway," which was published in his book *The Art of England* (1884). Ruskin praised Greenaway's pastoral, preindustrial settings: "There are no railroads in it, to carry the children away . . . no tunnel or pit mouths to swallow them up . . . no vestige of science, civilization, economic arrangements, or commercial enterprise" (152). In other words, this was an alternative world that was attuned to other priorities of place while at the same time to a certain nostalgia of lost youth, something attractive to a masculine as well as a feminine sentiment.

This vision resonated with many critics like Ruskin who helped to construct for the public eye a way of seeing. To Martin Hardie, a contemporary artist and art historian, Greenaway distinguished herself through "the directness of the pictorial motives" that create a particular idealized world:

a little kingdom of her own, a kingdom like the island-valley of Avilon, "deep-meadowed, happy, fair with orchard lawns," a land of flowers and gardens, of red-brick houses with dormer windows, peopled with charming children clad in long, high-waisted gowns, muffs, pelisses, and sun-bonnets. In all her work there is a "sweet reasonableness," an atmosphere of old-world peace and simple piety that recalls Izaak Walton's *Compleat Angler* and "fresh sheets that smell of lavender." The curtains and frocks of dainty chintz and dimity, the houses with the reddest of red bricks, the gardens green as green can be, the little lads and lasses "with rosy cheeks and flaxen curls," tumbling, toddling, dancing, singing—all make for happiness, all are "for the best in the best of all possible worlds." (277)

To William Feaver, Greenaway was appealing because of her "mob-capped infants playing adult in model villages" (17). Greenaway's world was securely in the past, the past of Blake's *Songs of Innocence*, of Jane and Ann Taylor's poetry, or of Maria Edgeworth's "The Cherry Orchard," which were some of Greenaway's favorite works from her childhood.

When Kate Greenaway was five years old, the family moved to the district of Islington, once a quiet rural village famous for its inns and swelling in the 1850s into a busy suburban commercial section of North London. Behind her mother's millinery shop was a large back garden that soon became "Kate's domain," although it was shared with two other families. While this small patch of ground was little more than abandoned flower beds beside makeshift sheds, the garden led into a pocket of pastureland where sheep idly grazed. To Kate, this rural retreat behind the busy Islington streets became her secret garden, a vision she recounted in a letter to a friend years later:

I often think just for the pleasure of thinking, that a little door leads out of the garden wall into a real old flowering garden, full of deep shades and deep colours. Did you always plan out delightful places just close and unexpected, when you were young? My bedroom used to look out over red roofs and chimney pots, and I made steps into a lovely garden up there with nasturtiums growing and brilliant flowers so near to the sky. There were some old houses joined ours at the side, and I made a secret door into long lines of old rooms, all so delightful, leading into an old garden. I imagined it so often that I knew its look so well, it got to be very real. (Engen 13)

The Greenaway children retreated to the country to relatives in Rolleston, an old rural village marked by a green around which nestled a number of thatched and red-tile-roofed cottages. Down the road lay an enclosed grassland for penning cattle, and beyond stretched fields of maize, corn, and wildflowers. Traveling by train 130 miles northwest from London, the children discovered the valley of the river Trent, a pastoral idyll vanishing from Victorian landscapes. Here she saw the commonplace sights of an old-fashioned England: villagers in antiquated eighteenth-century dress, men working in the fields in embroidered blue smocks, bonneted women wearing their Sunday-best lace, and primrose paths and fields of wildflowers and hay. Greenaway's brief, unfinished autobiography reveals her displaced delight in the sights, sounds, and smells of a romanticized rural setting.[2] Greenaway's Edenic bliss was always interrupted by a fall from grace, a return to the realities of mid-nineteenth-century urban life, the noisy streets of Islington, a solitary existence where she entertained her imaginative vision of beauty. In her journal of childhood reminiscence, Greenaway writes: "I have always had a curious feeling whenever I see or smell cowslips or apple blossoms—as if I had known them in some former existence—and I seem always trying to remember something I can't" (96).

Greenaway's earthly paradise was well received by the public. The Greenaway Vogue, as it was known, was launched with the publication of *Under the Window* (1879); many subsequent picture books, almanacs, and gift books followed in its path. Greenaway's delicate artistry was associated with the technical virtuosity of Edmund Evans (1826–1905), her color printer and commercial publisher. In the twenty-year span of Greenaway's publishing, from her first solo picture book to her last collaborative effort, Greenaway received persistent attention in the British and American press at a time when few figures maintained a high profile for so long and when there were no specialist journals devoted to children's literature. Her visibility was certainly linked to the status of Edmund Evans, whose work was associated with the pinnacle of book arts.

Greenaway was indeed fortunate to have Evans as her mentor, engraver, publisher, and commercial impresario. The distinctiveness of Evans's work lay in the quality of the wood engraving, a linear rather than a tonal process. Evans used separate woodblocks for each color and limited the use of inks to preserve the freshness of the colors. His care in designing her books (the extent of which is not yet known) and in executing the woodblock engravings, as well as his association with the distributor, Routledge, were instrumental to her success. Routledge, one of the leading publishers of children's books, frequently promoted her books as the lead juvenile of the season through selective listings, advertisements, and color inserts in the catalogs.

In a self-conscious "art culture," Greenaway was successful in impressing aesthetes, critics, book artists, and, most important, the consumer market of parents. Her books held a subtle message about the propriety of innocence and obedience to please the older generation, however enlightened or progressive they might be. Greenaway created or adapted texts that were familiar, even old-fashioned, and rendered them fresh, with a skillful blend of the old and the new. Her books were considered to belong to a new type of children's book, a harbinger of change in its romanticized portrayal of the child's world. Mrs. E. M. Field's *The Child and His Book* (1891) compared the costumes of Greenaway's children to the Georgian tales of a century before. To Field, the Greenaway children were only masquerading as historical. "They belong in real truth to our own age, which seems to own no dearer wish than that of making the children happy," she wrote (Field 314). What might be added to that intention was, also, to make parents happy.

Didactic messages were implicit in Greenaway's stylized designs. Gleeson White was one of the few contemporary critics who noticed a certain "priggishness" in her children's demeanor. To White, Greenaway's idealized children represented "the *beau-ideal* of nursery propriety—clean, good-tempered, happy small gentlefolk" (38). Their quiet acquiescence in a well-mannered and orderly nursery world suggested a foreordained universe of good taste and good behavior. At the same time, Greenaway offered a subversive vision, a view of childhood in which its values were not always those of the conventional adult world. Her imaginative landscapes where children cavort in unselfconscious play transgress the overbearing rational world, suggesting, by implication, their natural superiority. Her stylized figures suggest dolls created to please adults, yet the independence of these child figures belies adult artistry and reveals, instead, the subjectivities of childhood.

The fantastic and the real conjoin in Greenaway's major works to the public's pleasure. What Greenaway presented was England's idealized past—its national childhood—but fashioned into an eclectic contemporary style: eighteenth-century-styled children foregrounding Queen Anne architecture amid "England's green and pleasant bowers." The texts comprise a similar mix of historic and modern verse. Greenaway's two original works—*Under the Window* and *Marigold Garden*—depend textually on simple nursery rhyme morals and make-believe. Her other popular works—*Mother Goose, Pied Piper, A Apple Pie*—use traditional folklore texts. It is only in *Under the Window* that Greenaway displays a full range of fearsome elements (a goblin, a hooded character, and a procession of witches on broomsticks), a mixture of the terror and delight of childhood that never surfaces again in her work. John Ruskin's obsession with her young maidens led to expurgating such images from future editions. Thus, the culture industry around Greenaway perpetuated a singular vision that was well replicated in the popular culture. Her child figures, mostly female, were appropriated in advertising and commercial products; her books were copied outright by American publishers such as McLoughlin. While she suffered from this saturation economically and aesthetically, she triumphed in that most works were deemed by reviewers as "after Greenaway," thus perpetuating her style, her élan. The most serious and flagrant imitation of her work was *Afternoon Tea*, which appeared shortly after her first work, *Under the Window*.[3] While critics seemed to distinguish between the two, ignoring the derivations in style, Greenaway's name, not those of Sowerby and Emmerson, endured. In fact, one irony is that in the first substantive listing of children's books produced by the American Library Association, John F. Sargent's *Reading for the Young* (1890), the entry under Kate Greenaway lists, among other titles, *Afternoon Tea* (37).

Greenaway's prime was in the 1880s, and her fall from grace a decade later concluded a rather impressive longevity for a woman artist who shunned publicity. As the aesthetic fashion faded, her work began to appear outdated, along with its many imitations and commercial spinoffs. As Paula Connolly points out in her essay on A. A. Milne in this volume, an artist caught in the culture industry can feel trapped by his or her creations. Greenaway, unlike Milne, did not prosper from these by-products and was powerless to prevent their appropriation. The public, more in England than in America, tired of the ubiquity of her child figures, which seemed to appear on every imaginable commercial space. The advertisements that featured her figures stripped them of their context and heightened only their pose, transposed to a divergent marketing setting. The merchandising of the Greenaway image on incongruous products bears a similarity to the irony of Milne's reappropriated Enchanted Forest and its denizens. Milne's carefully controlled empire precluded the excesses that fractured the integrity of Greenaway's distinctive design. The British and American press referred to derivative works as belonging to the "School of Greenaway," which served euphemistically for the abusive imitation or outright plagiarisms at work. Her biographer, M. H. Spielmann, called her the "head of the school," by which he referred to the influence she held in shaping the development of children's book illustration (Spielmann and Layard 4).

Greenaway's stature was reaffirmed at the time of her death in 1901. She was accorded a great deal of attention, considering she had not been active for some time, almost a decade. Her last important works were the *Pied Piper of Hamelin* (1888) and *The Book of Games* (1889). The almanacs ceased in 1896, and her final work was the illustration of *April Baby's Book of Tunes* (1901), done without the artistic collaboration of Edmund Evans. Despite her absence from the field, her death was newsworthy and warranted coverage by leading critics. The most important commentary came from Austin Dobson and M. H. Spielmann, whose writing appeared in art magazines and was frequently reprinted. Spielmann's prose was incorporated into his biography of Greenaway, *The Life and Work of Kate Greenaway* (1905), which inspired a round of reviews and commentary on Greenaway that helped to propel her reputation further into the new century.

Kate Greenaway, along with Randolph Caldecott and Walter Crane, became mythologized as one of the patron saints of picture books, the founding artists who established new standards for the children's book as art. Martin Hardie, art librarian at the Victoria and Albert Museum, wrote *English Coloured Books* (1906), which contained an extensive chapter on Crane, Greenaway, and Caldecott, whom he dubbed "academicians of the nursery" (282). Later, F. J. Harvey Darton's *Children's Books in England: Five Centuries of Social Life* (1932) touted the "the triumvirate of Edmund Evans" as the artists "who made the modern picture book" (277). In the early twentieth century, their influence continued, ever strong in America, and constituted the ideal of illustration.

Greenaway benefited from the interest of John Ruskin in her work, from the artistic virtuosity and commercial genius of Edmund Evans, and from her consonance with the horizons of expectations of Anglo-American culture in the late nineteenth century. She also prospered into twentieth-century prominence through the agency of children's librarians and booksellers, two new enterprising professions for women.[4] Greenaway's style was reproduced and reinterpreted through the intervention of cultural purveyors such as Anne Carroll Moore (1871–1961), the legendary first children's librarian of the Pratt Institute and then of the New York Public Library whose work covered the years 1896–1941 (see also Sayers; Lundin). Moore was also the first American critic to write a sustained critical column on children's books: first in the *Bookman* (1918–1927), next in the *Herald Tribune* (1924–1930), and then in the *Horn Book* (1936–1960). Moore called her column "The Three Owls," which referred to the prominence of author, illustrator, and critic—all artists of the book. Moore was particularly close to her mentor, Caroline Hewins (1846–1926), the library director of the Hartford Public Library who made children's books and reading her passion. Hewins advocated for children's books at a time when children were not being served by public libraries; she fought for access to books for children and to a new professional commitment to their guidance. Hewins not only was the first woman to address the American Library Association at one of its annual conferences (asking "What are you doing to encourage a love of good reading in boys and girls?"), but she also wrote the first book of recommended readings, *Books for the Young: A Guide for Parents and Children* (1883), which included several Greenaway titles. Cautioning librarians not to rely on the scanty notices of children's books in the press, she urged her colleagues instead to develop a sufficent "body of doctrine"—critical judgments, knowledge of books—so that they could guide others in the selection of literature ("Sections" 164). This practice of knowing a body of literature rather than just knowing about it departed from the standards set by Melvil Dewey (1851–1931) for the new profession of librarianship. According to Wayne Wiegand, Dewey thought that librarians should select books based on reviews by experts in scholarly journals rather than make judgments themselves on literature (95).

Children's librarians, a feminized profession developing in the 1890s, were, by default, given province over children's literature, a subject considered appropriate for women, whose natural instincts were assumed to be authoritative. Thus Dewey, as professional progenitor, unwittingly created a special status for children's librarians: the power of cultural authority, the judgment to declare the value of literature, and the autonomy to create an institutional construct to further these values. The shaping of the field in this direction led children's librarians to become singularly powerful figures in the publishing world, wielding power through writing reviews, selecting and promoting recommended titles, training and guiding future children's book editors, and advocating a certain style in books for children.[5] Kate Greenaway was the beneficiary of such largess.

As a colleague of Dewey and mentor of children's librarians, Caroline Hewins inspired Moore with the impulse to write and promote literature through the media, which Moore embraced in a variety of long-standing columns in the popular press and commentary in professional literature, then in its infancy. Once Moore assumed leadership of the children's room at the New York Public Library in 1906, the first such position at this august institution, she freely promoted the literature she found most valuable for children. While not the first children's librarian, Moore became, over a career that spanned half a century, its most articulate arbiter of taste and a children's advocate. Moore earned a worldwide reputation as an outspoken pioneer in the field of children's books at a time when the number of volumes written and illustrated for children was slim indeed. For example, she had served as a librarian for twenty-two years before Macmillan inaugurated the first children's book division in 1918. To one contemporary critic, Josiah Titzell, Moore was "the yea or nay on all children's literature" in America (218). As Barbara Bader writes in her study of American picture books, "What we have then, for thirty or forty years, is Miss Moore endorsing (or tacitly damning) and, through New York Public Library programs, promoting; *The Horn Book* sorting and sifting and, through its selection of articles, sponsoring the *Children's Catalog*—joined later by the school-oriented ALA Graded Lists—making permanent the evaluations of *The Horn Book*, Miss Moore, and a few of her colleagues, many of whom made their own lists" (12).

As institution builder, Moore's influence was large. She organized the many boroughs of New York into one system, whose crown jewel was the children's room at Fifth Avenue and 42nd Street, with its carved mahogany bookcases, exhibit cases, Italian marble countertops, and Welsh quarry-tile floors. It was here that she constructed one of the world's largest collections of children's books, historical and contemporary. Known for her sense of celebration, Moore commemorated the birthdays of select children's book authors, illustrators, and storytellers—Kate Greenaway, Randolph Caldecott, H. C. Andersen, Walter de la Mare, L. Leslie Brooke, Marie Shedlock. These celebrations not only happened at the main library but were encouraged at the various branches. Moore publicizes the ways various librarians celebrated Greenaway in their libraries and the response of the children. One librarian on the East Side took apart her own copy of *Kate Greenaway's Pictures* (1921) and hung the pages about the reading room on a level with the eyes of the children. This exhibit also included not only Greenaway's books to admire but a picture of the artist accompanied by a wreath of rosebuds. At a Greenwich Village library, children were encouraged to dress up as Greenaway characters, even to the extent of one child striding down the sidewalk carrying a paper bag—an imitation of her favorite picture, "Girl with a Muff" (Century 15). In one of her "Three Owls" columns in the *Horn Book*, Moore recounted other Greenaway celebrations of the centennial and mentioned that one of her first administrative actions as supervisor of children's services for the New York Public Library was to provide a copy of Spielmann's biography of Greenaway for every children's room in the city ("Three Owls' Notebook" 128).

Moore's advocacy of Greenaway extended into the popular press. In her columns, most of which reappeared in book format, she often brought Greenaway to attention by evoking memories of Greenaway's titles, such as *Marigold Garden*, and Spielmann's biography of Greenaway, no longer in print, and urging their revival. In an early column in the *Bookman*, reprinted in *Roads to Childhood*, she espoused Greenaway's work in a column on "Some First Books," in which she heralded Greenaway not only as an artist but as a child psychologist, mentioning five Greenaway titles that "should be added very early to a child's library" (73). In *New Roads to Childhood* (1923), Moore romanticized Greenaway's landscapes as "next to being in England in springtime," cited several titles, and mentioned her influence in Boutet de Monvel's picture books (131). Her greatest encomium was *A Century of Kate Greenaway* (1946) (fig. 1), a mono-

FIGURE 1. The cover to Anne Carroll Moore's centennial tribute to Kate Greenaway, *A Century of Kate Greenaway* (Frederick Warne, 1946).

graph in which Moore surveyed Greenaway's contributions and her persistent appeal to contemporary children, noting the responses of urban children to her pastoral motifs through specific library programming. She compared Greenaway to William Blake, both of whom held "a golden key to the kingdom of childhood" and "record what is seen and felt with a truth and beauty that defy time and space" (*Century* 5).

Moore's strand of Romanticism was deeply embedded in images of the English countryside, something akin to Greenaway's settings. In his book on Margaret Wise Brown, Leonard Marcus distinguishes between Moore's flights of fancy and those more real-world images of Lucy Sprague Mitchell, Margaret Wise Brown, and others of the Bank Street College of Education, known for their progressive views and emphasis on the "here and now" in children's books. Marcus associates Moore with a Romanticism akin to the poetry of Walter de la Mare. Quoting Randall Jarrell, Marcus sees de la Mare's Romanticism as a desperate clinging to a nonindustrial world, one in which "what is real lies above (God, Beauty), or beneath (dreams, animals, children) or around (ghosts, all the beings of myth or Märchen)" (56). Marcus describes the prevalent style in children's books of the period as still rooted in nineteenth-century Romanticism, "with its idealized imagery of the happy child at home in harmonious natural surroundings," as opposed to the Bank Street reforms that foregrounded the cityscapes and modern technology (53). While Moore recommended fairy tales as the staple works for children, Mitchell and her followers resisted the fantastic for young children. Moore and Mitchell battled over "once upon a time" versus "here and now," with each expressing thinly veiled criticism of the other. Moore's novel *Nicholas: A Christmas Story* is construed by some as a rebuttal to Mitchell's *Here and Now Story Book*, in that Moore whisks her characters—a brownie, gnome, and the toy/child Nicholas—through fantastic happenings. Moore perceived that her high literary standards and aesthetics were being compromised by reformist educational works for children, which somehow lacked the power of earlier romanticized renderings of childhood. Feeling attacked by mediocrity, Moore spoke even more vehemently for the books that she espoused and the domesticated vision of the child in nature. In one of her earliest columns in the *Bookman*, Moore writes: "We are tired of substitutes for realities in writing for children. The trail of the serpent has been growing more and more clearly defined in the flow of children's books from publisher to bookshop, library, home, and school—a trail strewn with patronage and propaganda, moralizing self-sufficiency and sham efficiency, mock heroics and cheap optimism—above all, with the commonplace in theme, treatment, and language, with the proverbial stone in place of bread, in the name of education" (*Roads* 26).

The artistic ideal for Anne Carroll Moore and other cultural mediators of the period was the natural aesthetic of British children's books, exemplified in the works of Greenaway, Crane, and Caldecott. Barbara Bader speaks of the "Crane-Caldecott-Greenaway conflagration," in which the artistic European book prevailed in taste over the homelier American product (6–7). Americans were insecure in their conception of American book artistry and looked across the Atlantic for exemplars, with the British style the most dominant until after World War I. In a study of the Newbery and Caldecott awards, Irene Smith depicts the children's book landscape of the 1920s as one of "much looking backward," citing, in particular, the work of Boutet de Monvel, Leslie Brooke, Willebeek Le Mair, E. Boyd Smith, and ties to Crane, Greenaway, and Caldecott (34). Moore's artistic temperament was stimulated not only by the backward glance into historical children's books, which she emphasized in her collection development and library exhibitions, but also by her keen Anglophilia. She was a frequent European traveler and visited the British Isles many times, where she became friends with Beatrix Potter. In France she assisted in reestablishing a children's library structure after World War I. Moore extended her influence throughout the country (and internationally) by the librarians she trained, such as Lillian Smith, who became Canada's leading children's librarian and the author of a landmark critical work, *The Unreluctant Years* (1953; see Fasick, Johnston, and Osler). She was friend and advisor to many well-known children's authors and illustrators, such as James Daughtery, Ludwig Bemelmans, Stephen Vincent Benet, Carl Sandburg, Leslie Brooke, Kate Douglas Wiggin, Wanda Gag, Edgar d'Aulaire, Theodore Geisel, E. B. White, and Robert McCloskey.

Moore's influence was considerable. She was clearly the most active professional in the 1920s and 1930s, when children's book publishing in America was just emerging as a specialty. She knew all the major New York publishers, who brought her their manuscripts and sought her favor. Moore's endorsement of a book was more than just desirable; her annual Christmas exhibition of books, begun in 1911, accompanied by a booklist, became a highly visible commercial spot for publishers. Not only was the Christmas season the standard selling market for children's books (as it has traditionally been), but this seasonal showing also heralded "the best of the new," an endorsement of quality by a woman and an institution key to the sales and reputation of authors and illustrators. Her authority extended over the children's book editors and writers she trained as staff: Margaret McElderry, Marian Fiery, Eleanor Estes, Helene Forbes, Eugenia Garson, Pura Belpré, Florence Adams, Mary Gould Davis, Anna Cogswell Tyler, Harriet Wright, Maria Cimino, Ruth Hill Viguers, Alexandra Sanford, Ruth Giles Lontoft, Shirley Barker, Claire Huchet

Bishop, and Frances Clarke Sayers. Moore shaped these editors' aesthetics toward her own privileging of the imagination and romantic sensibilities, and their influence continues immeasurably into the present day.

Anne Carroll Moore's power extended into other facets of children's book commerce. She was the inspiration for the creation of children's bookstores and a professional journal on children's books, both the contribution of Bertha Mahony (1882–1969). Mahony (later Bertha Mahony Miller) originally wanted to pursue a library education, but the costs prevented her from proceeding. Instead, she happened upon a 1915 article in the *Atlantic Monthly* by educator Earl Barnes about a new field for women—bookselling—and adapted her children's library instincts to a bookselling practice by initiating a children's bookstore in Boston. Mahony had been working at the Women's Educational and Industrial Union (WEIU) and inspired it to support the establishment. Mahony was stimulated by the ambience of the children's room at the New York Public Library, which she visited early after its opening in 1911 and later, in 1916, used as a design for her bookstore. The bookshop's colophon was based on the bookplates Kate Greenaway had designed for children. Sidney Smith adapted Greenaway's art into a colophon that showed a girl and boy sharing a book under a shade tree, with the turrets of a fanciful castle in the background (fig. 2). A permanent exhibit in the bookstore included a dollhouse called "The Greenaway House."

The Bookshop for Boys and Girls in Boston began issuing recommended reading lists in its first year of operation, 1916, and these lists evolved into the *Horn Book* in 1924. Mahony worked closely with legendary Boston Public Library children's librarian Alice Jordan (1870–1960), who counseled Mahony on her bookstore and co-opted some of Mahony's ideas for her library. The editor of *Publishers Weekly*, Frederick Melcher, helped to train Mahony in the trade and became instrumental in creating the two children's book awards, the Newbery and the Caldecott medals. But clearly it was Moore's inspiration as a "mover and shaker" in the field who most shaped Mahony and her own distinctive contributions. Voluminous correspondence in the archives of Simmons College, Boston, which holds Mahony's papers, reveals that Moore and Mahony were closely aligned in the establishment of standards for children's literature and that Moore was particularly vocal in expressing her opinions on textual matters related to the journal and became a regular contributor

FIGURE 2. The colophon designed by Sidney Smith for Bertha Mahony's Bookshop for Boys and Girls was based on an earlier Greenaway bookplate design.

to the journal from 1936 until 1960. Mahony's writings on children's literature are recorded in two books: *Realms of Gold* (1929) and *Five Years of Children's Books* (1936), both of which became guidebooks to the creation of a children's collection. Her co-edited work, *Illustrators of Children's Books, 1744–1945* (1947), included a large section on Greenaway (75–86) as well as a chapter on "Foreign Children's Books in a Children's Library" (123–56), which intentionally draws on their use in the children's room of the New York Public Library. This scholarly work offers essays on text and image, biographies of living illustrators, and a bibliography of the works of many authors and illustrators of children's books.

Nevertheless, Mahony's greatest influence lies in the *Horn Book*. This landmark journal—the first professional American periodical devoted to children's books—grew in 1924 from Mahony's compilation of recommended lists that she prepared for her bookstore customers. The creation of evaluative lists and annotations is a distinctive professional practice that goes back to Caroline Hewins's work in the early 1880s and to Anne Carroll Moore's prolific reading lists and reviews. The first issue, with its depiction of the Caldecott jovial huntsmen, announced its intention "to blow the horn for fine books for boys and girls." The journal began publishing books under its own imprint, such as Paul Hazard's classic *Books, Children, and Men* and other historical and critical works.[6] The *Horn Book* also featured a special issue on the centennial of Kate Greenaway's birth in 1946 and marketed the issue for multiple copies. In a special fiftieth-year celebration of the *Horn Book* in 1974, Virginia Haviland, a longtime reviewer, commented on Mahony's attachment to picture books, citing Greenaway as one of her favorites (59). Mahony's *Horn Book* became a forum to promote children's books that exemplified characteristics associated with the classics. American children's book publishing was still in its infancy when the magazine began, and the backward glance and forward sights were toward England as the motherland of imaginative writing and illustrating for children.

The conjoined influence of Anne Carroll Moore and Bertha Mahony was instrumental in shaping a style of illustration in the burgeoning field of children's book illustration. Moore, through her presence in libraries, reviewing, and book publishing, and Mahony, through her pioneering in bookselling and professional journalism, had the means to construct a canon in the new business of American children's books—the privileging of a Romantic style as text and image. A company of artists can be distinguished who perpetuated a Romanticism in illustration that can be traced back to that of Kate Greenaway. While few of her following actually acknowledged her work, an intertextual thread can be traced in the domesticated image of the child and feminized settings of home and garden.

Greenaway's aesthetics were well received in France. Her work sold so well there that the French adopted the phrase "Greenawisme," which meant "all things Greenaway" (Spielmann and Layard 268). Evoking her work as embodying the heart of femininity, Alfred de

Lostalot writes in the *Gazette des Beaux-Arts* (1881): "Miss Kate Greenaway joint aux sentiments les plus délicats de l'artiste une nuance attendrie qu'elle doit à son coeur de femme" [Miss Kate Greenaway unites the most delicate feelings of the artist with a nuanced tenderness that she owes to her feminine sensibilities] (74). Other French art critics, such as M. Ernest Chesneau and Jeanne Doin, singled out her work for special attention in the press. Greenaway's work was also highlighted by her extensive contribution of drawings to the Paris Exhibition in 1889.

One of the first Europeans who became popularized in the United States was Maurice Boutet de Monvel (1850–1913), a French illustrator whose delicate depictions of French children reflected Greenaway's nursery world of English children. As an artist, Boutet de Monvel was especially drawn to Greenaway's fantastic creation of childhood, one independent of folktale renderings but a creation of her own imaginative vision. His work expressed a similar inventiveness and use of delicate but firm outlines highlighted by harmonious flat color washes. His first major success was *Nos enfants: Scènes de la ville et des champs* (1886) (fig. 3), in which he sensitively captured the essence of town and country children at play. His most spectacular subject was *Jeanne d'Arc* (1896), in which, in forty-five watercolors, Boutet de Monvel transformed her life into a picture book pageantry—a celebration of the feminine, the religious, and the patriotic. His work illuminated the lives of the young with a freshness of observation and a serious winsome rendering of the child. Modern illustrators Hilary Knight (illustrator of Kay Thomson's *Eloise*) and Maurice Sendak have acknowledged the influence of the French artist on their work (Trust 12).

Boutet de Monvel inspired many followers, including the celebrated Henriette Willebeek Le Mair (1889–1966). Born in Rotterdam, Le Mair published her first book, *Premiers rondes enfantines*, in France when she was only fifteen. She drew from experience running a nursery school in her early twenties. Le Mair had hoped to study with Boutet de Monvel, but he remained in the background as an advisor. Her fourteen picture books, such as *Little Songs of Long Ago* (1912), *Old Dutch Nursery Rhymes* (1917), and Robert Louis Stevenson's *A Child's Garden of Verses* (1926) (fig. 4), owe much to the French artist's song books and Greenaway's delicate child characters. An early bibliography in *Children's Library Yearbook* lists an article about Le Mair with the annotation: "A brief account of the art

FANCHON SAUTE DU LIT TOUT EN CHE-
MISE; ELLE OUVRE LA FENÊTRE ET VOIT
DANS LE JARDIN FLEURI DE ROSES, DE
GÉRANIUMS ET DE LISERONS, SES PETITS
OISEAUX, SES PETITS MUSICIENS DE LA
VEILLE QUI, RANGÉS SUR LA BARRIÈRE DU
COURTIL, LUI DONNENT L'AUBADE POUR
PRIX D'UNE MIETTE DE PAIN.

FIGURE 3. An illustration from M. B. de Monvel's *Nos enfants* (Librairie
Hachett, 1886) that evokes a sense of Kate Greenaway's *Under the Window*.

of an artist who resembles Kate Greenaway in many ways" (Committee 162). A contemporary critic, Arthur Reddie, writes of her work
in the *Studio*: "Since the days of Kate Greenaway, of whose work despite all its great charm one is often a little impatient—if it not be
heresy to say so—I know of no one who has caught so well the pure
spirit of childhood as Miss Le Mair; in her work one finds that the
naturalness, the simplicity of children is interpreted in its most attractive phase, with no suspicion of any attempt to ape the manners
of elders, no hint of precocity, no posing, no straining after an effect
of studied artlessness" (223). Long out of print, her works have recently been reprinted by Philomel Books.

FIGURE 4. The cover to a reprint of Le Mair's *Our Old Nursery Rhymes*
(Philomel, 1989).

E. Boyd Smith (1860–1943) was the first notable American illustrator who was influenced by Boutet de Monvel. Born in New
Brunswick, he was raised in Boston, educated in France, and returned to Boston, where he began illustrating picture books. He used
Boutet de Monvel's *Jeanne d'Arc* as a model for his *Story of Pocahon-
tas and Captain John Smith* (1906). Capturing much of the compo-
sition and decorative borders of Boutet de Monvel, Smith portrayed
domesticated scenes in works such as *The Farm Book* (1910) (fig. 5),
Chicken World (1910), and *The Railroad Book* (1913). His child figures
are distinctive in their delicacy of expression and movement, trans-
ported to an Americanized setting.

Swedish artists seemed sympathetic to the warm domestic sense
of childhood life. Carl Larsson's (1853–1919) paintings of family life,
luminous children, and homey interiors, decorated with bright Scan-
dinavian folk art, were first published in picture book form as *Ett
Hem* (*A Home*) in 1899. After prolonged art studies in Paris, Larsson
found a personal style which was derived from a weave of folk art,
Japanese prints, bright colors, and idyllic childhood scenes. One of
Anne Carroll Moore's book columns that focused on Swedish pic-

FIGURE 5. A scene from E. Boyd Smith's *The Farm Book*
(Houghton Mifflin, 1910).

ture books featured Larsson's work and also that of Elsa Beskow and
Ottilia Adelborg ("*Three Owls' Notebook*" 140–47). Bertha Mahony's
Illustrators of Children's Books also includes these artists in a chapter on foreign illustrators. Elsa Beskow (1874–1953) illustrated more
than thirty picture books in soft-toned watercolors. Her works were
distinguished by their design, color, and use of personified nature.
She creates illusions where elves and maidens become buds and
blossoms and play among ferns, a miniaturized, motherly world.
Beskow's child figures have much of the melancholic expression of
Greenaway characters and similar smocklike clothing. Her first picture book, *The Tale of the Little, Little Old Woman*, appeared in 1897,
followed by *Peter in Blueberry Land* (1901)—her best-known work—
and a host of other works well known, particularly, in Europe. An
artist with a related style is Ottilia Adelborg (1855–1936), who interpreted Swedish folk customs with naturalness and simplicity, her
best-known work in America being *Clean Peter* (1901).

Jessie Willcox Smith (1863–1935) was the most prolific and successful American illustrator of her time. While many art critics acknowledge her debt to Howard Pyle, with whom she studied, she
was clearly in the lineage of Greenaway with her Romantic visuali-
zation of child life. Her illustrations reflect a feminine view of the
joys of motherhood and childhood. Her children are often posed

FIGURE 6. An illustration of "Five little maidens all in a row" by Jessie Willcox Smith in *St. Nicholas Magazine* (May 1888).

with flowers, playing unselfconsciously in nature, reading in an overstuffed chair. S. Michael Schnessel, in his book on the artist, relates the formative influence of "European imports, books like *Kate Greenaway's Almanacks*, begun in 1883 and continued until 1897, or Greenaway's popular *Marigold Garden*, and the numerous books of nursery rhymes and other poems designed for children during the period" (28). Smith was also influenced by two leading American illustrators of the period, Maud Humphrey and Ida Waugh, whose works show Greenaway touches in their depiction of the child, alone or grouped, with little background. Smith's earliest work was as a kindergarten teacher, when she was exposed to picture books on a daily basis and, presumably, educated by their imagery. Smith's first published illustration (1888) was for *St. Nicholas*, a drawing of "Five little maidens all in a row" (fig. 6), which owes much to Greenaway's style of lining her figures in a poised and slightly animated manner, of toddlers in long dresses and bonnets. After studies with Howard Pyle at the Drexel Institute of Arts and Sciences in Philadelphia, Smith's style became more narrative, with figures outlined with a dark, contrasting border. She began to work for some of the leading periodicals of the day, such as *Collier's*, the *Ladies' Home Journal*, *Scribner's Magazine*, *Century*, *Harper's Weekly*, *Harper's Bazaar*, and *Good Housekeeping*, for which she designed covers for fifteen years. Her illustrations to *Rhymes of Real Children* (1903), written by Betty Sage, reveal Greenaway-like decorative borders reminiscent of the cover of *Under the Window* (1879). Smith also illustrated many of the great children's classics: *The Jessie Willcox Smith Mother Goose* (1914); *Little Women* (1915); Charles Kingsley's *Water-Babies* (1916); George MacDonald's *At the Back of the North Wind* (1919) and *The Princess and the Goblin* (1920); and *Heidi* (1922).

Rachel Field's (1894–1942) reputation is as an author as well as an illustrator. Her most celebrated book, *Hitty: Her First Hundred Years* (1929), a picaresque doll narrative, won a Newbery Medal; she was the first woman to receive the award. A novelist, nonfiction writer, poet, playwright, and artist, Field was friends with many in the burgeoning children's book world of the 1920s, including Anne Carroll Moore and Bertha Mahony. The *Horn Book* devoted a special memorial issue to Field in 1942, in which her editor, Louise Seaman Bechtel, noted that Field, in preparing to illustrate *Taxis and Toadstools* (1926), "pored over Kate Greenaway" (qtd. in Titzell 231). A special commemorative issue of the journal in 1946, honoring the centenary of Greenaway and Caldecott, included Mahony's editorial column "The Hunt Breakfast," in which she stated: "Of Kate Greenaway's influence in our own day, we could point to the drawings of Rachel Field and of Tasha Tudor" (74). Greenaway's influence in Field's art is most apparent in *Taxis and Toadstools* (1926); *An Alphabet for Boys and Girls* (1926) (fig. 7), with a poem and drawing for each letter, and its companion volume, *A Little Book of Days* (1926); and *Pocket-Handkerchief Park* (1929), of which a reviewer in the *Saturday Review* wrote, "Within a small compass, they have a character of their own, reminding one of that succession of charming little volumes of Kate Greenaway whose appearance so delighted another generation" ("Pocket" 431). Field's illustrations consisted of watercolor, black-and-white, and ink drawings and silhouettes, notable for a certain naïveté and playfulness characteristic of childhood.

Tasha Tudor (1914–) was influenced by both Kate Greenaway and Beatrix Potter, celebrative of the child and the natural animal world. Her fanciful style of dress—both in her person and in her art—recreates a fantasy world much like Greenaway's archaic style. Writing and illustrating more than seventy-five children's books, Tasha Tudor captures some of the diminutive size and delicacy of Greenaway's art of the book and, most visibly, her decorative page and borders. Tudor expands Greenaway's frame of flowers and children and evokes the sense of an innocent, older world of bucolic pleasures. Her first work was *Pumpkin Moonshine* (1938), followed by a host of other

FIGURE 7. A page from Rachel Field's *An Alphabet for Boys and Girls* (Doubleday, Page, 1926).

natural-child reveries and recollections. Her evocation of Greenaway is most present in illustrations to Robert Louis Stevenson's *A Child's Garden of Verses* (1981) (fig. 8), which, curiously, was done by Stevenson in 1885 in response to Kate Greenaway's *The Birthday Book for Children* (1880).

Kate Greenaway's influence persists in the work of a number of other modern illustrators. Note the style of Edward Ardizzone in his gentle and wistful children, the work of Marguerite De Angeli and Jane Dyer, and Satomi Ichilawa's romanticized, delicate portrayal of childhood. Despite the variance in individual style, a certain kind of line drawing evokes comparisons. Greenaway's resonance can be seen in decorative borders, innocent, pastoral childhood landscapes, and a timeless appeal—a sense of romanticized reverie for the past. This cultivation of childhood is not lost in the popular culture, with products created by Joan Walsh Anglund, Laura Ashley, and Mary Engelbreit that evoke an Anglocentric, hermetic paradise of domesticity. The debasement of Greenaway's invented world by commer-

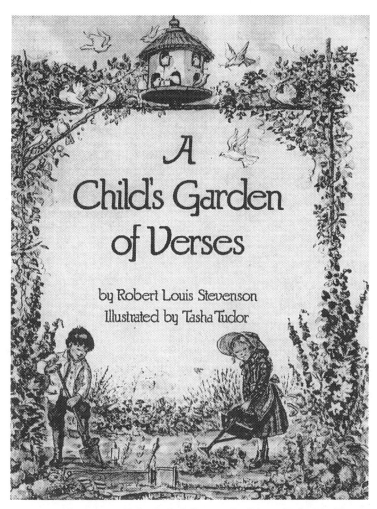

FIGURE 8. The cover to Tasha Tudor's illustrated edition of Robert Louis Stevenson's *A Child's Garden of Verses* (Rand McNally, 1981).

cial interests is reflected in the appropriation of the mass marketing of Beatrix Potter's *Peter Rabbit* artifacts. The text is altered, plasticene figures replace line drawings, colors compete with contents as products proliferate. Romanticism continues to be reinterpreted as consolatory fantasy, an idealized backward glance, refined by art or defined by commerce.

To what extent are these depictions "cultural work" and "sensational designs," in the words of Jane Tompkins? In the development of the picture book, they represent what cultural mediators like Anne Carroll Moore and Bertha Mahony envisioned and promoted as the ideal of children's literature and book arts, the aesthetic mimeticism of mother and child, conjoined. Greenaway as a phenomenon led to the construction of a canon that perpetuated her reputation and privileged a similar style of illustrating childhood. Kate Greenaway initiated a Romanticism that resonated with the early institutional founders and cultural mediators of twentieth-century children's literature—a domesticated glimpse into a younger world that in its sweetness and light allows a different reading. Greenaway was a children's book illustrator in a patriarchal culture that viewed her sentiment as safe nostalgia, a departure from the real and rational. The utopia is of another world—a feminine community of nurture and play, a fanciful quotidian. These designs evoke what some want to believe childhood is like—in the words of Northrop Frye, "the world we want rather than the world we have" (6–7). While this vision is fantastic, full of dreamy wish fulfillment, it also suggests "the promise of happiness," what Stendhal conceived to be the provenance of art and which Fred Inglis has construed, in his work by that name, as the right of childhood. Greenaway's strand of feminine Romanticism, with its depiction of a childhood idyll, suggests how intimate and distant such a peaceable kingdom might be. While others may contest the rightness of that image, the Romantic notion lingers. The experience of childhood, in Blake's terms, may yet be felt, but the still-life innocence remains a desideratum for artists and audience, an autobiographical trope of domestically cultured beginnings, a Romance of what could be in the best of all possible worlds.

NOTES

Portions of this essay were adapted from my earlier "In a Different Place: Feminist Aesthetics of the Picture Book," in *Ways of Knowing*, ed. Kay Vandergriff (Scarecrow, 1996).

1. This art, in the words of White in his landmark *Studio* essay on children's book illustration, is "part of the legend of the gentlefolk" (39–40).

2. For more on Greenaway's journal, see Lundin, "Writing."

3. For a discussion of Greenaway imitations, see Lundin, "*Under the Window.*"

4. See Coultrap-McQuinn for a summary of what she calls the late-nineteenth-century "Vision of New Womanhood."

5. See Karen Smith for a special journal issue of the role of children's librarians in children's book publishing.

6. For a discussion of the influence of Paul Hazard's Romantic sensibilities, see Nodelman.

Bader, Barbara. *American Picturebooks from Noah's Ark to the Beast Within.* New York: Macmillan, 1976.

Bourdieu, Pierre. *Distinction: A Social Critique of the Judgment of Taste.* Trans. Richard Nice. Cambridge: Harvard UP, 1984.

Carpenter, Humphrey. *Secret Gardens: A Study of the Golden Age of Children's Literature.* London: George Allen and Unwin, 1985.

Clayton, Jay, and Eric Rothstein. *Influence and Intertextuality in Literary History.* Madison: U of Wisconsin P, 1991.

The Committee on Library Work with Children of the American Library Association. *Children's Library Yearbook.* Vol. 4. Chicago: American Library Association, 1932.

Coultrap-McQuinn, Susan. *Doing Literary Business: American Women Writers in the Nineteenth Century.* Chapel Hill: U of North Carolina P, 1990.

Darton, F. J. Harvey. *Children's Books in England: Five Centuries of Social Life.* 3rd ed. Ed. Brian Alderson. Cambridge: Cambridge UP, 1982.

Doin, Jeanne. "Kate Greenaway et ses livres illustrés." *Gazette des Beaux Arts* 3 (1910): 5–22.

Engen, Rodney. *Kate Greenaway: A Biography.* New York: Schocken, 1981.

Fasick, Adele M., Margaret Johnston, and Ruth Osler. *Lands of Pleasure: Essays on Lillian H. Smith and the Development of Children's Libraries.* New York: Scarecrow, 1990.

Feaver, William. *When We Were Young.* New York: Holt, Rinehart and Winston, 1977.

Field, E. M. *The Child and His Book.* London: Wells Gardner, Darton, 1891.

Foucault, Michel. *The Archaeology of Knowledge.* Trans. A. M. Sheridan Smith. London: Tavistock, 1972.

Frye, Northrop. *The Educated Imagination.* Bloomington: Indiana UP, 1964.

Geertz, Clifford. *The Interpretation of Cultures: Selected Essays.* New York: Basic, 1973.

Girouard, Mark. *Sweetness and Light: The Queen Anne Movement, 1860–1900.* New Haven: Yale UP, 1990.

Greenaway, Kate. Holograph journal, unpublished. The Frances Hooper Collection, Hunt Institute for Botanical Documentation, Carnegie-Mellon University, Pittsburgh, PA.

Hardie, Martin. *English Coloured Books.* London: Methuen, 1906.

Haviland, Virginia. "Bertha Mahony Miller as a Booklover and a Bibliophile." *Horn Book* 50 (October 1974): 58–63.

Hewins, Caroline. *Books for the Young: A Guide for Parents and Children.* New York: E. Leypoldt, 1883.

————. "Section for Children's Librarians." *Library Journal* 26 (August 1901): 164.

Inglis, Fred. *The Promise of Happiness: Value and Meaning in Children's Fiction.* Cambridge: Cambridge UP, 1981.

Jauss, Hans Robert. *Toward an Aesthetics of Reception.* Trans. Timothy Bathi. Minneapolis: U of Minnesota P, 1981.

"Joies D'Enfants." *Illustrated London News*, December 13, 1890, 739.

Lostalot, Alfred de. "Les Livres anglais en couleur." *Gazette des Beaux-Arts* 1 (1881): 68–78.

Lundin, Anne. "Anne Carroll Moore (1871–1961): 'I Have Spun out a Long Thread.'" *Reclaiming the American Library Past: Writing the Women In.* Ed. Suzanne Hildenbrand. Norwood, NJ: Ablex, 1996.

————. "*Under the Window* and *Afternoon Tea*: 'Twirling the Same Blade of Grass.'" *Lion and the Unicorn* 17.1 (June 1993): 45–56.

————. "Victorian Horizons: The Reception of Children's Books in England and America, 1880–1900." *Library Quarterly* 64.1 (1994): 30–59.

————. "Writing Kate Greenaway: Carrier Bag Autobiography." *Children's Literature* 26 (1998): 169–84.

Maccunn, Florence. "Children's Story-Books." *Good Words* 44 (1904): 341–46.

Mahony, Bertha. "The Hunt Breakfast." *Horn Book* 22 (March–April 1946): 74.

Mahony, Bertha, Louise Latimer, and Beulah Folmsbee, eds. *Illustrators of Children's Books, 1744–1945.* Boston: Horn Book, 1947.

Marcus, Leonard. *Margaret Wise Brown: Awakened by the Moon.* Boston: Beacon, 1992.

Mellor, Anne K. *Romanticism and Gender.* New York: Routledge, 1993.

Moore, Anne Carroll. *A Century of Kate Greenaway.* New York: Frederick Warne, 1946.

————. *New Roads to Childhood.* New York: George H. Doran, 1923.

————. *Roads to Childhood.* New York: George H. Doran, 1920.

————. "The Three Owls' Notebook." *Horn Book* (March 1946): 126–28.

Myers, Mitzi. "Reading Rosamond Reading: Maria Edgeworth's 'Wee-Wee Stories' Interrogate the Canon." *Infant Tongues: The Voice of the Child in Literature.* Ed. Elizabeth Goodenough, Mark Heberle, and Naomi Sokoloff. Detroit: Wayne State UP, 1994. 57–79.

Nodelman, Perry. "Fear of Children's Literature: What's Left (or Right) after Theory?" *Reflections of Change: Children's Literature since 1945.* Ed. Sandra Beckett. Westport, CT: Greenwood, 1997.

Nunn, Pamela Gerrish. *Victorian Women Artists.* London: Women's P, 1987.

"Pocket Handkerchief Park." *Saturday Review of Literature*, November 16, 1929, 431.

"The Point of View: 'The Child's Garden'—and of Verses and Other
Literature." *Scribner's Magazine* 19 (April 1896): 519–20.

"The Point of View: The Golden Age: Second Childhood in Literature."
Scribner's Magazine 23 (January 1898): 123–24.

Radway, Janice. *Reading the Romance: Women, Patriarchy, and Popular
Literature.* Chapel Hill: U of North Carolina P, 1984.

Reddie, Arthur. "Miss Willebeek Le Mair's Illustrations for Children's Books."
International Studio 53 (September 1914): 223–28.

Ross, Eulalie Steinmetz. *The Spirited Life: Bertha Mahony Miller and Children's
Books.* Boston: Horn Book, 1973.

Ruskin, John. *The Art of England.* Orpington: George Allen, 1884.

Sargent, John F. *Reading for the Young.* Boston: Library Bureau, 1890.

Sayers, Frances Clarke. *Anne Carroll Moore.* New York: Atheneum, 1972.

Schnessel, S. Michael. *Jessie Willcox Smith.* New York: Thomas Y. Crowell, 1977.

Smith, Karen Patricia, ed. *Imagination and Scholarship: The Contributions of
Women to American Youth Services and Literature.* Special issue of *Library
Trends* (Spring 1996).

Smith, Irene. *A History of the Newbery and Caldecott Medals.* New York: Viking,
1957.

Spielmann, M. H., and G. S. Layard. *The Life and Work of Kate Greenaway.*
London: Adam and Charles Black, 1905.

Sutton, H. "Children and Modern Literature." *National Review* 18 (December
1891): 507–19.

Titzell, Josiah. "Rachel Field: 1894–1942." *Horn Book* 18 (July–August 1942):
216–25.

Tompkins, Jane. *Sensational Designs: The Cultural Work of American Fiction,
1790–1860.* New York: Oxford UP, 1985.

The Trust for Museum Exhibitions. *Maurice Boutet de Monvel: Master of
French Illustration and Portraiture.* Traveling exhibit catalog, 1987.

White, Gleeson. "Children's Books and Their Illustrators." *Studio* (Winter
1897–98): 3–68.

Wiegand, Wayne. *Irrepressible Reformer: A Biography of Melvil Dewey.* Chicago:
American Library Association, 1996.

Paula T. Connolly

THE MARKETING OF ROMANTIC CHILDHOOD: MILNE, DISNEY, AND A VERY POPULAR STUFFED BEAR

rom philosophy to business management, the foibles of literary criticism to the fundamentals of Latin, and shampoo to teacups, Winnie-the-Pooh is big business. As much as this well-known bear may seem like a cultural monolith, he and Christopher Robin have undergone myriad incarnations.[1] There are, in fact, several different Winnie-the-Poohs, not the least of which is that first created by A. A. Milne and E. H. Shepard and later re-created by the Walt Disney Company. The changes are more complex than a simple transference of genre from book to animation; they tell of different cultures, different times, and even different views of childhood. They speak, too, to differences in audience and marketing. The popularity of Christopher Robin and Winnie-the-Pooh has been secure since the 1920s, and as early as the 1930s "Pooh had already become an industry" (Thwaite, *A. A. Milne* 362). The merchandising of Milne's characters is not simply a phenomenon of today's often rabid marketing practices or of Disney Studio's new versions of those characters. Yet the proliferation of revisions and appropriations of Pooh, as well as the financial success of such merchandising (both today and in the 1930s), reveals quintessential ironies about the contrast of Milne's visions of childhood and the readers'/viewers'/marketers' sentimentalization and commodification of that vision.

Christopher Milne's death in April 1996 made international news, yet it was more the fictional character than the man himself that ever made Christopher Milne newsworthy. Even author A. A. Milne was surprised by the overwhelming attention afforded his son upon the publication of his children's verses. He later satirized that attention, complaining:

You can imagine my amazement and disgust . . . when I discovered that in a night, so to speak, I had been pushed into a back place, and that the hero of *When We Were Very Young* was not, as I had modestly expected, the author, but a curiously-named child. . . . It was this Christopher Robin, not I, whom Americans were clamouring to see; and . . . it was this Christopher Robin, not I . . . who was selling the book in such large and ridiculous quantities. ("End of a Chapter" 203–4)

That notoriety, which began with the introduction of the Christopher Robin character in "Vespers" (1923) and continued in the poetry collection *When We Were Very Young* (1924), only grew with the publication of the storybooks *Winnie-the-Pooh* (1926) and *The House at Pooh Corner* (1928) and one other collection of verses, *Now We Are Six* (1927).

Despite Milne's humorous recounting of how the fame of his authorship had been superseded by the public's interest in his real-life son, both father and son ultimately suffered from that attention, as did their familial relationship.[2] To defend both his own creativity and his son's privacy, A. A. Milne tried to differentiate between the two Christopher Robins, noting, for example, that the adventures of the fictional Christopher Robin came from three sources:

1. My memories of my own childhood.
2. My imaginings of childhood in general.
3. My observations of the particular childhood with which I was now in contact. ("End of a Chapter" 202)

Milne argued that although he "exploited" his son's toys, making up stories about the nursery playmates, "I have not exploited the legal Christopher Robin. All I have got from Christopher Robin is a name which he never uses, an introduction to his friends . . . and a gleam which I have tried to follow." Nonetheless, Milne realized that "the distinction, if clear to me, is not so clear to others," and "the dividing line between the imaginary and legal Christopher Robin [even for the author] becomes fainter with each book." His desire to protect his son from further public scrutiny was "one of the reasons why these verses and stories have come to an end" ("End of a Chapter" 205).

Milne may have stopped writing stories about Christopher Robin, but those stories would never stop affecting both father and son.

A. A. Milne felt trapped by his creations. A prolific satirist who wrote in a variety of genres, Milne was quickly typecast, and he later bemoaned, "I wrote four 'Children's books,' containing altogether, I suppose, 70,000 words—the number of words in the average-length novel. . . . [K]nowing that as far as I was concerned the mode was outmoded, I gave up writing children's books. I wanted to escape from them. . . . In vain. England expects the writer, like the cobbler, to stick to his last" (*Autobiography* 286). Critics inevitably compared Milne's later writing to his children's stories,[3] and the public expected each new play to evoke memories of the Enchanted Forest.

The father guessed well when he supposed Christopher Robin, too, would "soon feel that he has had more publicity than he wants for himself" ("End of a Chapter" 205). That the tremendous publicity he received was unwanted by the "real" Christopher Robin Milne is well known. Named one of the "six most famous children in the world" (Thwaite, *A. A. Milne* 218) in 1933, Christopher Milne suffered from the public's unrelenting interest. In his autobiography, *The Enchanted Places*, he wrote:

> Unfortunately the fictional Christopher Robin refused to die and he and his real-life namesake were not always on the best of terms. . . . Christopher Robin was . . . a sore place that looked as if it would never heal. . . . In pessimistic moments, when I was trudging London in search of an employer who wanted to make use of such talents as I could offer, it seemed to me, almost, that my father had got to where he was by climbing upon my infant shoulders, that he had filched from me my good name and had left me with nothing but the empty fame of being his son. (177, 178, 179)

Christopher Milne's "fame" was the public's confusion of him with what many saw as the idealized child of his father's literary creation.[4]

The sentimental conflation of this character with Christopher Milne has been misplaced especially because both the parody and praise of Christopher Robin have frequently missed Milne's often subtle ironies. A well-known satirist living during the age of the "Beautiful Child,"[5] A. A. Milne both deconstructs and reifies notions of Wordsworthian Romanticism in these depictions of childhood. Indeed, in the introduction to *When We Were Very Young*, Milne begins with a direct reference to Wordsworth: "At one time (but I have changed my mind now) I thought I was going to write a little Note at the top of each of these poems, in the manner of Mr. William Wordsworth, who liked to tell his readers where he was staying, and which of his friends he was walking with, and what he was thinking about, when the idea of writing his poem came to him." Milne further parodies Wordsworth when he admits, "If I had followed Mr. Wordsworth's plan I could have explained [the poem's speaker] . . . each time; but, as it is, you will have to decide for yourselves." The reader's choice of speaker includes a cryptic character "Hoo," who seemingly becomes an explanation to forestall further discussion of the matter. Not only in this introduction to his first collection of children's verses but also later in his writings about childhood and his work, Milne parodies and at times directly confronts Wordsworthian poetics and notions of childhood.

Despite such parody, the final scenes of *The House at Pooh Corner* clearly evoke the way "Shades of the prison-house begin to close / Upon the growing Boy" (Wordsworth 187, ll. 67–68). Although Christopher Robin and Winnie-the-Pooh journey to Galleon's Lap, where "they could see the whole world spread out until it reached the sky, and whatever there was all the world over was with them in Galleon's Lap," Christopher Robin is here caught in a transition between two worlds, "with his eyes on the world . . . [and his] hand . . . [on] Pooh's paw" (Milne, *House* 173, 179). In a poignant literary depiction of the loss of childhood, Christopher Robin realizes, "I'm not going to do Nothing any more. . . . They don't let you" (Milne, *House* 178). The boy knows he must leave the Forest because he is besieged by the necessity of learning about factors and kings and pounds and ounces and exports from Brazil. He also knows that this leave-taking is irrevocable. Although Christopher Robin begs that Pooh remember him, "even when I'm a hundred," his own promise is less certain: "'Pooh,' said Christopher Robin earnestly, 'if I—if I'm not quite—' he stopped and tried again—'Pooh, *whatever* happens, you *will* understand, won't you?'" (Milne, *House* 179).

Thus, Milne assures us in final paragraph of *The House at Pooh Corner*: "So they went off together. But wherever they go, and whatever happens to them on the way, in that enchanted place on the top of the Forest, a little boy and his Bear will always be playing" (*House* 180). That place, however, has become a remembered rather than a present place. In the "Contradiction" (that book's version of an introduction) Milne describes how he tells stories to Christopher Robin, but then he and the boy fall asleep and go "into the Forest.

There, still, we have magic adventures . . . but now, when we wake up in the morning, they are gone before we can catch hold of them" (*House* n.p.). For the Forest to become an eternal place to the growing boy it must also become more elusive, now waiting only in his dreams and memories.

Despite the poignancy of this final scene in *The House at Pooh Corner*, Milne more frequently uses the Christopher Robin character to parody Wordsworthian notions of childhood. The quintessential example, both of such parody and of the way the public has misread it, is "Vespers," a poem which Christopher Milne later claimed "has brought me . . . toe-curling, fist-clenching, lip-biting embarrassment" (*Enchanted Places* 42).

The first and last stanzas of the poem read:

> *Little Boy kneels at the foot of the bed,*
> *Droops on little hands little gold head.*
> *Hush! Hush! Whisper who dares!*
> *Christopher Robin is saying his prayers.*
>   (Milne, *When* 99–100)

A. A. Milne was mystified by the public's immediate appropriation of the fictive character as a paragon of innocence and spirituality. He acknowledged that the poem "has been more sentimentalized over than any other in the book" and that indeed, "the spectacle in real life of a child of three at prayers is one over which thousands have been sentimental" (*Autobiography* 285). Yet the crux of Milne's poem is not the reification but the castigation of such sentimentality. The saccharine depictions of the "gold" head and the repetitions of "little" in describing the boy satirize the fictive audience that idealizes him. In truth, the prayers the child recites are only those he's been told—"*God bless Mummy.* I know that's right. . . . And what was the other I had to say? . . . Oh! Now I remember. *God bless me*" (Milne, *When* 99–100).

Milne noted in his *Autobiography* that the sight of a child at prayers is "*calculated* to bring a lump to the throat" (285, emphasis added). That innocence, however, is only a guise. As Milne explained:

> Not "God bless mummy, because I love her so," but "God bless Mummy, I know that's right" . . . not even the egotism of "God bless Me, because I'm the most important person in the house,"

but the super-egotism of feeling so impregnable that the blessing of this mysterious god for Oneself is the very last thing for which it would seem necessary to ask. . . . [T]he Truth . . . [is] that prayer means nothing to a child of three, whose thoughts are engaged with other more exciting matters. (*Autobiography* 285)

In "Vespers" those "other more exciting matters" include the temperature of his bathwater and the fact that his cloak is better than Nanny's because it has a hood. The matters that truly interest this child are banally material and never rise to any level of spiritual insight.[6]

The tension between the appearance and the so-called Truth of children is a central issue in much of Milne's writings for children. In explaining this tension, Milne consciously responded to Wordsworthian visions of childhood:

In real life very young children have an artless beauty, an innocent grace, an unstudied abandon of movement, which, taken together, make an appeal to our emotions. . . . Heaven, that is, does really appear to lie about the child in its infancy. . . . But with this outstanding physical quality there is a natural lack of moral quality, which expresses itself, as Nature always insists on expressing herself, in an egotism entirely ruthless.

. . . [T]he writer who is trying to put a child upon paper must keep these two outstanding facts about children before him, and endeavour to preserve his sense of proportion. . . . A pen-picture of a child which showed it as loving, grateful and full of thought for others would be false to the truth; but equally false would be a picture which insisted on the brutal egotism of the child, and ignored the physical beauty which softens it. (*Autobiography* 283)[7]

Thus, in Milne's view, "the beauty of childhood seems in some way to transcend the body" (*Autobiography* 283), but that appearance of inherent spirituality is largely a sentimental projection by adult society.

The Christopher Robin of the storybooks is marked by such guise, although one that none of his companions puncture. In the Forest he is seen as both omniscient and omnipotent. Sitting in the tree above the circling Pooh and Piglet, Christopher Robin knows the signs of the Woozles the two seek are their own footprints; when Kanga realizes that Roo has been kidnapped, "she knew she wasn't [frightened] for she felt quite sure that Christopher Robin would never let any harm happen to Roo" (Milne, *Winnie-the-Pooh* 103); and later, when Rabbit needs to resolve a dispute, his trust is unwavering: "What does Christopher Robin think about it all? That's the point" (Milne, *House* 106).

The *point* that the toy characters never realize (and one that has escaped some readers) is that Christopher Robin is as duped by his insecurities as are many of his companions. Indeed, there are times when he knows remarkably little about those who look to him for answers. When Eeyore loses his tail it is found before Christopher Robin even learns it is missing, and when the donkey later loses his house, the boy admits he hadn't known either that Eeyore had a house or that he is sometimes cold without one. The boy's separation from the others is particularly evident in his relationship with nature. He "lived at the very top of the Forest. [When] [i]t rained, and it rained, and it rained, . . . the water couldn't come up to *his* house" (Milne, *Winnie-the-Pooh* 139). His insulation from the natural scene is also evident when he agrees to help Eeyore find the lost house but first puts on "his waterproof hat, his waterproof boots and his waterproof macintosh" (Milne, *House* 14). Even before the closing scene in *The House at Pooh Corner*, Christopher Robin's relationship with nature responds to but does not successfully reflect the Wordsworthian notion of nature and child. After a morning presumably spent at his studies,

> Christopher Robin came . . . feeling all sunny and careless, and just as if twice nineteen didn't matter a bit, as it didn't on such a happy afternoon, and he thought that if he stood on the bottom rail of the bridge, and leant over, and watched the river slipping slowly away beneath him, then he would suddenly know everything that there was to be known, and would be able to tell Pooh, who wasn't quite sure about some of it. But when he got to the bridge and saw all the animals there, then he knew that it wasn't that kind of afternoon, but the other kind, when you wanted to *do* something. (Milne, *House* 105)

Although the Forest is a place where Christopher Robin can escape school anxiety, the expectation that it can tell him "everything there was to be known" is not fulfilled. The wisdom of nature eludes Christopher Robin here, and if it had not, the boy would have used it as a means of power over a creature he assumes knows less than he.

Indeed, this focus on externally projected knowledge and the inability to learn from nature marks the Christopher Robin character through the two storybooks. The only adventure in either book initiated and led by Christopher Robin, the "Expotition to the North Pole," is a parody of man's attempt to conquer land and hence impress his ego upon nature.[8] Christopher Robin, wearing his "Big Boots," is determined to lead an expedition although he does not know what the North Pole is. Because Christopher Robin is unable to imagine that the North Pole can be anything other than an actual pole, his imagination here is strictly literal, his expedition strictly external.

Christopher Robin's lack of imagination is exacerbated in the narrative frame of *Winnie-the-Pooh*. There, the child is not father of the man but the reverse, for it is the father-storyteller, not the child, who makes up these stories and hence also has the imaginative sway to create the Forest world. Indeed, the metanarrative moments of the *Winnie-the-Pooh* frame story reveal the Romantic irony that Dieter Petzold discusses elsewhere in this volume. As Petzold defines this term,

> Side by side with the Romantic glorification of the imagination and of the naive child as its purest practitioner, we find the Romantic glorification of the author's supreme subjectivity. . . . While in the first case the implied authors/narrators try to efface themselves in order to facilitate the reader's secondary belief, in the second they remain in evidence . . . in order to remind the reader that in telling the story they are really playing a game. . . . The result is a deliberate deconstruction of secondary belief: the most prominent indication of a profoundly ironic attitude toward the text. (88–89)

In this case, however, Milne's narrative frame reveals not only an ironic attitude toward the text but also a deconstruction of Romantic notions of childhood. Here, the child's imagination is limited to a projection of the insecurities that riddle his ego — Christopher Robin assures the storyteller it is Pooh who would like to hear more stories, and that he only asks questions because *"Winnie-the-Pooh wasn't quite sure"* (Milne, *Winnie-the-Pooh* 4). At the close of the first and last chapters, Christopher Robin carries his toy *"bump-*

bump-bump" (Milne, *Winnie-the-Pooh* 161) head down up the stairs, as if the stories of a living bear companion have made little impression on him. This is a very real boy, after all.

Indeed, the supreme irony of Milne's children's stories is that it is Winnie-the-Pooh who becomes the emblem of Romantic notions of childhood. In the stories, the teller transforms Pooh so that he is still seen as a "Bear of Very Little Brain" by his companions, while he is the one who actually solves many of the problems of the Forest. In *Winnie-the-Pooh* it is the title character who realizes Eeyore has lost his tail and then finds and returns it; he who organizes Eeyore's birthday party; he who saves Roo from drowning (and inadvertently discovers the "North Pole"); he who comes up with the idea of how to save Piglet during the rainstorm.

Although Christopher Robin leads an "expotition" to the North Pole, Winnie-the-Pooh leads some adventures of his own, principally tracking down Woozles and setting a trap for Heffalumps. Christopher Robin may love Pooh especially because of how foolish the bear is (first, fearful of Woozle tracks, then caught in his own Heffalump trap), and in each scene it is Christopher Robin who proves omniscient as he sits in a tree high above the Woozle hunters and later identifies the pot-domed Pooh to a frightened Piglet. Yet these adventures differ considerably from the one led by Christopher Robin to the North Pole. Pooh and Piglet know no more of what they seek than does Christopher Robin, but what they find is quite different indeed. When Christopher Robin calls down from the tree, "Silly old Bear. . . . First you went round the spinney twice by yourself, and then Piglet ran after you . . . and then you were just going round a fourth time," Pooh holds up a paw to interrupt him, then he "sat down and thought, in the most thoughtful way he could think. Then he fitted his paw into one of the Tracks" (Milne, *Winnie-the-Pooh* 43) and realizes they are his. Winnie-the-Pooh, in short, ultimately realizes that *he* is the Woozle he seeks, just as later he becomes the Heffalump. His adventures may begin as external ones, but in the end they are internal journeys to hunt and tame his own fears.

In these stories Pooh creates his own imaginative world and landscape and learns his place in it. That discovery is ultimately a recognition of the symbiotic relationship between his imagination and the reality he creates for himself. Not finding it necessary to impose his ego on the land, he instead accepts the love of Christopher Robin.

When Pooh frees himself from his Heffalump trap, Christopher Robin tells him, "Oh, Bear! . . . How I do love you!" and Pooh responds rather cryptically, "So do I" (Milne, *Winnie-the-Pooh* 71).

Pooh often sees himself as "Foolish and Deluded . . . a Bear of No Brain at All" (Milne, *Winnie-the-Pooh* 43) and in doing so defines a central contest in the Forest. It is, throughout, the "lack of brain" which underpins characters' dismissals of each other. To claim his place in the Forest, Rabbit reasons that "Pooh and Piglet and Eeyore . . . haven't any Brain" (Milne, *House* 76). He later tells Owl, "You and I have brains. The others have fluff" (Milne, *House* 78).[9] Eeyore, too, when asked what the letter A means, tells Piglet, "It means Learning, it means Education, it means all the things you and Pooh haven't got" (Milne, *House* 88). Used in this way, acquiring "Brains" is a means of competition and establishing hierarchy that suggests a fragmentation of both the community and the individual. It is, after all, because Christopher Robin "learns. He becomes Educated. He instigorates" (Milne, *House* 90) that he must leave the Forest. Having "Brains," however, often shows a marked lack of insight. Pooh notes this in a discussion with Piglet:

> "Rabbit's clever," said Pooh thoughtfully.
> "Yes," said Piglet, "Rabbit's clever."
> "And he has Brain."
> "Yes," said Piglet, "Rabbit has Brain."
> There was a long silence.
> "I suppose," said Pooh, "that that's why he never understands anything."
> (Milne, *House* 131)

In the Forest, action, instinct, imagination, and emotion are most valued, and they are not—in the figure of Pooh—necessarily antithetical to intelligence, just to "Brain," which is the fracturing of reason from emotion. As Abrams has pointed out, in a Wordsworthian sense, the integration of reason with feeling bespeaks a unity of the individual.[10] Pooh exemplifies that integration; although dismissed as silly, his insights, which spring from his poetic sense and closeness to nature, show him to be much keener than those with "Brain" alone.

Further, "Brain" is an emblem of almost violent interaction with community or landscape. Rabbit, who is described as one "who never let things come to him, but always went and fetched them" (Milne,

House 83), masterminds two plots to conquer Forest newcomers. His first "PLAN TO CAPTURE BABY ROO" (Milne, *Winnie-the-Pooh* 95) entails an eleven-point list that details how Roo will be kidnapped and he and Kanga sent from the Forest; his plot to abandon Tigger as a way to unbounce him is also a carefully planned deception.

Pooh may "fetch" things for friends (setting out on a quest to find Eeyore's tail or birthday presents, building a home for what he fears is a homeless donkey, getting a pole to save Roo, or always being on the lookout for more honey), but he much prefers restful days of communing with nature. Although Christopher Robin is often isolated from nature and cannot hear what the stream might tell him, nature does speak to Winnie-the-Pooh—and Pooh listens. One "drowsy summer afternoon . . . the Forest was full of gentle sounds, which all seemed to be saying to Pooh, 'Don't listen to Rabbit, listen to me.' So he got into a comfortable position for not listening to Rabbit" (Milne, *House* 109). When a fir cone about which Pooh has been "trying to make up a piece of poetry" (Milne, *House* 93) falls into the river, Pooh is about to fetch another. "But then he thought that he would just look at the river instead, because it was a peaceful sort of day, so he lay down and looked at it, and it slipped slowly away beneath him . . . and suddenly, there was his fir-cone slipping away too" (Milne, *House* 94). What Pooh then "invents" is the Pooh-sticks game, a diversion both originating in and effecting a moment of rest in the Forest. For this bear, the "wise passiveness" of simply "being Pooh in the middle of the stream" (Milne, *House* 58) is activity enough.[11]

Pooh is the poet of the Forest, and his songs are certainly "the spontaneous overflow of . . . feelings," though those feelings are neither necessarily "powerful" nor frequently "recollected in tranquillity" (Wordsworth 448, 460). His poems include simple hums, pantheons to himself as in "Sing Ho! for the life of a Bear!" and "3 Cheers for Pooh" (Milne, *Winnie-the-Pooh* 111, 150), and, particularly in the second storybook, as counterpoints to the "busy" days and imminent leave-taking of Christopher Robin, songs of nature. As Pooh travels through the Forest he sings: "Oh, the butterflies are flying, / Now the winter days are dying, / And the primroses are trying / To be seen." The final lines of the song tell how "a Pooh is simply poohing / Like a bird" (Milne, *House* 82). Pooh becomes central here, not only because he is nature's chronicler and interpreter but also because he is an intrinsic part of it, one of the many Forest creatures listed in the song and through simile connected to those other and real creatures.

Pooh's songs reveal more insight than he or any of the others acknowledge. When Rabbit is trying to explain why Tigger is so bothersome, all the while blaming Tigger,

> Pooh tried to think, and all he could think of was something which didn't help at all. So he hummed it very quietly to himself.
>
> If Rabbit
> Was bigger
> And fatter
> And stronger,
> Or bigger
> Than Tigger,
> If Tigger was smaller,
> Then Tigger's bad habit
> Of bouncing at Rabbit
> Would matter
> No longer,
> If Rabbit
> Was taller.
>   (Milne, *House* 112)

Even nonsense like "*Tra-la-la, tra-la-la / Rum-tum-tiddle-um-tum*" proves a sign of transcendence, for as Pooh walks through the Forest and hums it, he wonders "what it felt like, being somebody else" (Milne, *Winnie-the-Pooh* 23, 24). The imaginative expansion and links with nature demonstrated by the songs privilege feeling over simple "Brain" and place Winnie-the-Pooh much more than Christopher Robin as Romantic poet of the Forest.

As much as Milne satirizes idealized elements of Wordsworthian childhood through the Christopher Robin character, he also espouses them, both through Christopher Robin in the conclusion of *The House at Pooh Corner* and in the central figure of Winnie-the-Pooh. This is problematic, however, for in choosing Winnie-the-Pooh to represent Romantic notions of childhood, Milne has shown how "real" children do not have access to the spiritual insights Wordsworth suggests. It may be fitting that a bear understands nature, but Christopher Robin's frequent insulation from nature offers little hope for a boy's understanding. This bear, though, is a toy; and stuffed, his head "full of fluff," his centrality as the Forest's Romantic poet provides incisive satire all its own.

Pooh's head becomes decidedly more filled with fluff in the Disney versions of these stories. *The Many Adventures of Winnie the Pooh*,[12] released as a full-length feature by Disney Studios in 1977, uses metanarrative strategies—from Tigger asking to be "narrated down" from a tree, to the characters jumping over the dividing margins between pages—that often allow intriguing explorations of intertextuality. Despite such sophisticated storytelling, the depictions of Christopher Robin and Winnie the Pooh are surprisingly *un*sophisticated, lacking much of the complexity of Milne's characters. While Christopher Robin never reveals the anxieties or inadequacies of Milne's character, it is the role of Winnie-the-Pooh which undergoes more of a transformation than simply his name's loss of hyphens. In the Disney version of these stories, he also loses his often central role in resolving the problems of others. The hero Pooh had once been (as during the rainstorm, when he finds Piglet's message and then suggests that Christopher Robin rescue him by floating in an overturned umbrella) becomes a hero only by default. In the Disney version, Roo finds Piglet's message, and the rescue is only effected when Pooh, afloat with his head stuck in a honey pot, and Piglet, afloat on a chair, mistakenly change places as they catapult over a waterfall. Christopher Robin's assertion that Pooh "was . . . very brave" and "our hero" only highlights the kindly foolishness of the bear.

What is perhaps more clear in the Disney transformation of Pooh is that he loses any sense of insight into either himself or the world around him. Indeed, the self-reflection inherent in Milne's Woozle hunt is thoroughly expunged. In the Disney version, Pooh and Piglet walk around a tree following footprints that the audience realizes are theirs, but the two are called away before they have a chance to realize that themselves. Similarly, when Tigger warns Pooh that Heffalumps and Woozles may steal his honey, the bear has an extended nightmare in which the animals transform into varied shapes and sizes, always chasing him about and searching for his honey. Although the Heffalumps become creatures of Pooh's dreams, the self-reflection Milne evokes is absent. At the end of the nightmare, a creature pours water on Pooh; he wakes and finds that a rainstorm is flooding his home. With no opportunity for more thought, the bear is soon headed downstream, his head caught in a honey pot.

Indeed, Pooh may go to his "thoughtful place" from time to time, but the joke is that Pooh can never really "think! think! think!" of anything at all. His interaction with nature is diminished as well. Milne's Pooh, who ignores Rabbit because he is listening to nature (*House* 209), becomes, in the Disney version, a bear who loses consciousness and sleeps and snores through Rabbit's discourse. When awakened, Pooh denies that he had been sleeping, saying that there had only been "fluff" in his ear.

What has changed in such later varied versions of Winnie-the-Pooh is the vision of childhood itself. Although Wordsworth's notions of the child become a means of both parody and sentiment in Milne's portrayal of childhood, Disney's *The Many Adventures of Winnie the Pooh* has escalated and redefined notions of sentimentality, for in this film Pooh is lovable precisely because he is as vacuous as others believe him to be. It is, finally, the fact that he *is* so full of "fluff" in the Disney feature that marks him as endearing—both to the fictive Christopher Robin and to the audience. Such often coarse sentimentalization moves Disney's Winnie the Pooh far from A. A. Milne's.

Both Milnes, father and son, had noted the importance of nostalgia, which provided motivation for Milne's writing the books as well as a key to the public's fascination with the Enchanted Forest. Christopher Milne had noted that nostalgia "was the only emotion that [my father] . . . seemed to delight in both feeling and showing" (*Enchanted Places* 160). Written during the decade following World War I and during a time of political, social, and technological upheaval,[13] *Winnie-the-Pooh* offers a world where characters may adventure but come to no harm, a place where companionship and the simple enjoyment of nature mark their days. In her study *When Toys Come Alive*, Lois Kuznets points out how animated toys in literature offer "consolation [of] . . . 'that enchanted place on the top of the Forest' . . . where living toys wait patiently for human return" (7). The enduring public and financial success of the Winnie-the-Pooh character has much to do with such nostalgia.

In the more recent *New Adventures of Winnie the Pooh*, a Disney animated series that creates new stories for the characters, the Forest world has become one that often cannot fully offer an alternative vision to the violence and upheavals of the present world. In many of these episodes, technological gadgets and even threats of violence intrude upon the Forest, as in "Sorry, Wrong Slusher!" when Christopher Robin and his toy friends have stayed up late watching television and become frightened that they are being stalked by a "Slusher," Tigger's version of a slasher. In these later Disney stories, Milne's vision of Romantic childhood and nostalgia for a pretechnological age collapse and are also largely replaced by a keen sentimentalization, even evident in the way Shepard's Winnie-the-Pooh is redrawn by Disney Studios. Audience, too, has come to determine the incarnations of marketing strategies for Winnie-the-Pooh.

The Enchanted Forest has always been a place defined by the privilege of money and social class. Christopher Milne describes the "real" Ashdown Forest as a place where he spent some of his most enjoyable childhood years. There he was able to "wander . . . freely" (Milne, *Enchanted Places* 71), always with Nanny nearby. That world was, in many ways, an extension of the nursery for the young Christopher Milne, a place of play and protection.[14] A. A. Milne's Forest of the storybooks is likewise an insulated world where the child is protected and, at least in his own illusions, holds sway. The role of the nursery is evident even in the narrative frame of *Winnie-the-Pooh* where the father (in place of Nanny) tells his child a series of stories. What is essentially ironic about not only this use of the Forest as metaphor for the middle-class insulation of the nursery but also the continued and successful merchandising of these characters is the close relationship between Romantic visions of the child (or bear, in this case) and very real financial success. Winnie-the-Pooh, in this way, both is created from and engenders worlds marked by financial status and material concerns.

David Leonhardt has reported in *Business Week* that Disney is "carefully marketing two distinct Poohs. The original line-drawn figure [by Shepard] appears on fine china . . . found in upscale specialty stores. . . . The plump, cartoonlike Pooh, clad in a red T-shirt and goofy smile, adorns plastic key chains . . . and animated videos. It sells in Wal-Mart stores and five-and-dime shops. Except . . . at Disney's own stores, the two Poohs do not share the same retail shelf" (82).[15] This two-tiered marketing strategy points out not-so-subtle ironies about these characters—the original creatures of the Enchanted Forest drawn by Shepard still represent a protected, more affluent world; hence, these products reify the intersection of Romantic childhood with issues of class, a connection Alan Richardson explores in this volume. The less romantic and more overtly sentimentalized Winnie-the-Pooh, now Americanized and not as insightful as his earlier counterpart, becomes the icon for the less affluent, those who shop at Wal-Mart and not, as Leonhardt points out, Nordstrom and Bloomingdale's.

In "Vespers," Milne had parodied a child concerned with material matters, not with God, although many in his audience did not notice such implicit irony. In *Winnie-the-Pooh* and *The House at Pooh Corner*, Milne has created a world of childhood that Christopher Robin must leave behind, a world where Pooh may remain with his simple pleasures and insights into nature. Yet while Pooh's only real materialism is a constant concern for honey, the simplicity of his world has provided fodder for big business enterprises that have lasted over half a century.

Kinder to appropriations of his father's work than he would be at other times, Christopher Milne argued in his second autobiography that "every child who, at some future date, reads about Pooh—whether in the original text or in translation or even in Disney's version—will be holding a personal truth about my father. Disney's Pooh may have little resemblance to the original Pooh, but this in no way . . . makes this personal truth less truthful" (*Path through the Trees* 247–48). Followed throughout his life by his father's creation, Christopher Milne was mistaken for Christopher Robin largely because the public yearned to believe the "enchanted place" existed. But it was not even his fictive character who held the key to that world. While Christopher Robin must leave the Forest, Pooh will not; A. A. Milne promises in the book's "Contradiction": "of course, it isn't really Good-bye, because the Forest will always be there . . . and anybody who is Friendly with Bears can find it" (*House* n.p.). That hope that the memories of childhood await us all is perhaps the central Romantic tenet of Milne's stories. In recent revisions more banally sentimentalized, it is still a hope that has survived to make the characters eminently popular, not only despite but as a foundation for the current range of incarnations and cavalcade of merchandise that has, after all, taken Winnie-the-Pooh far from Milne's Forest.

NOTES

1. For a range of appropriations made of Winnie-the-Pooh, see Hoff, *The Tao of Pooh* and *The Te of Piglet*; Allen, *Winnie-the-Pooh on Management*; Crews, *The Pooh Perplex*; and Lenard, *Winnie ille Pu.* See Connolly (8–13) for a discussion of appropriations of Milne's works. Also see Thwaite for pictures of

early merchandising of Pooh products such as board games, paper dolls, and bookends (*The Brilliant Career* 138–39). Pooh products currently outsell the books: in 1985, for example, U.S. sales of nonbook Pooh merchandise exceeded $100 million, yet worldwide a million copies of *Winnie-the-Pooh* were purchased ("Now We Are Sixty" 14). See Haring-Smith for a detailed bibliography of Milne appropriations and adaptations. The books themselves are still big business, particularly as artifacts. In 1995 a first edition of *Winnie-the-Pooh* that had belonged to Christopher Robin's Nanny sold for $10,780, "six times the amount expected and the highest price paid at auction" for one of Milne's books ("'Pooh' Book Sets Record").

2. See *The Enchanted Places* (esp. 177–83) for a discussion of the problems Christopher Milne encountered living as "Christopher Robin." He especially notes the jealousy inherent in his relationship with his father. Also see Thwaite's biography of A. A. Milne.

3. Biographer Ann Thwaite points out that "even his detective story *The Red House Mystery* carried the inappropriate addition: 'By the author of *Winnie-the-Pooh*'" (*The Brilliant Career* 132). It was difficult if not impossible for Milne to recoup a varied writing career after the publication of his children's books, although some suggest that was not merely due to the public's attention. Christopher Milne would later note that "*The House at Pooh Corner* was to mark his meridian. After that came the decline. He was writing just as fluently, just as gracefully. But fluency and grace were not enough: the public wanted stronger meat" (*Enchanted Places* 180). Another critic was more direct: "Milne blamed Pooh for overshadowing his later plays. But Pooh was blameless. Through the 1930's, Milne produced nothing to overshadow" (Swann in Thwaite, *A. A. Milne* 378).

4. This confusion by the public continued through Christopher Milne's life. He eventually opened a bookshop but in *The Enchanted Places* recounts how people sought him out even there so they could "say how-do-you-do to Christopher Robin" (182). For a discussion of the public and critical reception of these books, see Connolly (14–22). Perhaps one of the best-known parodies was that of Dorothy Parker, who describes how "Tonstant Weader Fwowed Up." For a parody of "Vespers," see Morton.

5. For a discussion of the "Beautiful Child," see C. Milne, *Enchanted Places*; Carpenter; and Cunningham (151–63).

6. Christopher Milne discusses "Vespers" and points out how his view of Wordsworthian childhood differs from his father's (*Enchanted Places* 43–45). He further points out that his father was an "Unbeliever," and Christopher was never christened (*Enchanted Places* 156–57), which suggests further ironies in the depiction of the worshiping child in this poem.

7. Milne states that "it is possible to give what one might call 'an air of charm' . . . to any account of a child's activities, and . . . this 'charm,' if one can convey it, should have as much chance in the printed page as in real life of hiding from the sentimentalist the uncharming part of a child's nature: the egotism and the heartlessness" (*Autobiography* 284).

8. See Moynihan, who argues that this "Expotition" to the North Pole parodies exploratory polar expeditions, especially those of Adm. Robert E. Peary.

9. Rabbit is right in some sense; he and Owl were the only two characters not based on Christopher Milne's actual toys and hence the only "real" toy-characters in the book. In his illustrations for Milne's children's books, Shepard draws Rabbit and Owl as real animals to differentiate them from the characters based on Christopher Milne's toys.

10. Abrams argues of Wordsworth: "Prominent . . . is his version of the great commonplace of the age: unity with himself and his world is the primal and normative state of man, of which the sign is a fullness of shared life and the condition of joy; analytic thought divides the mind from nature and object from object, and this division, if absolute, kills the object it severs and threatens with spiritual death the mind from which it has been severed" (278). Also see Abrams for a discussion of the image of "journey" in Wordsworth's poetry (284–92). The violent images in Abrams's discussion above are also relevant to the historical context of Milne's time, when the aggressive and dangerous possibilities of technology became evident, particularly in the development of weaponry during World War I. For Milne's horror of the war, see his *Autobiography* (esp. 249). For a discussion of the development of technology in the early twentieth century, see Thomson.

11. See Wordsworth's "Expostulation and Reply" (106), which provides a similar debate between "seeking" and "dream[ing] . . . time away."

12. *The Many Adventures of Winnie the Pooh* was originally released as three separate "featurettes." Critics' responses to the adaptations (or appropriations, depending on one's view) varied widely. The title of the *Daily Mail*'s review, "Massacre in 100 Aker Wood: . . . Or How Disney the Walt Said Pooh to Winnie," largely summarizes the tone of the article (April 16, 1966, rpt. in Thwaite, *The Brilliant Career* 164–65). Jack Gould of the *New York Times* later described the same featurette, *Winnie the Pooh and the Honey Tree*, as "an enchanting half-hour" (March 11, 1970). Disney later produced a children's television series, *The New Adventures of Winnie the Pooh* (1989), which created, as the title suggests, "new" stories not written by Milne. For a discussion of Disney's revisioning of Milne in that series, see Connolly (111–16).

13. See Thomson for an overview of the historical context of the time. For a discussion of the nostalgia of Milne's stories, see Connolly (3–7). Kuznets

points out that the nostalgia for childhood "seems to stem from the late nineteenth century, when people . . . were inclined to idealize the differences between childhood and adulthood and to internalize a view of childhood promulgated by the Romantic poets" (45).

14. Several critics have pointed out how the Forest world is informed by Milne's sense of class. Townsend argues that "the world of Pooh and Christopher Robin is undoubtedly a comfortable, bourgeois, nanny-protected world" (896). Also see Mackenzie (19–20). In *The Enchanted Places* (esp. 68–78) Christopher Milne describes Cotchford Farm and Ashdown Forest as prototypes for Pooh's Forest. For further discussion of the Forest as metaphor of the nursery, see Connolly (esp. 58–70, 101–4).

15. I am grateful to Lauren Peak, who alerted me to this *Business Week* article.

WORKS CITED

Abrams, M. H. *Natural Supernaturalism: Tradition and Revolution in Romantic Literature*. New York: Norton, 1971.

Allen, Roger E. *Winnie-the-Pooh on Management*. New York: Dutton, 1994.

Carpenter, Humphrey. *Secret Gardens: A Study of the Golden Age of Children's Literature*. Boston: Houghton Mifflin, 1985.

Connolly, Paula T. *Winnie-the-Pooh and the House at Pooh Corner: Recovering Arcadia*. New York: Twayne-Macmillan, 1995.

Crews, Frederick. *The Pooh Perplex: A Freshman Casebook*. New York: Dutton, 1963.

Cunningham, Hugh. *The Children of the Poor: Representations of Childhood since the Seventeenth Century*. Oxford: Blackwell, 1991.

Gould, Jack. "Winnie the Pooh Film Is Shown on N.B.C." *New York Times*, March 11, 1970, 95.

Haring-Smith, Tori. *A. A. Milne: A Critical Bibliography*. New York: Garland Publishing, 1982.

Hoff, Benjamin. *The Tao of Pooh*. New York: Dutton, 1982.

———. *The Te of Piglet*. New York: Dutton, 1992.

Kuznets, Lois Rostow. *When Toys Come Alive: Narratives of Animation, Metamorphosis, and Development*. New Haven: Yale UP, 1994.

Lenard, Alexander. *Winnie ille Pu*. New York: Dutton, 1960.

Leonhardt, David. "Two-Tier Marketing." *Business Week*, March 17, 1997, 82–90.

Mackenzie, Compton. *Literature in My Time*. 1934. Freeport, NY: Books for Libraries P, 1967.

The Many Adventures of Winnie the Pooh. Walt Disney Studios. 1977.

(Previously released as separate short featurettes: *The Honey Tree, The Blustery Day, Winnie the Pooh and Tigger Too*.)

Milne, A. A. *Autobiography*. New York: Dutton, 1939.

———. "The End of a Chapter." *By Way of Introduction*. London: Methuen, 1929.

———. *The House at Pooh Corner*. Illus. Ernest H. Shepard. 1928. New York: Puffin-Penguin, 1992.

———. *Now We Are Six*. Illus. Ernest H. Shepard. 1927. New York: Puffin-Penguin, 1992.

———. *When We Were Very Young*. Illus. Ernest H. Shepard. 1924. Puffin-Penguin, 1992.

———. *Winnie-the-Pooh*. Illus. Ernest H. Shepard. 1926. Puffin-Penguin, 1992.

Milne, Christopher. *The Enchanted Places*. 1974. New York: Dutton, 1975.

———. *The Path through the Trees*. New York: Dutton, 1979.

Morton, J. B. "Now We Are Sick." *The Best of Beachcomber*. Ed. Michael Frayn. London: Heinemann, 1963. 60.

Moynihan, Ruth B. "Ideologies in Children's Literature: Some Preliminary Notes." *Children's Literature* 2 (1973): 166–72.

"Now We Are Sixty." *Money*, December 15, 1986, 14.

Parker, Dorothy. "Far From Well." *New Yorker*, October 20, 1928, 98.

"Pooh Book Sets Record." *Boston Herald*, June 12, 1995, 55.

"Sears Gets Merchandising Rights to Disney Characters." *Marketing News*, December 18, 1987, 1.

"Sorry, Wrong Slusher!" *The New Adventures of Winnie the Pooh*. Walt Disney Co., 1990.

Thomson, David. *England in the Twentieth Century*. 2nd ed. Ed. Geoffrey Warner. New York: Viking, Penguin, 1981.

Thwaite, Ann. *A. A. Milne: The Man behind Winnie-the-Pooh*. New York: Random House, 1990.

———. *The Brilliant Career of Winnie-the-Pooh: The Story of A. A. Milne and His Writing for Children*. London: Methuen, 1992.

Townsend, John Rowe. "Milne." *Twentieth Century Children's Literature*. 2nd ed. Ed. D. L. Kirkpatrick. New York: St. Martin's Press, 1983.

Wordsworth, William. *Selected Poems and Prefaces*. Ed. Jack Stillinger. Boston: Houghton Mifflin, 1965.

PART FOUR

Romantic Ideas in Cultural Confrontations

William J. Scheick

THE ART OF
MATERNAL NURTURE
IN MARY AUSTIN'S
THE BASKET WOMAN

s the American literary canon has undergone re-
assessment in recent years, Mary Austin (1868–
1934) has emerged from the shadows of cultural
memory. The renewal of interest in Austin, who
was born in Illinois and taught in southern California, has mainly focused on three of her many books: *The Land of
Little Rain* (1903), which indicts the American desecration of land
and self sacrificed for progress; *Lost Borders* (1909), which critiques
the boundaries constructed by cultural stereotypes; and *Earth Horizon* (1932), which relates the author's personal struggle with various
constraints upon female identity. Although these concerns also inform *The Basket Woman: A Book of Fanciful Tales for Children* (first
published in 1904 and reissued in 1932), this collection of tales has
never attracted much attention. Perhaps its designation as a children's
book and especially its republication in 1910 as a school text (entitled
The Basket Woman: A Book of Indian Tales for Children) have contributed to this oversight. Whatever the reason, this work deserves
reconsideration not only for its demonstration of Austin's clever use
of Paiute myth and ritual (Hoyer, "Weaving" 139) but also for its
exhibition of her adroit adaptation of the Victorian construction of
childhood in Romantic terms. Austin's book, moreover, anticipates
modern attempts to intersect art and ethos in children's literature.

When *The Basket Woman* appeared, a Romantic literary inclination was no longer fashionable among the literati. For these high-
culture pundits, who were largely inattentive to children's literature,
literary realism and naturalism were in vogue. The cost of resisting
this development could be substantial, as Sarah Orne Jewett (1849–
1909) intimates at the end of "A White Heron" (1886), an allegorical
tale about a nine-year-old girl's loyalty to a beautiful symbol of nature. This impecunious child need only relate "the story she can tell"

to the ornithologist (Jewett 2: 20), who wants to kill the rare heron for an exhibit, and she will then receive a substantial sum of money. The child's refusal to do so expresses Jewett's personal refusal to betray nature for financial gain as an artist. Instead of writing fashionably, instead of "the story she can tell," Jewett conserves a now outmoded and financially unrewarding Romanticism in "The White Heron." The manner of tales like Jewett's short story was influenced in part by the conventions of romance, a form often favored by Romantic authors that turn-of-the-century cultural pundits particularly identified as the antithesis of their revered literary modes of realism and naturalism. Over time this snubbed genre was judged to be at best suitable for youthful and working-class readers (Scheick, *Ethos* 11–30).

Mary Austin was, as we will see, as keenly aware of this literary divide as was Jewett. Like Jewett, she wrote both romance and realistic fiction. In fact, two sketches collected in *The Basket Woman* that first appeared in the *Atlantic Monthly* conform to the conventions of literary realism. *Atlantic* editor Bliss Perry doubtless thought that the Native American and western matter of these tales suited his emphasis on current affairs in the periodical or satisfied his audience's related appetite for "local color" narratives. The prior appearance of these tales, moreover, amounted to advance publicity for Austin's book, which was published by Houghton Mifflin, the Boston owner of the *Atlantic*.

If Austin's tales contained local color matter of current public interest, they also evidenced a continuity with New England tradition. The writings of such Transcendentalists as Ralph Waldo Emerson and Henry David Thoreau provided a wellspring for Austin's Romantic thought (Smith 18; Stineman 12). She openly admitted Emerson's impact not only on her ideas but also on her literary style (Austin, *Earth* 165). She may have qualified some Transcendentalist beliefs, but generally these concepts reinforced her personal sense of life, which included occasional mystical experiences (Pearce, *Beloved* 64–77). If her work shares the Keatsian notion that human salvation begins and ends in the phenomenal world, it does so precisely because of her Transcendental faith in a pervasive divine force imparting to humanity capacities as yet temporally unrealized. This faith informed her version of a fundamental emphasis of Romantic thought, the need for humanity to undergo a radical transformation of consciousness if it is to end its "divided state" and discover a new relationship to self, nature, fellow humans, and history (Abrams 56–65).

The critical necessity of a therapeutic revolution of mind, a new consciousness, is the guiding principle of *The Basket Woman*. This collection participates in an early-twentieth-century pattern defined by Anita Moss: the representation of the child as an agent of human transformation (245). In "The White-Barked Pine" sketch, for example, Austin pertinently advocates the metamorphic potentiality of childlike wishing: "What one desires with all one's heart for a long time finally comes to pass in some fashion or other" (*Basket Woman* 167). Behind such a claim is Austin's belief in a divinely inspired organic principle that informs and unites physical and mental human experiences. Austin's notion of wishing with the faith of a child expresses an Emersonian confidence that mind and matter reciprocally "aspire to the highest" (Emerson 1: 107).

In "The White-Barked Pine" and other sketches, however, Austin indicates that the heart may err in its desire. In making this concession she involuntarily engages the darker Romantic perspective that observes the historical gap between revolution as thought and as action (Farrell 28–38) or between the heroic ideal as vision and as experience (Wilson 189–96). At this point Austin's reader might wonder: if a divine principle suffuses all creation, how can the human heart ever err? But like her Transcendentalist predecessors, Austin elides this problem of how Western humanity can be, in fact came to be, so out of touch with its true desires. Instead, like them, she simply prophesies remediation.

The Basket Woman is, accordingly, designed to assist in a therapeutic revolution of mind. It is fashioned as a speculum through which viewers may become aware of the presently forgotten openness of human options. *The Basket Woman* encourages its readers to further the progressive manifestation of the innate divine force in both nature and the human self. This resultant new consciousness, Austin's book indicates, must include (1) the reclamation of the child perspective, (2) the recuperation of humanity's relation to nature, (3) the recognition of reality as protean, (4) the transformation of ideology through myth, (5) the redefinition of women's social identity, and (6) the revitalization of storytelling.

The title of Austin's book designates children as its primary readers. The schoolbook edition, which differs from the other editions in its prefatory matter, states that these tales are designed to "appeal to the child mind" (Austin, *Basket Woman* iii). Austin endorses the Romantic idea, as summarized by Emerson, that "infancy is the perpetual Messiah" (1: 71). She hopes to nurture the child's sense of wonder. Like the intention behind the trope of the child in Blake's poetics of resistance, Austin strives to enlist her audience's imagination against the current version of reality. If she succeeds, the young readers of her book may in their adult lives transform the present-day delimiting perception of reality.

Nurturing the child's sense of wonder, Austin explains, requires the recuperation of humanity's "normal intimacy with nature" (*Basket Woman* iii). When in "The Stream That Ran Away" a rivulet thinks, "That baby and I understood each other" (*Basket Woman* 41), Austin points to a mode of Wordsworthian first-knowing, in which childhood imagination merges with sublime nature. Still more radical is her post-Darwinian assertion, after the manner of Chauncey Wright (31–38), that human "consciousness and personality [are] by-products of animal life only" (Austin, *Basket Woman* iii). Such a belief recalls totemic cultures whose myths about creation present humans and animals interacting as members of a social unit (Shepard 125). For Austin, in short, the human self, or soul, is utterly natural in origin. And, as defined in terms of her Transcendentalist perspective, this site of origin entirely accounts for whatever is divine in humanity.

Austin, however, does not indicate that we can rationally comprehend this origin. In the first sketch, for example, a man receives the ability to tell stories from a wolf (nature). This wonderful gift is simply one of the "by-products of animal life" (Austin, *Basket Woman* iii). When this ability is reclaimed by the wolf during the man's dream, the gift is temporarily lost to humanity. It merely returns to its source, nature itself, whence it will once again renewingly reemerge as a gift. This mysterious process exhibits a fundamental Transcendentalist tenet: that "there is never a beginning, there is never an end, to the inexplicable continuity of this web of God, but always circular power returning into itself" (Emerson 1: 85).

This divinely inspired, self-generating circular pattern is implied elsewhere in *The Basket Woman*. For instance, a stream is unable to give any "account of itself except that it crept out from under a great heap of rubble far up in the cañon"; and a sugar pine is similarly bewildered, as if "in a dream," over "what he was to be" even as he "felt within himself the promise of what he was to be" (Austin, *Basket Woman* 34, 134). These allegorical occasions apply to humanity, which likewise can never cognitively understand or close with its origin in nature. Recognition of this inability is a complex Romantic theme (Brisman 11–20), but put simply it means that humanity, as a part of nature, cannot know the whole of which it is a part. At best, Austin suggests, human origination can only be sensed through a childlike intuitive faith. In the apt latter-day Romantic phrasing of Theodore Roethke, we "learn by going where [we] have to go" (Allison 1119).

In *The Basket Woman*, Austin's sketchlike manner of rendering natural settings conveys this mysterious elusiveness of the divine origin of creation. In the first paragraph of the opening tale, for example, nature characteristically entices and recedes from human attention: "The hills had a flowing outline and melted softly into each other and higher hills behind, until the range broke in a ragged crest of thin peaks white with snow" (Austin, *Basket Woman* 3). To observe the natural world in this way is to glimpse more than physical terrain. It is to perceive in a manner similar to the specially sighted Weaving Woman, who envisions "an *enchanted* mesa covered with *misty* bloom and gentle creatures moving on trails that *seemed* to lead to places where one had always *wished* to be" (Austin, *Basket Woman* 47, emphasis added). To perceive in this manner is to notice, with disoriented Alan (the little boy appearing in many of these tales), that "the high mesa, with the water mirage rolling over it, was a kind of enchanted land . . . where almost anything might happen" (Austin, *Basket Woman* 74).

Here and elsewhere Austin's imagery challenges conventional notions of empirical reality. Her imagery, characteristic of the genre of romance, intimates that the world we take for granted as the bedrock of our existence is instead as mutable and capricious as an enchanted dream. Pertinently, "as if he had dreamed" (Austin 84) functions like a refrain in *The Basket Woman*. This Romantic motif undercuts the commonplace perception of the quotidian as a fixed and firm foundation for arriving at meaning about the world and about ourselves. It implies that a reader's current sense of reality may be only one dreamlike version among a host of latent dreamlike alternatives open to human discovery.

The first tale, "The Basket Woman," establishes this motif. In this story, little Alan mistakenly fears a mahala (a female Native American) who comes periodically to his home to wash his family's laundry. He worries that she will kidnap and conceal him in one of her baskets. One night he dreams that he voluntarily climbs into such a basket and that she carries him into the past to visit her people's bygone village. Within his dream he hears various legends, including one concerning a primal episode of dreaming. In this episode a Native American (while asleep) has his ability to tell stories stolen by the same wolf which had originally given it to him.

Just as this man's dream is invaded by a representative of nature (a wolf), so too Alan's dream (encompassing this inner dream episode) is invaded by a similar representation (a coyote). The howl of the coyote outside his window awakens Alan at the same time as "the spaces in between the words" of the mahala's song about a coyote become "filled with long howls" (Austin, *Basket Woman* 15). Alan does not awaken to quite the same world he left when he went to sleep. This feature of the story insists that while divine nature remains an elusive ontological constant, "reality" as experienced by humanity in time is always as fluid and open-ended as is a dream.

Austin's association of the idea of the past with a dream within a dream pertains to her apprehension of both the elusiveness of human origins and the absence of any real boundary between the empirical (rational) and the fantastic (imaginative). In terms of her Romantic correlation of Native American beliefs and of child perception, Austin depicts the world of matter as inextricably interwoven with the world of mind. In fact, as we saw in her claim about the generative desires (wishes) of the human heart, Austin radically contends that the material world is in a significant sense only a manifestation of the mental perception—the spirit—of a people.

This conviction especially informs "The Coyote-Spirit and the Weaving Woman." In this story the protagonist transforms an animal into a man by convincing it to believe that it is already human. "According as they think man-thoughts or beast-thoughts," Austin writes in this narrative, people "can throw over them[selves and others] such a change that they have only to choose which they will be" (Austin, *Basket Woman* 54). What is experienced as empirically real, in short, is in actuality fundamentally mutable. It is always potentially another temporal possibility. This Transcendental belief in life as infinitely protean provides the fountainhead of Austin's attempts to educate her audience about alternative possibilities for human perception and behavior.

As the examples of Alan and the coyote spirit illustrate, what matters is the process of successive wakening from one dream version of the actual to ever-better eventualities. What matters finally in this Romantic paradigm is an ongoing self-education and self-discovery. The coyote spirit awakens to his latent power to be more than he has been both in mind and in life, just as Alan awakens (we are told at the start of the second tale) to being not "nearly so much afraid" of the basket woman (Austin, *Basket Woman* 19). In the penultimate story Alan, whom the mahala had saved from death in the sixth sketch, undergoes a further development in his perspective when he realizes that "since the time of his going out to see the buzzards making a merry-go-round, he knew he should never be afraid of the Basket Woman again" (Austin, *Basket Woman* 173). This successive unfolding of perception in both Alan and the coyote spirit reflects the mysterious asymptotic character of nature; that is, the way everything in nature infinitely emanates from some elusive divine source and always approaches but never arrives at any endpoint. This is the Transcendentalist notion expressed by Thoreau when he speaks metaphorically of an eternity of dawns or wakenings: "only the day dawns to which we are awake. There is more day to dawn. The sun is but a morning star" (221).

This paradoxical concept of an infinite succession endlessly renewed through a circular refunding—"the inexplicable . . . circular power returning into itself" described by Emerson—is also expressed in "The Fire Bringer." Set during the time when "men and beasts talked together," this Paiute story concerns a young boy's determination to save his "people from the cold" (Austin, *Basket Woman* 111, 113). With the assistance of Coyote, the young boy journeys to the Burning Mountain. There Coyote snatches a flaming brand and passes it to the boy, who (like Prometheus in Greek myth) gives it to his people. In time, however, the appellation Fire Bringer passes from the boy to Coyote, just as in "The Basket Woman" the human ability to sing reverts to a wolf.

This transference of name not only stresses the circularity of humanity's interaction with nature, it also relatedly insists that human health—here represented as the need for warmth against the cold—depends upon a vital collaboration, even an intimacy, with nature. This ideal state, Austin urges, is characterized by the vanishing of any boundary between therapeutic legends such as "The Fire Bringer" and the everyday experience of its audience. Such an erasure of the apparently resolute borders between fact (matter) and fiction (mind) is similar to how the seemingly firm "rim of the world [is] hidden in a [dissolving] bluish mist" (Austin, *Basket Woman* 115) in the story. Such is the lesson Alan unconsciously learns after hearing this tale many times. As a result he is able to appreciate in a new way something as simple as the "backward-streaming" sparks of a burning brand that now strikes him as "shining star-like" (Austin, *Basket Woman* 117). The images here hint that distant cosmic wonder (stars) and near quotidian wonder (sparks) coalesce because Alan's eyes (body) and his imagination (mind) are mutually allied. So likewise he marvels at a falling star "trailing across the sky" and also at the close representation of a similar wonder in a coyote's flanks, "singed and yellow," as if by backward-blowing flames (Austin, *Basket Woman* 118).

Although his mother tells him "he must have dreamed it," Alan believes that "he had been part of the story himself," that "he was the boy of the story who was afterward to be called the Fire Bringer" (Austin, *Basket Woman* 109–11). Alan *is* indeed part of this dream-like story. The Fire Bringer symbolizes his and every other child's archetypal potentiality just as, for Shelley, Prometheus represents humanity's latent destiny. Austin believes that such mythic stories convey the rich, protean dream matrix of human existence. In this matrix the child's perspective, represented by the young Fire Bringer in myth and by Alan in the story, expresses something of the timeless fire of Promethean imagination that has the capacity to melt the temporal frigidity caused by the unhealthy prevailing ideologies of the early twentieth century.

As presented in *The Basket Woman*, this salutary work of the imagination is impeded when people so forget the human past that, as the mahala tells Alan, history seems to matter only "in dreams" (Austin 15). The repudiation of humanity's past as an infantile stage of civilization is a related impediment. The Anglo American perception of Native American cultures as inferior, or primitive, is presented in Austin's book as such a hindrance. Austin was aware of how this cultural construction was featured in arguments for the U.S. policy of manifest destiny, which included the steady displacement of the indigenous peoples of North America. In *The Basket Woman* Austin resisted this ideological reading of reality and history by attempting to reinstate, in nearly Coleridgean terms, the value of the child as the representative of a mythic mode of perception.

Her maneuver here is very precarious. Austin concedes, in effect, the propriety of conventional early-twentieth-century applications of the trope of the child to Native Americans. She suggests, however, that such an attribution is proper for reasons forgotten by her contemporaries. Austin attempts to awaken her contemporaries' deep comprehension of the child trope; she aims to revise their response to Native American culture by reinstating the Romantic mythic valuation of the child. Contributing to the later Romantic version of the Noble Savage motif prevalent in her time (Berkhofer 73–80), Austin reminds her audience that Native Americans are to twentieth-century civilization what childhood is to adulthood. But, she contends, neither is merely an early stage left behind in maturity, for the later period is always in an organic sense defined or determined by the earlier phase. Once again, Austin confronts the standard linear sense of time of her day and fosters an appreciation of the "circular power returning into itself" described by Emerson, a power of nature that always coalesces the past and the present. Her sentiment here recalls Wordsworth's "The Child is father of the Man" in "My Heart Leaps Up" (Allison 551). For Austin, in short, the childlike intuitive knowing evident in Native American mythic beliefs is a feature of humanity's past that ideally—as the heuristic example of little Alan indicates—also provides redemptive medicine for humanity's future.

"There is a period in the life of every child," Austin writes in the preface to *The Basket Woman*, "when almost the only road to the understanding is the one blazed out by the myth-making spirit, kept open to the larger significance of things long after he is apprised that the thunder did not originate in the smithy of the gods nor the Walrus talk to the Carpenter" (v). Austin stresses the "educative value" of her Paiute tales of the "broadly human," romance tales presenting "certain aspects of nature as they appear in the myth-making mood" (*Basket Woman* iii, viii). Referring to something allied to the Wordsworthian first-knowing, Austin pits the mutual dreamlike mythic perceptions of Native Americans and of children against the conventional ideology of her day, a materialistic period of conspicuous wealth and power concentrated among a few industrialists who exploit both natural and human resources.

Austin's critique of ideology is especially featured in "The Christmas Tree," which appears exactly midway in *The Basket Woman*. The title of this tale, originally "The Kiss of Niño Dios" when it first appeared in *Out West* (Pearce, *Literary* 10), suggests an authorial desire to attract the attention of prospective youthful readers. It is not, however, a customary Christmas story. It not only coalesces certain Paiute and Christian beliefs (Hoyer, "Weaving" 141–43), it also in particular condemns Christianity's ideological sacrifice of the natural world.

The name of the protagonist of this story alludes to the author of the first book of the New Testament, a detail that heightens Austin's challenge to Christianity. The Mathew of "The Christmas Tree" first becomes a devoted Christian convert, but later, unlike his namesake, he serves as a witness to a different gospel. As a child, Mathew loves a silver fir, which serves as a maternal influence on him after the death of his mother: "When at times there was a heaviness in his breast which was really a longing for his mother, though he did not understand it, he would part the low spreading branches and creep up to the slender trunk of the fir. Then he would put his arms around it and be quiet for a long beautiful time. The tree had its own way of comforting him; the branches swept the ground and shut him in dark and close" (Austin, *Basket Woman* 94). Mathew's attachment to this tree, which "seemed to him" to possess "a soul," is narratively presented as fitting, especially since the result is his own healthy development into "a great lad, straight and springy as a young fir" (Austin, *Basket Woman* 92, 93).

Eventually Mathew is sent away from his mountain home to be educated in town. The town is the antithesis of his mountain forest nurturance. As seen from the mountain (a prospect device drawn from Romantic tradition), the town is an ugly industrialized place characterized by "the red smoke, the glare, and the hot breath of the furnaces" (Austin, *Basket Woman* 89). It is also a place dominated by the Christian doctrine of sacrifice. "Believing what he had been told" by the minister about "giving the best beloved," Mathew eventually offers up his silver fir—"beauty," in his approving father's words— so that it may serve as a Christmas tree in the town church (Austin, *Basket Woman* 101).

During the Christmas Eve service, however, Mathew undergoes a reverse conversion: "he heard the minister talking, and it was all of a cross and a star; but Mathew could only look at the tree, for he saw that it trembled, and he felt that he had betrayed it" (Austin, *Basket Woman* 102). Austin's imagery, moreover, reinforces his conviction.

It implies that a prior, more benign doctrine of the Christmas star and the Christian cross is already expressed in nature. For "the topmost sprig" of the fir "rises above all the star-built whorls in a long and slender cross, until by the springing of new branches it becomes a star" (Austin, *Basket Woman* 95). After his reverse conversion experience, Mathew leaves town and returns to the wilderness, where "stately star-built firs rose up like spires, taller than the church tower, each with a cross on top" (Austin, *Basket Woman* 103). Austin carefully expresses Mathew's resolution: "that he might find more in the forest than he ever thought to find, now that he knew what to look for, since everything speaks of God in its own way" (Austin, *Basket Woman* 104).

This nuanced passage apparently allowed some of Austin's contemporaries to think that Mathew learned in church how to find God in all of life; for other readers, however, the passage may insinuate that Mathew has adopted nature as the true church. That nature is depicted in terms of female nurture and that Mathew never again returns to the town's church both reinforce Austin's emphasis on the need to restore humanity's "normal intimacy with nature" as the origin of human religious sentiment. In this respect, including the feminization of the natural, the story may be read as an allegorical representation of an Emersonian observation: "The aspect of Nature is devout. Like the figure of Jesus, she stands with bended head, and hands folded upon the breast. The happiest man is he who learns from nature the lesson of worship" (Emerson 1: 61). In "The Christmas Tree" this message contrasts with the demand of both the Christian church and civilization to sacrifice what is natural in humanity and in the world. Here too, in related Blakean terms, Austin has pitted liberating mythic knowledge against the mind-forged manacles of ideology.

"The Christmas Tree" not only rejects the triple sacrifice of natural beauty, child perspective, and mythic knowledge; it also specifically identifies these sacrificed values with female power. As Shelley's reference to "our great Mother" in *Alastor* (1816) (71) and as Emerson's kindred reliance upon the female pronoun throughout *Nature* (1836) exemplify, the Romantics often gendered nature as female. It is likewise a characteristic gesture in Austin's writings (O'Grady 137–38). In *The Basket Woman*, the fir is as much a maternal influence on Mathew as the Weaving Woman is on the coyote spirit and as (in five sketches) the Basket Woman is on little Alan. This gendered representation of nature is not merely a rhetorical convention for Austin but a matter of feminist ethos that informs *The Basket Woman* just as it does *The Land of Little Rain* (Ammons 86–97) and *A Woman of Genius* (Graulich 13–16).

Austin's feminist thought expands Romantic arguments—such as Mary Wollstonecraft Shelley's revision of the Prometheus myth (Veeder 197–203) and Margaret Fuller's revision of the domestic angel convention (Scheick, "Angelic" 297)—that were designed to foster a new consciousness concerning women. And like Fuller, Austin specifies speech as a particular province of the female principle. But Austin seems to surpass Fuller's Transcendental effort in *Woman in the Nineteenth Century* (1845) to reinstate women by defining them as distinct from men in the unified essential dualism of creation. For in the final story in Austin's collection, "Mahala Joe," female garb is worn by a male as a badge of faithfulness. And relatedly, as we noted, "The Basket Woman" recounts how men lost a natural gift and also implies that women may potentially repossess it.

To observe this thrust in *The Basket Woman*, however, is not to suggest that Austin escapes the perils of Romantic feminism. Associating female identity and nature is as risky a move for her as is associating Native American identity and childhood. The latter association may only reinforce the stereotype of the puerile Native American if Austin's Romantic claims for the redemptive status of the child fail to prevail, and so likewise the former association may only reinforce the stereotype of the body-oriented (reason-deficient, immature) woman if Austin's Romantic claims for the essential divinity of nature fail to prevail. Indeed, Austin's feminism has been found wanting by those who conclude that her essentialist imputation of female spirituality and marginality is confounded by her endorsement of women's special identification with nature, the very connection that has traditionally disempowered women (Karell 156).

Even in light of characteristic nineteenth-century Transcendentalist attempts to reveal a higher truth secreted within a mistaken human perception, Austin's attempt to metamorphose negative cultural constructions into profound Romantic insights is nothing less than daunting and was not likely to convince the skeptical adult readers of her day. *The Basket Woman*, however, is designed for children, young minds already intuitively inclined (in Austin's opinion) to discover the deeper truth at the core of the cultural stereotypes that have yet to incapacitate their imagination. This purpose behind *The Basket Woman* is important to recall, even if the book finally cannot break free from the hazards of Romantic feminism.

In the dream within Alan's dream in the first sketch, the Basket Woman notes that "the old men told tales one after the other, and the children thought each one was the best" (Austin, *Basket Woman* 12–13). In yesteryear, apparently, men were the primary storytellers, the primary agents of deriving words from human encounters with nature. Through carelessness men lost this faculty, which returned to its source, Mother Nature. Women, according to Austin's Romantic feminism, have remained closer to nature than have men. Even women's language reveals this closeness: the "mellow voices" of Native American women are "like smooth water flowing over stones," and the "words of their song are always the same," like "the cheerful water [that] comes out of the foot of the nameless peak" (Austin, *Basket Woman* 52, 70). Such imagery likely recalls the Transcendental notion that in "its infancy" language was "all poetry," its every word "borrowed from some material appearance" (Emerson 1: 25). More importantly, this imagery attests that female artists are especially advantaged in reclaiming this nature-inspired Logos capacity of language.

In our present state of alienation from our divine source, Austin reflexively indicates, the female storyteller is like a maternal Prometheus. She has the power to bequeath life-sustaining warmth and nurture, implications likely to appeal to Austin's designated youthful audience. This female capacity is represented in the effect of the basket woman on Alan, the weaving woman on the coyote spirit, the maternal silver fir on Mathew, and the female dress on its male wearer, who thereby becomes "well thought of among his people" (Austin, *Basket Woman* 185). Such Promethean power is also implicitly attributed to Austin's own relationship with her readers, especially since "the narrator/writer and the Basket Woman merge at certain points in the narrative" (Stineman 79). Such representations of female aesthetic power, Austin implies, may preserve the Native American/child perspective and thereby repatriate humanity to the natural, the mythic, and the protean dream of human destiny. Specifically, women's narrational powers can foster humanity's recuperation of what has been temporarily lost—"man's normal intimacy with nature" (Austin, *Basket Woman* iii). The nurturing warmth of this female-rehabilitated intimacy is Austin's version of "the vital heat in us" that Thoreau identified as "the grand necessity" of life (8).

The Basket Woman and the Weaving Woman represent Austin's ideal of the female artist. They transform legends and baskets into an art that is at once aesthetic and educational, the dual aim of Austin's own tales as announced in her preface. Containing food and water (Austin, *Basket Woman* 4–5), the mahala's baskets potentially provide life-sustaining nourishment for others. In the mahala's narrative evocation of the Native American village of the past, women weave baskets and then use them to toss corn "like grains of gold" (Austin, *Basket Woman* 11). Moreover, one of these containers of nurture, as valuable as gold, transports Alan to a legendary time, also as valuable as gold. The mahala's basket is like female storytelling, both (similar to Austin's art) potential agents of therapeutic nurture and natural wealth.

Austin's concept of art is most fully presented in "The Coyote-Spirit and the Weaving Woman." In this tale, the Weaving Woman's peculiar manner of seeing "everything with rainbow fringes" sets her apart from others. Her baskets, as a result, are "such wonderful affairs" that people, as they stroke "the perfect curves" or trace "out the patterns," think "how fine life would be if it were so rich and bright as she made it seem" (Austin, *Basket Woman* 46–47). The Weaving Woman's romancelike art envisions "the places where one had always wished to go" (Austin, *Basket Woman* 47). More importantly, in her transformation of the coyote into a man through mere language, the Weaving Woman also reaffirms that art and life are not separate experiences. Her performance reveals that human society may in fact be crafted just as creatively as an artist can imagine or dream an aesthetic vision.

In a certain sense, then, Alan's initial fear, that the mahala would conceal him in one of her baskets, is indeed warranted. It is through the visionary art of her stories that the mahala kidnaps Alan and transforms his fear, even as in her own sketches Austin attempts to transmute the stereotypes of Native Americans as being more like children than like adults and women as being determined more by the body than by the mind. As early as the second sketch, Alan has changed and now craves more of the mahala's stories (Austin, *Basket Woman* 29–30). Alan has become a captive of her woven tales— intertwined romancelike narratives mingling fact and fantasy—even as Austin seeks to carry off the imaginations of any young readers possibly enchanted by the intricately woven baskets that are her own stories.

The weave of a basket corresponds to Austin's narrative technique of combining dream, fiction, legendary history, and the present moment. Austin's sketches expose their audience, as Austin said of ideal art in her preface, to "successive layers of insight and purport" that intimate something wonderful concealed within their "passing experience" (*Basket Woman* viii). In other words, Austin indicates that her seemingly simple children's stories may contain interwoven layers of subtleties designed, like the artistic "wonderful affairs" of the Weaving Woman, to make an audience imagine "how fine life would be if it were so rich and bright as she made it seem." This artistic technique of layering replicates a pattern of nature, as is evident in the scene (observed earlier) where tiered or layered mountains instructively dissolve their form and recede before Alan's and the reader's searching vision: "The hills had a flowing outline and melted softly into each other and higher hills behind, until the range broke in a ragged crest of thin peaks white with snow" (Austin, *Basket Woman* 3).

The Basket Woman not only insists on the repatriation of humanity to nature, it also insists on the reclamation of art as a sacramental medium for reinvigorating humanity's sense of wonder in response to the elusive mystery of existence. Austin particularly values romance as a genre open to the artful expression of a strangeness that "implies a criticism of the familiar of which we lack any criterion of authenticity other than it is ours" (*Earth* 230). In America this strangeness had long been suspected as a feature of the alleged socially subversive nature of romance as a genre (Bell 25–36), but Austin seeks to revise this stereotypical response to romance even as she aims to reform stereotypes of Native Americans and women. For Austin, romance is an apt vehicle for a "mythic" art maternally offered to children, who as future adults might, as a result of that nurturing art, make a difference in realizing another, more spiritually fulfilled version of human existence.

Austin's Romantic valuation of language as the primary instrument for instating the ontological divinity of nature possibly participates in the Romantic mode of Humean skeptical self-affirmation identified by Andrew M. Cooper (7–34). This feature may especially be evident in the substantial number of references to death in her book, including one tale of persistent faith, "The Golden Fortune," in which a prospector dies never knowing the truth about his "worthless lode" (Austin, *Basket Woman* 160). The instability of the ground for her affirmation through language notwithstanding, Austin implicitly advances the nineteenth-century literary examples of Maria Edgeworth (Myers 110) and Frances Hodgson Burnett (Bixler 209) by advocating a maternal art that offers alternative values for future adults. Austin believed that this nurture, like the mahala's saving of Alan's life in "The Merry-Go-Round," could potentially rescue humanity from the premature death of spirit and body that ensues as a result of the loss of humanity's "normal intimacy with nature" (*Basket Woman* iii).

Without making any claim for Mary Austin's influence, one can observe the longevity of many of the ideas she expressed in *The Basket Woman*. The novelist John Gardner certainly shared her late-Romantic belief that "real art creates myths a society can live instead of die by, and clearly our society is in need of such myths" (126). Such a belief, as well, seems to inform a number of later twentieth-century books for children. Jean Craighead George's *Julie of the Wolves* (1972) and Whitley Strieber's *Wolf of Shadows* (1985), as merely two later instances of children's books reflexively concerned with the ethos of storytelling, illustrate the endurance of the Romantic beliefs expressed in Austin's book.

In *Julie of the Wolves*, a thirteen-year-old Eskimo girl flees an unsuccessful contract marriage and becomes lost in the Alaskan wilderness. Her biological father had become involuntarily separated from her when she was nine and, as she later discovers, has adopted the ways of white civilization, including marrying a gussak (a white woman) and owning his own plane. After she finds him she must choose between two ways of life, American culture or Eskimo culture. The contrast between the two is as dramatically dualistic in George's novel as is the perceived conflict between civilization and nature in Romantic tradition. Whereas Miyax (Julie) associates "fire and blood and . . . flashes and death" with American culture, she associates "peace and Amaroq," a wolf pack leader who becomes her "adopted father" (George 152, 170), with Eskimo culture.

Miyax survives the tundra by learning the "wolf language" of her adoptive lupine family (George 125). The meaningless death of Amaroq at the hands of sportsmen not even interested in his pelt reinforces Miyax's sense of the contrast between the natural "brotherly . . . love" among the wolves and the unnatural ethos of "men . . . taught to kill without reason" (George 78, 156). Besides her sympathy with the wolves, who "did not like civilization" (George 133), Miyax's preference for the wilderness includes, as well, cherished childhood memories of her biological father. She often recalls how "walking the tundra with Kapugen was all laughter and fun" (George 79).

Throughout *Julie of the Wolves* the word *fun* and its derivatives encode Miyax's valuation of this mythic past. At one point she imagines that what a wolf pup is "dreaming about . . . must be funny" (George 50), at least in part because she associates the wolves' natural state with her childhood memories, both constructed as halcyon. Indeed, if the past seems like a dream to her, so does the present: "her wide-awake dream was hardly amusing—it was desperate" (George 51). George seems to share Austin's Romantic concept of human experience as being as mutable as a dream, with the past associated with animal/child knowing. In one version, the paradisiacal version, human and animal existed in some form of wonderful reciprocity, a cooperative equality. This notion, most evident in Miyax's relationship with the wolves, informs the introductory description of her as being "like the beautifully formed polar bears" and the subsequent description of an owl as looking "like a funny little Eskimo" (George 8, 45). In a later version of the dream work of life this totemic relationship, celebrated in Eskimo myth, has vanished. Only a vestige of it remains in Miyax's reverent, if forlorn, devotion to a totem of Amaroq, symbol of an Eskimo ancestral dream past.

For, as both Amaroq's senseless death and her father's new life indicate, the world she knew as a child and more recently among the wolves has rapidly changed. The "new attitudes of the Americanized Eskimos" are replacing the "old ways," and now "the hour of the wolf and the Eskimo is over" (George 85, 89, 170). This realization, the final lesson of Miyax's story as she decides to live with her Americanized father, is presented by George in terms of a Romantic nostalgia for a paradise lost. Whatever problems existed with the old ways, such as Miyax's miserable experience as a contract bride, are overlooked in the haze of this nostalgic impulse positing such a distinct dualism between the pleasant past and the unpleasant present in *Julie of the Wolves*.

Humanity, George's book suggests, does not "adjust . . . to nature" and so now cannot "understand the earth" (George 121, 81). No longer "familiar with" how "the plants and birds point . . . the way for wanderers," out of touch "with the rhythm of the beasts and the land," humanity has forgotten its "wolf language" (George 11, 169, 125). Humanity has lost a primal way of experiencing nature and so no longer appreciates, typically, "the simplicity" of "the scheme of the moon and stars and the constant rise and fall of life on the earth" (George 130). It is this loss of a mythic childlike first-knowing, more than Miyax's specific past, that is finally Romantically elegized in *Julie of the Wolves*.

Wolf of Shadows depicts the world as it might become if Miyax's young and female sensibility were ultimately vanquished by the male-dominated ethos of meaningless killing. Strieber's book relates how a woman, an animal ethologist, and her remaining daughter survive a nuclear holocaust by becoming "members of [a wolf] pack" (90). As her daughter pertinently observes with the clarity of a child's intuition, "If we weren't in the pack we'd be dead" (Strieber 100). The pack's ability to endure postholocaust conditions significantly depends on "their instincts" (Strieber 52), a way of knowing that the human survivors learn to appreciate. Through this suprarational understanding, the pack leader senses the elusive origins of nature as he listens "for the stillness . . . behind the murmuring scents of the world" (Strieber 11).

Insofar as the wolves in Strieber's story "know what's best" (54), they symbolize humanity's need to be repatriated to nature. Accordingly, they "guide" the mother and her surviving child "away from people" (Strieber 75, 79) and into the wilds. Similar to Mary Austin's use of the legendary past to suggest an antecedent way of knowing that must be reexperienced if humanity is to imagine/create a more salutary version of human existence, Strieber instructively returns his survivors to primitive conditions, in which humanity is "shown [its] place" (78). Among the wolves in the wilderness the "rebelliousness" of the human survivors is "vanquished" (Strieber 78), leaving them (like Alan in Austin's book) more receptive to the guidance of instinct, as represented by the pack leader.

To be led away from civilization and deep into nature, *Wolf of Shadows* suggests, would provide humanity with an opportunity to recover some understanding that is presently close to being fatally lost. Such an understanding is vital to human survival. Through a more intimate relationship with nature, humanity could ideally discover an abiding regenerative principle, "the urgency of life to be reborn" (Strieber 80). Then, too, humanity might better appreciate the degree to which any particular manifestation of human existence is merely one dream version among alternative possibilities, some of which are distinctly preferable to the present nuclear variant. Because of the regenerative capacity of nature, it is possible "to awaken . . . from the dream of death," the present existence threatened by nuclear destruction, to "a dream of snuffling in green ferns" (Strieber 94, 96). In short, humanity can live closer to paradise, to the elusive stillpoint of nature, than it does at present.

Just as Mary Austin uses Paiute myth and George uses Eskimo myth to embody this message about the mutability of what we think of as reality, Strieber uses Native American voices, each presented as an epigram to the four divisions of *Wolf of Shadows*, to assist his Romantic allegory of humanity's need to rediscover its natural origins. The first of these voices, Chief Luther Standing Bear, is most revelatory of Strieber's design: "The old Lakota was wise. He knew that man's heart away from nature becomes hard; he knew that lack of respect for living, growing things soon led to lack of respect for humans too" (3). In the context of Strieber's tale this observation becomes a prophecy. It implies that the nuclear holocaust world in the story is the likely outcome for the reader's world if the human heart continues to harden in relation to nature and to humanity itself. Chief Luther Standing Bear should know, for what happened to his people was a significant stage in the development of the human disaffection from nature that results in the destroyed world depicted in *Wolf of Shadows*. Humanity vitally needs to reconnect to nature's nurture, and so the wolves (as representatives of nature) lead the mother and her children "away from people" (Strieber 79). At the symbolic end of the story, "wolves and humans twined close" as "the little clutch of creatures sought one another" (Strieber 102–3).

Strieber, like George, has some trouble managing his Romantic themes. Unlike George, he gives the wolves certain cognitive capacities designed to justify to the reader the need for the hierarchical and violent behavior of the pack. These features, which conflict with his attempt to revise his reader's acceptance of humanity's sense of superiority of place and humanity's acts of violence toward nature and itself as a species, are far less successful than George's related sleight of hand in having Miyax reassuringly inform the reader that the wolves attack only "the old and sick" (40). Strieber even has the pack leader mimic Native American ritual in giving thanks to his life-sustaining "gift of the hunt" (42). But even these shortcomings, viewed in terms of the design of *Wolf of Shadows*, reinforce Strieber's point (like Austin's and George's) that conventional notions about relationships between humans and animals (nature) are insufficiently totemic. Just as the mother and her family learn to depend on the leader of the wolf pack, so too humanity should surrender its ideological self-construction as the dominant life form. To recover a relationship with nature requires cooperation with nature, including an acknowledgment of an equality of value and place among living creatures.

In *Wolf of Shadows* the remnant of humanity—all females, significantly—is potentially headed toward such a recovery. Strieber shares Austin's belief in this potentiality to dream a different version of existence, to live closer to the elusive regenerative core of nature. To do so, for both Strieber and Austin, requires the reclamation of a Wordsworthian intuitive "first knowing" that, in the Romantic terms informing their works, is utterly crucial if humanity is to discover a more elevated and healthy human identity. George may point to the loss of this understanding, but the poignant nostalgia of her novel in effect conveys the same wish as Austin and Strieber: that something of this primal knowing be restored and revered, even as at the end of her story Julie regards her totem of Amaroq. "Patience with the ways of nature" is Kapugen's advice to his daughter (George 8), and it is George's, Strieber's, and Austin's Romantic recommendation, too, as the first step in humanity's recovery of a vital connection to nature. As Gary Snyder similarly observes, "We should be patient, and give the land a lot of time to tell us" about its sacredness (96).

WORKS CITED

Abrams, M. H. *Natural Supernaturalism: Tradition and Revolution in Romantic Literature*. New York: Norton, 1971.

Allison, Alexander W., et al., eds. *The Norton Anthology of Poetry*. New York: Norton, 1983.

Ammons, Elizabeth. *Conflicting Stories: American Women Writers at the Turn into the Twentieth Century*. New York: Oxford UP, 1991.

Austin, Mary. *The Basket Woman: A Book of Indian Tales for Children*. Boston: Houghton Mifflin, 1910.

———. *Earth Horizon*. New York: Literary Guild, 1932.

Bell, Michael Davitt. *The Development of American Romance*. Chicago: U of Chicago P, 1980.

Berkhofer, Robert F., Jr., *The White Man's Indian: Images of the American Indian from Columbus to the Present*. New York: Knopf, 1978.

Bixler, Phyllis. "Gardens, Houses, and Nurturant Power in *The Secret Garden*." *Romanticism and Children's Literature in Nineteenth-Century England*. Ed. James Holt McGavran, Jr. Athens: U of Georgia P, 1991. 208–24.

Brisman, Leslie. *Romantic Origins*. Ithaca: Cornell UP, 1978.

Cooper, Andrew M. *Doubt and Identity in Romantic Poetry*. New Haven: Yale UP, 1988.

Emerson, Ralph Waldo. *The Complete Works of Ralph Waldo Emerson*. Boston: Houghton Mifflin, 1903–4. 12 vols.

Farrell, John P. *Revolution as Tragedy: The Dilemma of the Moderate from Scott to Arnold*. Ithaca: Cornell UP, 1980.

Gardner, John. *On Moral Fiction*. New York: Basic Books, 1978.

George, Jean Craighead. *Julie of the Wolves*. New York: Harper and Row, 1972.

Graulich, Melody, ed. *Western Trails: A Collection of Short Stories by Mary Austin*. Reno: U of Nevada P, 1987.

Hoyer, Mark T. "Prophecy of the New West: Mary Austin and the Ghost Dance Religion." *Western American Literature* 30 (1995): 235–55.

———. "Weaving the Story: Northern Paiute Myth and Mary Austin's *The Basket Woman*." *American Indian Culture and Research Journal* 19 (1995): 133–51.

Jewett, Sarah Orne. *The Best Stories of Sarah Orne Jewett*. Ed. Willa Cather. Boston: Houghton Mifflin, 1923. 2 vols.

Karell, Linda K. "*Lost Borders* and Blurred Boundaries: Mary Austin as Storyteller." *American Women Short Story Writers: A Collection of Critical Essays*. Ed. Julie Brown. New York: Garland P, 1995. 153–66.

McGavran, James Holt, Jr., ed. *Romanticism and Children's Literature in Nineteenth-Century England*. Athens: U of Georgia P, 1991.

Moss, Anita. "E. Nesbit's Romantic Child in Modern Dress." *Romanticism and Children's Literature in Nineteenth-Century England*. Ed. James Holt McGavran, Jr. Athens: U of Georgia P, 1991. 225–47.

Myers, Mitzi. "Romancing the Moral Tale: Maria Edgeworth and the Problematics of Pedagogy." *Romanticism and Children's Literature in Nineteenth-Century England*. Ed. James Holt McGavran, Jr. Athens: U of Georgia P, 1991. 96–128.

O'Grady, John P. *Pilgrims to the Wild: Everett Ruess, Henry David Thoreau, John Muir, Clarence King, and Mary Austin*. Salt Lake City: U of Utah P, 1993.

Pearce, T. M. *The Beloved House*. Caldwell, ID: Caxton, 1940.

———, ed. *Literary America 1903–1934: The Mary Austin Letters*. Westport, CT: Greenwood P, 1979.

Scheick, William J. "The Angelic Artistry of Margaret Fuller's *Woman in the Nineteenth Century.*" *Essays in Literature* 11 (1984): 293–98.

———. *The Ethos of Romance at the Turn of the Century*. Austin: U of Texas P, 1994.

Shelley, Percy Bysshe. *Shelley's Poetry and Prose*. Ed. Donald H. Reiman and Sharon B. Powers. New York: Norton, 1977.

Shepard, Paul. *Thinking Animals: Animals and the Development of Human Intelligence*. New York: Viking, 1978.

Smith, Henry. "The Feel of the Purposeful Earth: Mary Austin's Prophecy." *New Mexico Quarterly* 1 (1931): 17–33.

Snyder, Gary. *The Practice of the Wild: Essays*. San Francisco: North Point P, 1990.

Stineman, Esther Lanigan. *Mary Austin: Song of a Maverick*. New Haven: Yale UP, 1989.

Strieber, Whitley. *Wolf of Shadows*. New York: Knopf, 1985.

Thoreau, Henry David. *Walden and Civil Disobedience*. Ed. Owen Thomas. New York: W. W. Norton, 1966.

Veeder, William. *Mary Shelley and Frankenstein: The Fate of Androgyny*. Chicago: U of Chicago P, 1986.

Wilson, James D. *The Romantic Heroic Ideal*. Baton Rouge: Louisiana State UP, 1982.

Wright, Chauncey. "The Evolution of Self-Consciousness." 1873. *American Thought: Civil War to World War I*. Ed. Perry Miller. New York: Holt, Rinehart and Winston, 1954. 27–45.

Teya Rosenberg

ROMANTICISM AND ARCHETYPES IN RUTH NICHOLS'S *SONG OF THE PEARL*

eter Hollindale suggests that "since 1970 a highly intelligent and demanding literature has emerged which speaks with particular directness to the young adult mind" (86). He calls this literature "the adolescent novel of ideas" and, borrowing a phrase from Betsy Hearne, says that such novels "grow the mind a size larger" (86). *Song of the Pearl* (1976), by Ruth Nichols, certainly deserves to be included in this category. An intricately plotted novel, *Song of the Pearl* has the added complexity of dealing with sophisticated matters of death and eschatology as well as drawing upon a variety of philosophies and theologies to create setting, characters, and themes. It is a complex and intellectually challenging novel that Nichols herself has said probably has as its audience adults or "precocious adolescents" ("Ruth Nichols: An Interview" 3).

The main character of *Song of the Pearl*, Margaret Redmond, dies at the end of the first chapter after remembering her short life in nineteenth-century Toronto, a life affected by her debilitating asthma, her rape by her uncle, and her continuing sense that she has been somehow responsible for the unfortunate nature of her life. The remainder of the novel traces her experiences after her death as she undergoes a journey toward self-understanding and healing. Ultimately, Margaret realizes that the events of her most immediate past life are the result of actions she took in an incarnation thousands of years before as a young Sumerian prince, Tirigan. In succeeding lives, some of which she remembers during her journey, she has repeated those actions or been living out the effects of them. The journey depicted in *Song of the Pearl* is crucial for Margaret, a time when she must come to some understanding of herself if she is to grow beyond a sort of perpetual adolescence.

I first read the novel as an adolescent, and, although it intrigued me, I did not really understand it. It was not until I read interviews with Nichols, in which she discusses fantasy's affiliations with Romanticism, and then read M. H. Abrams's *Natural Supernaturalism* that the novel's ideas began to make more sense. My understanding developed further after I became familiar with Jung's writings about archetypes and the process of individuation. Finally, I became aware of shortcomings in the novel as I encountered feminist critiques of archetypal criticism. Achieving an understanding of the novel in the light of these theories worked in two ways: I understood the novel because of the theories I was learning, but I could understand the theories because I had a specific example to which to apply them. Thus, *Song of the Pearl* served to grow my mind larger by encouraging me to ask questions and by providing a frame in which to understand the answers. It has also served as a template upon which to understand the very process of interpretation.

Interpretation of *Song of the Pearl* begins with acknowledging the effect of genre. The obvious archetypal elements in the novel are partially a result of Nichols's choices of expression but also of the form of fantasy, which lends itself to such expression. Myth is the cornerstone of the genre and of Abrams's and Jung's theories: fantasy uses both content and structure of myth. Abrams traces the biblical myth and typology as revised by Romantics, and Jung draws many of his ideas and examples from myth. Archetypal interpretation, however, tends to downplay the significance of some of the more disturbing elements of *Song of the Pearl*, elements that have particularly strong sociological resonance, such as the responsibility of the victim for her victimization and the seeming acceptance of the role of women as submissive. Thus, although I find Abrams's and Jung's theories useful for understanding *Song of the Pearl*, I am also aware of some drawbacks to using such theory, drawbacks I will touch on as I examine Nichols's use of reconstituted theology, the affinities of Margaret's journey to Abrams's Romantic hero's journey and to Jung's process of individuation, particularly in the use of archetypal characters and of motifs from the occult, and finally, the weaknesses of the novel that correspond to feminist critiques of archetypal interpretation. Abrams's theories of Romanticism provide a beginning point with which to explore both the complexities of *Song of the Pearl* and the strengths and weaknesses of archetypal theories.

The first connection to examine is Nichols's views of fantasy expressed in a number of interviews and articles which support the connection between *Song of the Pearl* and *Natural Supernaturalism*, in particular, Abrams's theory of reconstituted theology.[1] One of Abrams's chief points is that "characteristic concepts and patterns of Romantic philosophy and literature are displaced and reconstituted theology, or else a secularized form of devotional experience" (65). Abrams's term "reconstituted theology" suggests that those feelings are reperceived and presented anew, a process Nichols recognizes: "[modern fantasy] is an attempt to recover certain values, values which have not been taken with full seriousness in the West since before the rise of rationalism and of scientific materialism" ("Fantasy and Escapism" 21). Although I would argue that the values Nichols wants to "recover" have not been lost and that the better word is "reconstitute," this comment states Nichols's view of the role of fantasy as well as her close connection with a part of Romantic tradition, a connection she herself acknowledges: "If I am arguing the worth of fantasy, I am also arguing the worth of Romanticism" ("Fantasy and Escapism" 23). For Nichols, the importance of Romanticism lies in its attempt to find spiritual and moral meaning in a world which has largely accepted what she calls "Rationalist Materialism," a view of reality in which "moral values are a sophisticated rationalization of elemental drives like hunger, sex, and the herd-instinct" and in which "human suffering is meaningless" ("Fantasy and Escapism" 24). In opposition to this view of the world, Nichols proposes the Romantic worldview, which she identifies as being "very close to the religious world-view" ("Fantasy and Escapism" 24). In that view, "human values—courage, love, nobility, compassion—represent a direct participation in the numinous reality which is the basis of our own being" ("Fantasy and Escapism" 23). Nichols's definition of "human values" bears a striking resemblance to Abrams's description of Romantic "humane values": "life, love, liberty, hope, and joy" (431). Of course, Abrams and Nichols discuss one type or vision of Romanticism; critics have pointed out for some time that there are Romanticisms, plural.

Viewing *Song of the Pearl* as providing "reconstituted theology" depends on understanding how Nichols "reconstitutes" theology. The basic premise of the afterlife's existence creates a religious framework, but Nichols's portrayal of the afterlife secularizes that framework. Margaret Redmond's death as the starting point of her journey reinforces the religious and spiritual nature of the story. Figurative deaths, such as Bilbo's loss of consciousness after fighting and killing the spider in Mirkwood (Tolkien 152), often appear in children's literature to represent the protagonist passing from one stage of growth to another. Actual physical death, followed by experiences in the afterlife, is rarer, occurring in only a handful of fantasies since George MacDonald's "The Golden Key." The physical death of the protagonist at the beginning of the novel places Margaret's journey in the realm of the metaphysical, a realm that in previous centuries was the territory of religious assurance. Religion itself may well have developed from attempts to come to terms with death. As David Stannard points out in *The Puritan Way of Dying*, it is "the limited knowledge that men necessarily have of [death] that Malinowski and other early anthropologists saw as the primary source of religion" (4). Certainly, the religious nature of *Song of the Pearl* is clear in its vision of death as productive, which counters the common twentieth-century view of it as destructive, and in its proposal that death leads to another life, which remedies the twentieth-century lack of religious assurance about immortality. Such reassurance is, of course, rooted in centuries of religious belief, but the Romantic element of this reassurance lies in the ways in which Nichols revisions the nature and purpose of the metaphysical realm.

The depiction of the afterlife in the novel draws on many different religions but espouses none in particular and blurs the lines between different religions and beliefs. Thus, it proposes that all religions are expressions of what Nichols calls "the numinous reality" ("Fantasy and Escapism" 23). The multiplicity begins with the book's epigraph from an apocryphal Christian gospel and continues with the different people and places Margaret encounters. Margaret travels through Heaven, which most readers in Western society automatically associate with the Christian idealized afterlife; in *Song of the Pearl*, the many references to Chinese literature and culture indicate that this Heaven belongs more to the Chinese traditional Heaven, which is a pagan otherworld or fairyland. Heaven in *Song of the Pearl*, however, has no single cultural affiliation but is what each individual makes it. Margaret's Heaven consists of a small pavilion on a lake hidden in the mountains, a Renaissance English village, and an Iroquois village, whereas that of her guide, Paul, is a Chinese family estate, the Compound, which Margaret visits. The people she meets include Paul, a Chinese man, and his relatives: the Matriarch, Phoenix, Hope, and Compassion Jade. She also meets Meri-ka-ra, an Egyptian priest, and Inanna, a Sumerian goddess. All these people have embraced different religions during different incarnations, yet they all return to Heaven, although they shape their immediate surroundings differently. This multiplicity allows Nichols to portray Margaret's journey as transcultural and transhistorical. She has belonged to many cultures at many times, but her essential self remains the same. Such a portrayal certainly connects with Jungian theory of the self and serves to emphasize the magnitude and importance of Margaret's growth during this particular journey as she struggles to overcome problems thousands of years in the making. As Nichols points out in an interview, "The whole point of *Song of the Pearl* was that it took Margaret about seven thousand years to recognize that she had actually constructed the events that victimized her in life after life" (Stott, "Nature of Fantasy" 42).

The use of multiple sources to create the transcultural nature of *Song of the Pearl* continues with another premise of the story: Margaret has lived many lives. In order to create multiple lives across many centuries for Margaret, Nichols draws upon the traditionally Eastern belief of reincarnation, the belief that souls assume differing bodily forms over time. Reincarnation is usually associated with Hinduism and Buddhism, but Nichols alters the doctrine to suit the purpose of her novel. There are many schools of thought about and many interpretations of reincarnation within Hinduism and Buddhism, so general statements are problematic, but some elements of the doctrine do not allow for *Song of the Pearl's* focus on self-knowledge. As David Christie-Murray points out in *Reincarnation: Ancient Beliefs and Modern Evidence* (1981), neither Hinduism nor Buddhism clearly states that the personality developed in one incarnation continues as an independent, self-aware unit: "whereas [Hinduism] postulates an eternal individual self, the *atman*, to which the illusory separate individuals that are incarnated relate, [Buddhism] denies the existence of a permanent self or soul that transmigrates from life to life" (41).[2] While the Hindu *atman* may sound like an independent, continuous self, the "illusory" nature of individual incarnations indicates that those incarnations are not significant personalities in their own right.

In *Song of the Pearl*, the characters have continuing self-aware personalities; thus, Nichols changes Eastern beliefs so that Margaret can remember past lives and thereby achieve an understanding of her actions in the past and of how those actions affect her present and future. This modification creates the spiral nature of Margaret's development, the constant revisiting of the past and attempts to learn from it, connecting her journey to Abrams's description of the Romantic hero's journey. The revised presentation of the doctrine of reincarnation is not unique to Nichols. Such revisions are apparent in a number of nineteenth- and twentieth-century Western movements such as theosophy, anthroposophy, and spiritualism which modify the doctrine to focus more clearly on the individual personality and the cycle of reincarnation as a cycle of growth and learning (Christie-Murray 69–93). Such movements were undoubtedly influenced by Romantic attention to the development of the self. A further modification exists in the fact that events from her past life affect Margaret's current life, a fact that suggests the existence of karma, the belief that what souls do in one life can affect the quality of the next life. Because, traditionally, people cannot remember their past lives, karma may seem a sort of predestination that negates the purpose or meaning of any sort of growth (Christie-Murray 43). Margaret's ability, finally, to remember her many past lives subverts the possibility of predestination and thus emphasizes individual responsibility.

Thus, Nichols draws upon elements of established religious doctrine to support secularized beliefs about individual development. She fulfills the need to emphasize growth as ongoing by portraying development taking place over many lives but, in so doing, connects with a problem Edward Said identifies in *Orientalism* (1978). As Said points out, "a very influential Romantic idea" was that "it was Indian culture and religion that could defeat the materialism and mechanism (and republicanism) of Occidental culture," allowing that culture to regenerate (115). His point is that the Romantics were not interested so much in Asia as in "Asia's *use to* modern Europe" (Said 115). In *Song of the Pearl*, Nichols's attention to details of setting and custom in the Compound demonstrates a fascination with Chinese-Oriental customs of the seventeenth century, but she does continue that Romantic tradition of using Asian theology that Said protests. Thus, although Nichols's aim of using fantasy to recover or reconstitute theology does create a productive, and thus reassuring, vision of death and the afterlife, the way in which she accomplishes that aim is problematic. [3]

The reconstituted theology is one parallel between Abrams's theory of Romanticism and *Song of the Pearl*; a second parallel is the concentration upon the development of a unified and aware self. A large portion of the novel is devoted to Margaret's torturous journey to understand herself. As the title and the central image of the pearl suggest, much of the novel is symbolic or allegorical.[4] There are many descriptions, and Margaret has many experiences and encounters that seem, on initial readings, cryptic and confusing. I have found that starting with Abrams's idea of the Romantic hero's pilgrimage as a beginning point of understanding Margaret's journey is helpful, but the Jungian theory of individuation and the steps of that process have helped me better understand the significance of many elements of the novel.

Song of the Pearl portrays the necessity for spiritual and psychological self-development that leads to the "human values" Nichols lists. The focus corresponds directly to Anne K. Mellor's description of masculine Romanticism, a description that addresses Abrams's ideas in *Natural Supernaturalism*. Romanticism, she says, "has traditionally been identified with the association of a self that is unified, unique, enduring, capable of initiating activity, and above all aware of itself as a self" (Mellor 145). It is important to note that Mellor does not feel that masculine or feminine ideas of the self belong to men or women, respectively, but are "different modes of subjectivity that can be shared by males and females alike" (168). Although Nichols and her character, Margaret, are women, *Song of the Pearl* belongs to this masculine tradition of Romanticism rather than to a feminine Romanticism.

In *Song of the Pearl*, Nichols uses elements of reincarnation and the image of the pearl to present Margaret's journey through the layers of herself to find her inner "seed" (66), the self that expresses the important "human values" and has divine potential. Margaret's overall, multilife journey of development, as she circles between Heaven and Earth, has the capacity to be either an ironic circle, in which she continues to repeat the same mistakes and not grow, or a successful upward spiral, in which she realizes her inner potential. Abrams describes the Romantic hero's journey as "an education in experience through stages of awareness which culminate on the level of intellectual maturity—a stage of integrity, power, and freedom in which the protagonist finally learns who he is, what he was born for, and the implicit purpose of all that he has endured on the way" (193–94). The successful spiral Margaret achieves by the end of *Song of the Pearl* as she leaves Heaven to return to Earth is part of a continuous process of education that will eventually lead to immortality and divinity. The novel clearly proposes a purpose to life, and that proposal corresponds directly with the spiral pattern of self-development outlined by Abrams. As Abrams implies and Nichols states, that development is moral as well as spiritual. In discussing the self, in discussing development as moral, and in the sense of teleology inherent in the process of development, Abrams and Nichols have much in common with Jung's ideas of psychic development.

The interconnections are hardly surprising, since Romantic thought and writing affected Jung's theories, a point he himself acknowledges (*Symbolic Life* 771, 774–75). Martin Bickman, in *American Romantic Psychology*, discusses Jung's thought as "largely determined by intellectual and artistic currents in Jung's background and time, currents that in the broader sense can be called Romantic" (xii). For Bickman, such association contextualizes and historicizes Jung's ideas, providing a balance for the claims of the "universal, transhistorical patterns" (xii) that Jungian psychology makes and that are under attack today for their seeming lack of recognition of the influence of society and culture on individuals.

As Estella Lauter and Carol Schreier Rupprecht point out in *Feminist Archetypal Theory*, archetypal interpretation can be essentialist (5–6), but they regard such essentialism as arising from the practitioners of the theory rather than the theory itself. In the feminist process of revisioning archetypal theory, there is "a reluctance to regard the archetype as absolute or transcendent . . . [but] the concept of the archetype remains useful even when it is removed from the essentialist (Platonic) context from which it was originally formulated" (Lauter and Rupprecht 13). Thus, a critic such as Annis Pratt suggests a series of archetypes more clearly representative of the patterns that appear in women's writing than do those originally associated with archetypal theories such as Jung's or, to take a more literary example, Northrop Frye's. In the case of Nichols's writing, one might think that Pratt's archetypes of enclosure, escape, the green world, and the green world lover, which she perceives in women's fiction, would be useful because Nichols is a woman. However, just as Mellor's ideas of feminine Romanticism do not apply to *Song of the Pearl*, neither do Pratt's patterns. While Margaret is caught for some time in a pattern of self-loathing that arises from her transgression of feminine norms (Pratt, *Archetypal Patterns* 75), few of Pratt's patterns are present. This lack of conformity to Pratt's archetypes supports the point Pratt and other feminist archetypal critics make: the patterns are not absolute.

In *Song of the Pearl*, Margaret's journey to self-knowledge follows a clear pattern, one that corresponds in many ways to stages of Jung's pattern of individuation, though it does not include all that Jung outlines. Although Nichols says in "An Interview with Ruth Nichols" that she is not a Jungian, later in the interview she acknowledges that she "was drawing on those [archetypal symbols Jung discusses,] unaware" that she was doing so (Stott 8, 10). While journeying in the afterlife, Margaret is essentially exploring her unconscious and encountering her shadow. Although Jung suggests that encountering the shadow occurs in middle age, Ursula Le Guin points out that "when in pre-adolescence and adolescence the conscious sense of self emerges . . . the shadow darkens right with it" (65). Margaret has lived many lives on Earth, but her continuing self is caught in a stage at which it needs to recognize and acknowledge its darker side. In her incarnation as Margaret, her growth on Earth ceases completely when she is still an adolescent, a condition that indicates the stasis of her larger development. Her feeling that, because her pain is so great, "so . . . must her evil and her unworthiness to be loved" (Nichols, *Pearl* 13), darkens her short life. She senses the presence of her shadow but cannot yet identify it. She does not know the source of this unease, and, until she does, she cannot grow or achieve any sort of integration, either within herself or with the society surrounding her.

Nichols uses reincarnation to concretize the encounter with the suppressed elements of the psyche. Margaret cannot recognize her shadow because she cannot remember her past lives. Once she does begin remembering, the painful process that occupies most of this story, then she can encounter and integrate her shadow. As Nichols says, "the story of growing up . . . is the story of recognizing one's own proper power, recognizing that power inside one is innate and that if one denies its existence it will not be made nonexistent but will merely destroy others" (Stott, "Interview" 15). This statement owes a great deal to Romantic thought about the inner self, and it also recalls Jung's warning that "it is dangerous to suppress [the unconscious] because [it] is life . . . and turns against us if suppressed" (*Archetypes* 288). Margaret suppresses memories of her past, part of her unconscious and her shadow self, and that suppression results in an abuse of her inner power. She projects that abuse outward as a hatred of others and also turns it inward in self-hatred. Before she can mature, Margaret has to recognize her projection of her shadow upon others and come to terms with the power that shadow possesses. She can only do so by becoming aware of the contents of her unconscious and coming to terms with her inner self.

In Jung's theory of individuation, the process of encountering archetypes such as the shadow takes place in the unconscious, and people are only aware of it as a change or sense of unease and have access to that process chiefly through analysis of their dreams. Heaven in *Song of the Pearl* is clearly connected to dreams and the unconscious. Margaret's first stop in Heaven is a pavilion on a small island in the middle of a ring of mountains. She traces her initial sense of the familiarity of the place to her dreams (Nichols, *Song* 17, 18). Paul, her guide and mentor, calls Heaven "the land of dreams . . . where imagination at once becomes reality" (Nichols, *Song* 32). In the Jungian schema, dreams are thought to be the conscious manifestations of the unconscious (Jung, *Structure and Dynamics* 77). Furthermore, Margaret is unsure whether Heaven is not, in some way, her own creation, which adds to the sense of Heaven as the realm of the unconscious. If she has created it, "the process had not been conscious" (Nichols, *Song* 37), which is entirely the point: Margaret is in the realm that, from the perspective of the living, is the realm of the unconscious. That realm must be consciously acknowledged, for such acknowledgment is a necessary part of growth, as the epigraph that opens the novel asserts: "*the Kingdom is both outside you and within you. And whosoever* knows himself *shall find it*" (Nichols, *Song* n.p.). During Margaret's journey, the incidents and encounters that occur force her to explore her past, but they also represent necessary psychological moments that lead to her spiritual and psychological growth.

Song of the Pearl's Heaven certainly has this Jungian interpretation, but it can be understood in Romantic terms also. The emphasis upon Heaven as the unconscious connects with a Romantic idea of the divine as immanent rather than as transcendent, as Abrams notes (91) and as Northrop Frye discusses in "The Drunken Boat": "the metaphorical structure of Romantic poetry tends to move inside and downward instead of outside and upward, hence the creative world is deep within, and so is heaven or the place of the presence of God" (16). Heaven in *Song of the Pearl* is simultaneously an external place of journeying and an inner place of exploration, and as such it is Romantic.

As well as the references to dreams and the unconscious, a central motif of the novel—images and ideas of the occult in general and of the Tarot in particular—further supports Heaven as the realm of the unconscious and Margaret's journey as that of individuation. The motif works on the level of plot to provide Margaret with clues to the ultimate purpose of her journey, but it also works to support the Jungian interpretation of her process. Again, the connection to Romanticism is a matter of shared interests and of Jung's own historical context. Nichols makes specific reference to Giordano Bruno (*Song* 75), and many of the occult references can be tied to Gnostic and Hermetic traditions, traditions that Abrams notes as influential in Germanic and English Romanticism (169–72). References to the occult occur early in the novel with mentions of Tarot cards, but the motif becomes strongest during the second stage of Margaret's journey, when she leaves the limitations of the isolated pavilion in the mountains and seeks the Oracle, someone or something that "will instruct [her]" (Nichols, *Song* 34). When she finds it, the elements of the setting establish a connection with the occult. Richard Cavendish, in *A History of Magic* (1977), writes that the Jungian journey of individuation "is directly related to the magical concept of the true self and the principle of the harmonious synthesis of opposites" (162) upon which occult philosophy is based. Within the place of the Oracle, Margaret finds a circular room with a white marble floor, marked by a black pentagram in the center (Nichols, *Song* 59–60). According to Lewis Spence in *An Encyclopedia of Occultism* (1960), modern occultists interpret the pentagram "as symbolic of the human soul and its relation to God" (262). The ascendant point of the pentagram represents a struggle upward. In Margaret's case, her struggle is to a higher plane of existence, one that unites the conscious and unconscious. The room physically represents her struggle and thus herself. Next to the pentagram is a mummified hand nailed to a post (Nichols, *Song* 60) that Margaret afterward identifies as the Hand of Glory, another symbol from the occult. Thought to have powerful magical properties (Leach and Fried 477), it represents, from a psychological point of view, the power of the unconscious. Margaret thinks that by clasping the hand, perhaps "all her questions would be answered . . . deeper questions, as yet hardly acknowledged, would be laid to rest" (Nichols, *Song* 60). Her questions are answered, but just as the "hardly acknowledged" questions are obscure to her, so is the Oracle's answer. It puts to rest only Margaret's sense that she can quickly end her journey. A surge of power transfixes her before she can touch the hand, and the voice of the Oracle speaks through her:

> "Stay where you stand!
> For the Hanged One's hand
> Alone may grasp the Hanged One's land."
> (Nichols, *Song* 60)

That the voice speaks through her reinforces the idea that Margaret encounters her own unconscious, something she later realizes for herself: "The Power of the Oracle . . . was in some way herself; but a self so ancient it was not yet human in her terms. It was a well of vitality from which she drank in her deepest sleep" (Nichols, *Song* 131), a very apt description of the Jungian collective unconscious.

The reference in the verse to the Hanged One further reinforces that Margaret's journey is through the unconscious, but it also contributes to the reconstituted theology of the novel. The Hanged One, or the Hanged Man, is a card in the Tarot. Throughout the novel there are a number of references and images that can be connected to the Tarot, creating a motif that helps unify Margaret's various experiences. The images used in Tarot are highly archetypal, and Jung sees them as "descended from the archetypes of transformation" (*Archetypes* 38). According to Margaret's uncle, the Hanged Man is "the symbol of revolution," the person who has the "courage to fall out of time" (Nichols, *Song* 131) and face chaos. Thus, the Hanged Man represents "the deepest spiritual endeavour and the highest triumph" (Nichols, *Song* 132). Fred Gettings, in *The Book of Tarot*, says, "On an ordinary level, we must read the significance of the card as relating to an inner crisis that needs an inner decision; . . . on a higher level of interpretation we may regard the Hanging Man as a sublime statement of cosmic truth, that man must die to be reborn on a higher plane" (71). To understand herself at her deepest levels, Margaret must become like the Hanged Man; she "must let go . . . of time, . . . of the comforts of intellect" (Nichols, *Song* 132) and search her memory, trusting her inner self to provide the answers, which she does at the end of her journey.

The importance of the Tarot to the novel is clear in the many other references that create this key motif throughout the story.

Meri-ka-ra, one of Margaret's guides, in his role as the Sun Priest, invokes another connection, the nineteenth card of the Major Arcana, the Sun. It is often interpreted as representing rebirth, especially spiritual rebirth (Gettings 100; Walker 127), and Meri-ka-ra oversees Margaret's ultimate memory journey, in which she remembers her life as Tirigan, the Sumerian prince. Also, the chair Margaret sits in during her final memory journey has lions carved on the end of the arms; these lions are mentioned a number of times (Nichols, *Song* 127, 131, 142), and they recall the eleventh Major Arcana card, Strength, which depicts a woman struggling with a lion and represents the endeavor to integrate the conscious and unconscious (Gettings 65–66; Walker 100). Inanna, who has watched over Margaret since before she was Tirigan, is also the evening star and, as such, connects with the seventeenth card of the Major Arcana, the Star. The card signifies inspiration and creativity (Gettings 89) or renewal of life (Walker 120), all elements Inanna brings to Margaret.

Not all of these connections are equally convincing because the symbolism is not exclusive to the Tarot, and so it is possible to argue, for example, that the connection between Inanna and the Tarot card the Star is coincidental. Stars are common symbols of guidance and of new beginnings. However, the Tarot is highlighted at the beginning of *Song of the Pearl* by Margaret's uncle's fascination with it (Nichols 9), and it plays an important role in Margaret's crucial encounter with herself, so its significance within the novel cannot easily be dismissed. As well, the Tarot is a system of divination in which the unconscious of the person using the cards endows them with meaning (Watson 344). The allusions to the Tarot, however slight some may be, support Margaret's process of encountering her unconscious. Furthermore, as a system of spiritual guidance, it is an alternative to traditional Christian forms and contributes to the multiple spiritual systems creating both the afterlife and the spiritual nature of the journey in *Song of the Pearl*.

The first half of *Song of the Pearl* establishes that Heaven is the realm of the unconscious. As well, it works very like a suspense novel, hinting at the mysteries of Margaret's past and her need to recover those memories she cannot or will not recall. The second half begins to answer the questions, to explain the mysteries, and in this latter half, the significance of Margaret's encounters with various characters becomes clearest when those characters are viewed as archetypes. The characters tend not to be developed in any depth; they are quickly sketched, and their chief importance lies in how they affect Margaret. There are a number of such characters: the Matriarch, Paul's grandmother and the ruler of the Compound, is one. Her title alone, *the* Matriarch, encourages an archetypal reading. The Matriarch embodies the Jungian mother archetype in both its aspects, the nurturing mother and the devouring mother, and as such she pushes Margaret to the next stage of growth, as that archetype frequently does in Jung's schema. Another is Meri-ka-ra, the Egyptian priest who pushes Margaret to take her final memory journey. The descriptions of him and his actions correspond to the Jungian wise old man. Both of these characters, Margaret eventually realizes, are actually the same person in different guises: they are both Inanna, the final character Margaret encounters in Heaven.

Inanna is a Sumerian goddess and guide of Margaret's journey from Tirigan to her present situation, and she corresponds to the Jungian archetype of the self. According to Jung, the self is the archetype of wholeness that unites the conscious and the unconscious (*Archetypes* 187) and is the final archetype encountered and accepted in the process of individuation. It, in a sense, encompasses and includes all the archetypes of the psyche, much as Inanna in *Song of the Pearl* plays many different roles. Jung notes that frequently a quaternity that unites light and dark, masculine and feminine, identifies the self (*Aion* 64). Inanna, in *Song of the Pearl*, is "both man and woman," and, in her identity as a star (Nichols, *Song* 149, 34), she unites light and dark, shining most brightly in a dark sky. As well, she appears to Margaret and Paul dressed in white with long black hair, thus uniting the two opposing colors. In Sumerian mythology, Inanna makes the descent to the Underworld, which furthers her connection to the self because the "scope of the integration" of the self archetype is, according to Jung, "suggested by the *descensus ad inferos*, the descent of Christ's soul to hell, its work of redemption embracing even the dead. The psychological equivalent of this is the integration of the collective unconscious which forms an essential part of the individuation process" (*Aion* 39). Diane Wolkstein, in *Inanna: Queen of Heaven and Earth* (1983), says Inanna's descent is a way to increase her power: "the Great Below, and the knowledge of death and rebirth, life and stasis, . . . will make . . . Inanna an 'Honoured Counselor' and a guide to the land" (Wolkstein and Kramer 156). Thus, Inanna's descent to and return from the underworld in Sumerian mythology signifies her full individuation in the Jungian interpretation of that mythology, and as such, in *Song of the Pearl*, she functions as an example and a guide for Margaret.

Furthermore, Inanna has been Margaret's guide for a very long time, a point that reinforces the connection to the archetype of the self. Marie Louise von Franz, in *Individuation in Fairy Tales*, notes that "the Self that exists at the very beginning of and generally in the process of individuation is what guides or regulates the process of inner growth" (116). Inanna has been part of Margaret's journey since the start of her larger spiral journey, which began with Tirigan (Nichols, *Song* 141). She was the "Holy Mother" for Zawumatec, an earlier incarnation of Margaret, who tells Margaret/Zawumatec, "You must turn your hate into suffering and your suffering into wisdom" (Nichols, *Song* 55–56). As well, she has been a part of Margaret's smaller journey in Heaven, which began on the island in the mountains when Paul placed Margaret under Inanna's protection (Nichols, *Song* 34, 150). As the Matriarch and Meri-ka-ra, she pushes Margaret farther along on her journey. Thus, there is much in the description and actions of Inanna that encourages seeing her as the important archetype of the self.

The encounter with Inanna reintroduces the connections to Abrams's theory of Romanticism. *Song of the Pearl* suggests that humankind is on a very large journey of individuation, collectively moving from primitive childhood to maturation, just as each person moves individually. This is an idea Jung suggests (*Civilization* 80), but it also has affiliations with Abrams's theory of Romanticism: "the history of mankind, as well as the history of the reflective individual, was conceived . . . as a process of the self-formation, or self-education, of the mind and moral being of man from the dawn of consciousness to the stage of full maturity" (187–88). As well as personifying an archetype within Margaret, Inanna also represents what Margaret can become. Inanna speaks of herself as a goddess, but she emphasizes that she is different from mortals not in kind but in development: "I was a goddess in the eyes of children. Someday my worshippers will understand that I am what they themselves can be" (Nichols, *Song* 150). Inanna assures Margaret and Paul that they have not finished their journeys: "Your story is vaster than you can conceive, and your adventures are just beginning," but they also have the potential to achieve the sort of individuated wholeness she has achieved, for they may well be among the "new gods," guiding "the struggling creatures of new worlds" (Nichols, *Song* 151). Thus, every individual has the potential for immortality and divinity. Continuing to grow and learn is the key to realizing that potential. This progress bears striking resemblance to the Christian pilgrimage, which Abrams sees as the model for the Romantic spiral (192–95).

Another important figure who fulfills an archetypal role in *Song of the Pearl* is Paul, Margaret's companion and guide during her journey in Heaven. He pushes her to confront and understand the mysteries surrounding her, although he is yet another mystery, and, in doing so, he personifies the animus, the archetype that is "a mediator between the conscious and unconscious" (Jung, *Aion* 16). He has knowledge of her most recent incarnation, he has been her lover and husband in past lives (Nichols, *Song* 152), and thus he knows both her conscious and her unconscious. As a personification of her animus, he prods her to "a capacity for reflection, deliberation, and self-knowledge" (Jung, *Aion* 16). He questions her and pushes her to look for answers: "I know you . . . better than you know yourself. And *until* you know yourself, you will not understand my love" (Nichols, *Song* 33). Margaret finally recalls that he was her husband in several lives (Nichols, *Song* 152–53), but their marriages were brief and always ended with his death preceding hers, leaving her to grieve and resent losing him.

Throughout her lives, numerous failed or painful relationships with men represent Margaret's failure as a developing self. As Elizabeth, a woman of Renaissance England, she mourns the death of her first husband and hates her second husband "for his masculine freedom, his use of her, his indifference to her pain" (Nichols, *Song* 50). As Zawumatec, a Mixtec woman kept as a slave by an Iroquois master, she hates her slavery and the man who holds power over her, and yet she feels she deserves that slavery and subjugation (Nichols, *Song* 114). The culmination of these relationships with their unfortunate power dynamics is her life as Margaret and her relationship with her Uncle Matthew. Her uncle rapes her and then abandons her by moving from Canada to England. Margaret both hates and longs for him and, in essence, wills her own death because she cannot forgive herself or him. Ultimately, she realizes that Matthew is the incarnation of Utuhegal, Tirigan's enemy and captor. They have been bound together throughout centuries and many incarnations, embodying continuously the power struggle established in ancient Sumer. She must forgive him and withdraw the curse Tirigan placed upon him before she can continue to develop; that is, she must move beyond the childish control of her shadow.

Understanding the archetypal and Romantic elements of *Song of the Pearl* does help clarify the nature of Margaret's journey and of the characters and events of this complex novel. However, such understanding can allow glossing over troubling elements of the novel. The point of trouble arises often in archetypal interpretations when the symbolic collides with the realistic or sociological in such a way that it becomes difficult or irresponsible to ignore the social implications of the symbolic. For me, this point arises in *Song of the Pearl* with the symbolic uses of rape to represent a dynamic of power, of being a woman to indicate submission and slavery, and of marriage as the sign of successful development. The novel draws upon traditional gender associations and seems not to question them.

To return to the discussion of Margaret's relationship with her uncle, the implication is that Margaret's rape is an act she brought upon herself. Read symbolically, the rape is another realization of the power struggle between Margaret's continuing self, beginning with Tirigan, the Sumerian prince, and her uncle's self, starting with his life as Utuhegal. Rape is the equivalent of Utuhegal placing Tirigan in a "hut made of mud and reeds" (Nichols, *Song* 137) and then taking his life. With the rape, Margaret is imprisoned by her sense of guilt and has her childhood taken from her. The symbolic equations can be made, but the use of rape to represent that power struggle is troubling, particularly in the context of other implications about rape and being female in the story.

The idea that the victim is responsible for the rape is a key point in the story. As Margaret, she feels that she has caused the rape: "She had excited him, and had done it without touching him, without moving. . . . She had known for some time that she could do this. Power—the first she had tasted—enthralled her. Its existence seemed sufficient reason for its use" (Nichols, *Song* 11). Ultimately, in remembering her life as Tirigan, she realizes her tie with her Uncle Matthew is attributable to Tirigan's final actions. When Utuhegal offers Tirigan a poison that will give him a quick death rather than the slow, painful drowning set as Tirigan's sentence, Tirigan rejects this act of compassion. Instead, he pronounces the curse on Utuhegal that will tie them together for centuries: "I will take . . . the death you first decreed. I will consecrate my hate with pain. And I will follow you, I swear before my soul" (Nichols, *Song* 139). As Tirigan says this, his voice is "passionate and intimate, almost the wooing voice of a lover" (Nichols, *Song* 139). Thus, Tirigan establishes the hatred and associated lust that plagues all his succeeding incarnations, manifested in Margaret's life as an incestuous relationship with her uncle.

Reading Margaret's relationship with her uncle archetypally explains the rape, but there is still a nagging discomfort: to what extent is the victim feeling responsible for being raped a culturally constructed effect, one that releases the rapist from responsibility? Nichols may be unconsciously fulfilling the demands of a patriarchal culture, as Annis Pratt suggests many women authors do: "Because gender norms are often unconsciously internalized by women authors, their writings are adulterated to a great degree with patriarchal cultural material" ("Spinning" 158). Pratt's argument, however, does deny the writer control over her creation. Nichols clearly meant to be provocative in opening what is ostensibly an adolescent novel with a rape and a premature death. Margaret's life in nineteenth-century Toronto has to be read through her other lives; the structure of the novel insists upon such reading. The opening prologue, where Margaret's mother and her uncle see her ghostly presence years after her death, indicates that Margaret's afterlife is the focus of the story. Furthermore, in March 1978, Nichols said in an interview with Susan Cooper and Maurice Sendak that "the whole book is about moral responsibility, which is why I think some people dislike it, because we want to blame our parents, we want to blame anything but ourselves. Cooper: That's right. If you're the victim of anything, you're the victim of your own nature, aren't you? Nichols: Absolutely" (Stott, "Nature" 42). All these factors indicate that, in the case of *Song of the Pearl*, Margaret is responsible for her rape, just as she has been responsible, since her life as Tirigan, for her unhappiness.

This point about the symbolic use of rape connects with the use in *Song of the Pearl* of being a woman as signifying entrapment and slavery. The sense throughout the novel is that being a woman is in some way a punishment. Margaret was a man once; because of a mistake in using her power, she spends her subsequent lives as a woman trapped by men and by her body. Paul comments that Margaret's uncle "will know in his own body what it is to be a woman at the mercy of a man" (Nichols, *Song* 144), a comment which seems to reinforce the point that being a female is a sort of punishment. This idea has, of course, its biblical precedent in Eve, and it is a pattern that exists throughout literature. While it reflects traditional beliefs about women and their role in life, it is disturbing because such belief remains largely unchallenged in this novel, despite the focus on Margaret's strength and independence.

The final troubling element that results from the collision between the symbolic and the sociological is the emphasis placed on the male-female union as signifying reward. Upon their reunion after she remembers her life as Tirigan, Margaret and Paul both foresee their meeting and marriage (Nichols, *Song* 154, 152) in their next lives on Earth. And the promise is that this next life will be rich and fulfilling in ways that none of her previous lives have been. So in forgiving the man who subjugated her and in being able to take happy and fruitful part in marriage, Margaret will finally be developing in the appropriate manner. Margaret's identity and happiness, then, are connected with being part of a marriage. In Jungian terms, marriage is symbolic of integration and the achievement of balance between conscious and unconscious realms, and in Romantic terms, according to Abrams, it is a signal of integration, achievement, and successful completion of the journey: "the achievement of the goal is pictured as a scene of recognition and reconciliation, and is often signalized by a loving union with the feminine other, upon which man finds himself thoroughly at home with himself, his milieu, and his family of fellow men" (255). Again, there is biblical precedent, in the Old and New Testaments, which both Jung and Abrams note (Jung, *Archetypes* 175; Abrams 194).

In sociological terms, however, the promise of marriage as the chief indicator of a successful journey and of growth is disturbing because it implies that marriage is the ultimate goal of female development. In this case, the collision between symbolic and sociological readings of a text becomes clearest. In Romantic and in Jungian systems, it should be noted, marriage is envisioned as the masculine element (the conscious, the journeying hero) encompassing and possessing the feminine (the unconscious, the passive lover/wife); such interpretation is based on the traditional role of women within marriage as the acquired rather than the acquiring. Of course, the fact that Margaret is the hero of this story might be considered an overturning of that tradition, but the similarity of Margaret's reward to the endings of so many popular folk tales and romance stories in which women's growth is marked chiefly by achieving marriage is hard to ignore.

These disturbing elements of the novel, around which archetypal readings fail to accommodate sociological concerns, bring me back to considerations of genre: there is much about *Song of the Pearl* that is mythic and encourages interpretation through archetypal theories, and yet there are also elements that are realistic and encourage sociological reading. How then to reconcile these elements of the novel? Perhaps they cannot be reconciled but only acknowledged. Although Pratt's assertion that women writers unknowingly transmit negative elements of the patriarchal culture has its own disturbing implications of passivity, she does supply a useful tip for literary critics and interpreters: "Feminine aspirations, exisiting in dialectical relationship to societal prescriptions against women's development, create textual mixtures of rebellion and repression that can be discerned by careful textual critics" ("Spinning" 101). In endeavoring to be a careful textual critic, I have to be aware of the challenges a text offers. *Song of the Pearl* does require that its readers have the curiosity to pursue its mysteries and accept its suspense. As a fantasy, it makes generic demands of its audience, demands which require a certain theoretical bent, a willingness to read symbolically. The reader who accepts that in literature marriage, for example, can be symbolic of successful development may leave *Song of the Pearl* satisfied. The reader who does not accept such a construct and sees Margaret's future as conditioned by the patriarchal culture of her author will not be satisfied.

The debate does have ramifications for the study of children's and adolescent literature as a whole, particularly fantasy. The Romanticism Abrams outlines, the psychic journey Jung developed, both owe a great deal to myth, as does fantasy. Archetypal criticism, then, with its basis in myth, can be a useful way to examine a fantasy, and, in the case of *Song of the Pearl*, discovering Abrams's discussion of Romanticism became my key to understanding Margaret's development, just as Jung's description of individuation and the archetypes encountered became my key to understanding the supporting characters of the novel. However, feminist awareness makes me very uneasy with the use of rape, of being female, of marriage in *Song of the Pearl* because that use seems to reinforce stereotypes rather than to realize archetypes. Feminist archetypal critics point out that awareness of the limitations of much archetypal theory is key to understanding and countering those limitations, and feminist critiques contribute to becoming aware of the limitations. My understanding of *Song of the Pearl* has its beginnings, however, in encountering and understanding a particular view of Romanticism that is, in essence, an archetypal approach: *Natural Supernaturalism* and its vision of Romanticism provide a useful paradigm by which to examine and achieve an understanding of *Song of the Pearl,* but the novel's complexity demands exploring other theories and ideas and, ultimately, helps to understand the strengths and weaknesses of a number of archetypal theories.

NOTES

1. These articles and interviews date from the time *Song of the Pearl* was written and published and so have bearing on that work, despite the fact that they are now some twenty years old.

2. See also Chennakesavan (32–33, 114); Kalupahana (41).

3. Unless, of course, one does not agree with Said that such use of other cultures is problematic. Using other cultures to define one's own culture or oneself is not solely the prerogative of the Western world. As well, so much of fantasy involves looking to and mining, if you will, other cultures to create the secondary world that it is practically a convention of the genre in the twentieth century. Whether such use is appropriate is another essay entirely.

4. Nichols states, however, that she was not aware of the medieval allegorical poem, *The Pearl*, until after she completed *Song of the Pearl* ("Ruth Nichols: An Interview" 4).

WORKS CITED

Abrams, M. H. *Natural Supernaturalism: Tradition and Revolution in Romantic Literature*. New York: Norton, 1971.

Bickman, Martin. *American Romantic Psychology*. Dallas: Spring Publications, 1988.

Cavendish, Richard. *A History of Magic*. New York: Taplinger, 1977.

Chennakesavan, Saravati. *A Critical Study of Hinduism*. Bombay: Asia, 1974.

Christie-Murray, David. *Reincarnation: Ancient Beliefs and Modern Evidence*. London: David and Charles, 1981.

Filmer, Kath. *Scepticism and Hope in Twentieth-Century Fantasy Literature*. Bowling Green: Bowling Green State U Popular P, 1992.

Frye, Northrop. "The Drunken Boat: The Revolutionary Element in Romanticism." *Romanticism Reconsidered*. Ed. Northrop Frye. New York: Columbia UP, 1963. 1–25.

Gettings, Fred. *The Book of Tarot*. London: Triune, 1973.

Gray, Eden. *The Tarot Revealed*. New York: Bell, 1960.

Hollindale, Peter. "The Adolescent Novel of Ideas." *Children's Literature in Education* 26.1 (1995): 83–95.

Jung, C. G. *Aion: Researches into the Phenomenology of the Self*. Trans. R. F. C. Hull. 2nd ed. Bollingen Series 20. Princeton: Princeton UP, 1967. Vol. 9.2 of *The Collected Works of C. G. Jung*. 20 vols. 1957–79.

———. *The Archetypes and the Collective Unconscious*. Trans. R. F. C. Hull. 2nd ed. Bollingen Series 20. Princeton: Princeton UP, 1968. Vol. 9.1 of *The Collected Works of C. G. Jung*. 20 vols. 1957–79.

———. *Civilization in Transition*. Trans. R. F. C. Hull. 2nd ed. Bollingen Series 20. Princeton: Princeton UP, 1970. Vol. 10 of *The Collected Works of C. G. Jung*. 20 vols. 1957–79.

———. *The Structure and Dynamics of the Psyche*. Trans. R. F. C. Hull. 2nd ed. Bollingen Series 20. Princeton: Princeton UP, 1969. Vol. 8 of *The Collected Works of C. G. Jung*. 20 vols. 1957–79.

———. *The Symbolic Life: Miscellaneous Writings*. Trans. R. F. C. Hull. 2nd ed. Bollingen Series 20. Princeton: Princeton UP, 1976. Vol. 18 of *The Collected Works of C. G. Jung*. 20 vols. 1957–79.

Kalupahana, David J. *Buddhist Philosophy: A Historical Analysis*. Honolulu: UP of Hawaii, 1976.

Lauter, Estella, and Carol Schreier Rupprecht, eds. *Feminist Archetypal Theory: Interdisciplinary Re-Visions of Jungian Thought*. Knoxville: U of Tennessee P, 1985.

Leach, Maria, and Jerome Fried, eds. *Funk and Wagnall's Standard Dictionary of Folklore, Mythology, and Legend*. San Francisco: Harper, 1972.

Le Guin, Ursula K. "The Child and the Shadow." *Language of the Night*. Ed. Susan J. Wood. New York: Putnam's, 1979. 59–71.

Mellor, Anne K. *Romanticism and Gender*. New York: Routledge, 1993.

Nichols, Ruth. "Fantasy and Escapism." *Canadian Children's Literature* 4 (1976): 20–27.

———. "Fantasy: The Interior Universe." *Proceedings of the Fifth Annual Conference of the Children's Literature Association, 1979*. Ed. Margaret P. Esmonde and Priscilla Orde. Villanova, PA: Villanova UP, 1979. 41–47.

———. *Song of the Pearl*. Toronto: Macmillan, 1976.

Pratt, Annis. *Archetypal Patterns in Women's Fiction*. Bloomington: Indiana UP, 1981.

———. "Spinning in the Fields." *Jungian Literary Criticism*. Ed. Richard P. Sugg. Evanston: Northwestern UP, 1992.

"Ruth Nichols: An Interview." *Children's Literature Association Newsletter* 2.2 (Summer 1977): 1–4.

Said, Edward. *Orientalism*. 1978. New York: Vintage, 1979.

Spence, Lewis. *An Encyclopedia of Occultism*. New York: University, 1960.

Stannard, David. *The Puritan Way of Dying: A Study in Religion, Culture, and Social Change*. New York: Oxford UP, 1977.

Stott, Jon C. "An Interview with Ruth Nichols." *Canadian Children's Literature* 12 (1978): 5–19.

———. "The Nature of Fantasy: A Conversation with Ruth Nichols, Susan Cooper, and Maurice Sendak." *World of Children's Books* 3.2 (Fall 1978): 32–48.

Tolkien, J. R. R. *The Hobbit*. London: Unwin, 1951.

von Franz, Marie-Louise. *Individuation in Fairy Tales*. Rev. ed. Boston: Shambhala, 1990.

Walker, Barbara G. *The Secrets of the Tarot*. San Francisco: Harper, 1984.

Watson, Donald. *A Dictionary of Mind and Spirit*. New York: Avon, 1992.

Wolkstein, Diane, and Samuel Noah Kramer. *Inanna: Queen of Heaven and Earth*. New York: Harper, 1983.

Notes on Contributors

Paula T. Connolly is associate professor of English at the University of North Carolina at Charlotte. She has published articles on children's literature and a book on A. A. Milne, *Winnie-the-Pooh and The House at Pooh Corner: Recovering Arcadia*.

Richard Flynn is associate professor in the Department of Literature and Philosophy at Georgia Southern University, where he teaches contemporary poetry and children's literature. He is the author of a critical study, *Randall Jarrell and the Lost World of Childhood*, a collection of poems, *The Age of Reason*, and articles about contemporary poetry and children's literature. He is currently writing a book about contemporary poetry and childhood tentatively titled *Postmodern Poetries, Postmodern Childhoods*.

Anne Lundin is on the faculty at the University of Wisconsin–Madison School of Library and Information Studies, where she teaches children's literature, storytelling, and youth services. She has published articles and reviews in children's literature and is the author of *Victorian Horizons: The Critical Reception of the Picture Books of Walter Crane, Randolph Caldecott, and Kate Greenaway*.

James Holt McGavran is professor of English at the University of North Carolina at Charlotte. He is the editor of *Romanticism and Children's Literature in Nineteenth-Century England* and numerous articles on Romantic writers.

Mitzi Myers teaches writing, children's literature, and young adult and adolescent literature at the University of California, Los Angeles. She has published extensively on historical literature for the young and historical pedagogy and has held fellowships from the National Endowment for the Humanities, the American Philosophical Society, the American Council of Learned Societies, and the John Simon Guggenheim Memorial Foundation. Her specialties are women writers of the later eighteenth century, including Maria Edgeworth, Mary Wollstonecraft, and Hannah More; Irish studies; women's fiction; and cultural criticism. She has guest-edited special issues of several academic journals concerned with these topics, including *Children's Literature*. She is the coeditor of the Pickering and Chatto twelve-volume reprint of Maria Edgeworth's selected works with special responsibility for four volumes, including the adult novel *Belinda* (1801), *Practical Education* (1798), and the tales for children and young adults. She is also finishing a critical study of Edgeworth and progressing on a literary life of Edgeworth.

Dieter Petzold is an associate professor (*ausserplanmaessiger Professor*) of English at the University of Erlangen-Nuremberg, Germany. Among his publications are books on nineteenth-century nonsense literature, nineteenth-century fairy tales, J. R. R. Tolkein, and Robinson Crusoe, plus numerous articles, especially in nonmimetic fiction and children's literature.

Alan Richardson is professor of English at Boston College. He is the author of *Literature, Education, and Romanticism: Reading as Social Practice, 1780–1832* and is coeditor of *Romanticism, Race, and Imperial Culture 1780–1834*. He has also published numerous articles on Romantic-era literature and culture, particularly in relation to gender, colonialism, and the social construction of childhood.

Teya Rosenberg is on the faculty of the English Department at Southwest Texas State University, where she specializes in children's and young adult literature.

William J. Scheick is the J. R. Millikan Centennial Professor of American Literature at the University of Texas at Austin. His most recent books include *The Ethos of Romance at the Turn of the Century* and *Authority and Female Authorship in Colonial America*.

Index